D1084643

STRATEGIC SUPPLY MANAGEMENT

Creating the Next Source of Competitive Advantage

Robert J. Trent, Ph.D.

Supply Chain Management Program Director
Lehigh University

ISBN-10: 1-932159-67-3
ISBN-13: 978-1-932159-67-7

Printed and bound in the U.S.A. Printed on acid-free paper
10   9   8   7   6   5   4   3

Library of Congress Cataloging-in-Publication Data

Trent, Robert J.
  Strategic supply management : creating the next source of competitive
advantage / by Robert J. Trent.
       p. cm.
  Includes index.
  ISBN 978-1-932159-67-7 (hardcover : alk. paper)
  1. Business logistics. 2. Strategic planning. 3. Teams in the workplace.
4. Competition, International. I. Title.
  HD38.5.T74 2007
  658.7--dc22   2007018287

Phone: (954) 727-9333
Fax: (561) 892-0700
Web: www.jrosspub.com

This book is dedicated to my wife Jan,
my daughter Ellen,
my son Jack,
and my daughter-in-law Natalie

CONTENTS

PREFACE

In 1994 an executive vice president for telephone products at AT&T made a comment that was widely repeated by supply managers and widely discounted by others. He said that "purchasing is by far the largest single function at AT&T. Nothing we do is more important."[1] A comment like that surely raised the eyebrows of more than one executive leader. Could this guy be serious? Was purchasing, the perennial Rodney Dangerfield of the corporate world, finally going to get some respect? Is it really that important?

Over the last 10 years, it has become evident that there just might be something to this gentleman's comment. Certain trends and changes almost guarantee that the supply group needs to be at the forefront of change and value creation. As firms rely on fewer suppliers to design complex systems instead of providing simple components, and as the amount of sales passed along to suppliers for purchased inputs exceeds 60 percent and sometimes 70 percent of total revenue, this process we call supply management begins to look pretty important. A shift from a regional to a global perspective also makes supply management an important place to be. But are we ready to move to the forefront?

Welcome to the exciting (and sometimes frustrating) world of strategic supply management. It's a world where the legacy function called purchasing is replaced with a proactive process called supply management. It's a world that requires shifting from a focus on transactions, short-term relationships, and price to developing leading-edge supply strategies, pursuing early supplier involvement, practicing cross-enterprise relationship management, and striving to achieve the lowest total cost for goods and services. And it's a world where the performance contributions made by supply managers are on par with or even greater than those made by any other organizational group.

While most observers would agree strategic supply management is probably relevant for large, global companies, is it all that relevant for smaller and medium-size companies? Consider the supply challenges facing a producer of process xii Strategic Supply Management

equipment for the cement industry. After reading the purchasing director's comments that follow, ask if strategic supply management shouldn't be one of the most important things on this company's radar screen.[2]

> *Our company is a worldwide engineering company headquartered in Europe. We design and sell rock crushing and processing equipment for the cement industry. Our U.S. unit normally books about $250 million annually in sales—this year we will likely double that figure. Our other offices and group companies are also enjoying large sales increases.*
>
> *Unfortunately, we cannot find enough supplier capacity for placing our work. It's gotten so bad that our own groups are competing, sometimes viciously, against each other for shop and foundry space, even in China! Many of our key suppliers are booked solid. Lead times have more than doubled, with some even tripling. Bearings and large casting suppliers are quoting one- and two-year lead times. Metal supply is getting tighter, steel distributors are monopolizing mill runs of steel plate, and the military is eating up a lot of special plate capacity. Steel structurals are also in big demand and in short supply. The cost of nickel for stainless steel and related cast alloys is also greatly affecting us. And to make matters worse, much of the world's capacity in casting, fabrications, and gear reducers is being controlled by the wind turbine industry, which is expected only to grow over the next 25 years. If this is not bad enough, we are seeing the overall supply base shrink as other companies buy or consolidate with their suppliers to ensure they have access to supply.*

This company and its industry are far from unique. The popular press is loaded with stories about supply issues that are affecting the aerospace, automotive, and electronics industries, to name but a few. And the pressure to reduce costs across almost every industry will continue to be relentless and severe.

This book is about creating a supply management organization that can be relied on to deliver reliable sources of supply and, eventually, competitive advantage. It is targeted to supply managers and executive leaders at firms of all sizes. It is also targeted to non-supply leaders who want a deeper appreciation of the supply management process.

Each chapter presents information about specific concepts, processes, best practices, tools, and company examples. The information presented here is derived from extensive research, experience with hundreds of leading companies, and information available from public sources. At times company names are identified in the chapters; at other times they are not. Omitting names is done at the company's request or to avoid embarrassment. All examples throughout the book are real.

Each chapter begins with a short vignette that introduces that chapter's topic and concludes with a summary of key points. Many of these vignettes are not feel-good stories. In fact, some are real horror stories. Realistically, not everything turns out as intended. Did you hear about the company that sourced its finished product from China only to see its designs duplicated by other Asian companies? Or about the company that entered into a 10-year contract to assure its source of supply only to find market changes left it with a burdensome contract? Or the company that formed global supply teams only to find it did not know how to manage these teams? And let's not forget about the company that created a sophisticated scorecard system only to find it rewarded underperforming suppliers with new business. These examples are not presented to be negative or to imply that supply managers are incapable of achieving some impressive performance gains. They are presented to provide some valuable learning lessons.

Airbus provides a good example of the opportunity to learn from mistakes. In its overhaul of its entire procurement operation, the new chief of procurement said the company's A380 (its double-deck jumbo jet) design and production problems offered a "mine of lessons" on designing, sourcing, and assembling components. He said, "You learn more when something is not working, and we are learning a lot." Airbus will attempt to apply these lessons to the company's new A350 XWB, the plane that will compete directly with Boeing's 787 Dreamliner.[3]

This book provides a systematic journey through the world of strategic supply management. The first two chapters fully define strategic supply management, as well as provide a better understanding of the leadership required to achieve a set of demanding supply objectives. Chapter 2 also summarizes what a leading supply management organization looks like today. Chapters 3 to 6 address four critical enablers underlying strategic supply management: organizational design, measurement, information technology, and human resources. Attention to these four areas is essential before a firm can realistically expect to pursue more sophisticated supply activities.

Chapter 7 discusses how to develop supply strategies, while Chapters 8 to 15 present the leading-edge supply approaches and strategies that can lead to sustained competitive advantage. The last chapter provides a topic-by-topic look toward the future. While the chapters could be read out of sequence (the underlying plot will not be too disrupted), the chapters are best approached in the sequence they appear.

Each chapter is not intended to be a comprehensive presentation of that topic. Entire books have been written about many of the subjects covered here. The challenge is to present a large domain of information in a way that works for rather than against the reader. The chapters are designed to present some of the more important aspects of each topic so the reader can take a holistic approach that focuses on breadth rather than depth. It is about seeing how the different elements that compose strategic supply management come together to create a hard-to-duplicate source of competitive advantage. Let the journey begin!

ENDNOTES

1. S. Tully, "Purchasing's New Muscle," *Fortune* (February 21, 1994): 56–57.
2. A special thanks to Robert Agonis for generously sharing his perspectives about the challenges facing his industry.
3. D. Michaels, "Airbus Opens Overhaul by Looking at Procurement," *Wall Street Journal*, September 25, 2006, A3.

ABOUT THE AUTHOR

Robert Trent is the supply chain management program director and the Eugene Mercy associate professor of management at Lehigh University. He holds a BS degree in materials logistics management from Michigan State University, an MBA degree from Wayne State University, and a Ph.D. in purchasing/operations management from Michigan State University.

Prior to his return to academia, Bob worked for the Chrysler Corporation. His industrial experience includes assignments in production scheduling, package engineering with responsibility for new part packaging setup and the purchase of nonproductive materials, distribution planning, and operations management at the Boston regional parts distribution center. He has also worked on numerous special projects.

Throughout his academic career Bob has authored or coauthored numerous articles appearing in the *International Journal of Purchasing and Materials Management,* the *Journal of Supply Chain Management*, the *International Journal of Physical Distribution and Logistics Management, Total Quality Management, Supply Chain Management Review, Inside Supply Management, The Purchasing Handbook, Academy of Management Executive, Business Horizons, Team Performance Management, Supply Chain Forum: An International Journal,* and *Sloan Management Review*. His coauthored study on cross-functional sourcing team effectiveness was published through the Center for Advanced Purchasing Studies (CAPS) in 1993. A research report on purchasing/sourcing trends was published through CAPS in 1995. He completed a third coauthored CAPS project in 1999 that investigated how organizations reduce the effort and transactions required to purchase low-value goods and services. A fourth CAPS Research project on global sourcing was published in 2006. He is also the coauthor of a textbook titled *Purchasing and Supply Chain Management*, now in its third edition. Bob has also worked with dozens of companies in a consulting and professional development role.

Bob is a recipient of an Institute for Supply Management (ISM) research grant for the study of cross-functional sourcing team effectiveness. He has also been awarded the Class of 1961 Professorship and the Eugene Mercy Professorship at Lehigh University. Bob is also active with the ISM, serving for many years as the Professional Development Director of the NAPM of the Lehigh Valley and, at the national level, as a member of the *ISM Educational Resources Committee*. He and his family reside in Lopatcong, New Jersey. He can be reached at rjt2@lehigh.edu.

Free value-added materials available from
the Download Resource Center at www.jrosspub.com

At J. Ross Publishing we are committed to providing today's professional with practical, hands-on tools that enhance the learning experience and give readers an opportunity to apply what they have learned. That is why we offer free ancillary materials available for download on this book and all participating Web Added Value™ publications. These online resources may include interactive versions of material that appears in the book or supplemental templates, worksheets, models, plans, case studies, proposals, spreadsheets, and assessment tools, among other things. Whenever you see the WAV™ symbol in any of our publications, it means bonus materials accompany the book and are available from the Web Added Value™ Download Resource Center at www.jrosspub.com.

Downloads for *Strategic Supply Management: Creating the Next Source of Competitive Advantage* include tools to assess supply management and human resource policies and practices, organization design, processes, leadership, and performance measures.

UNDERSTANDING STRATEGIC SUPPLY MANAGEMENT

Imagine being called a hog—and liking it! That's exactly how the owners of Harley-Davidson motorcycles feel about the company and its bikes. But this feeling was severely tested during the 1980s and 90s. As with many once-proud brands, Harley-Davidson sold products that no longer met the standards of demanding customers. Global competitors entered Harley's markets with high-quality and innovative products, and like too many other U.S. manufacturers, the brand lost its luster.[1]

Today, Harley-Davidson again stands tall. In its analysis of the world's best brands, *BusinessWeek* said the company is "still the king of the hogs. Growing sales to women augment the loyal customer base of baby boomers and hard-core bikers."[2] Harley's successful turnaround is as much a triumph of strategic supply management as it is engineering and marketing. For years the company kept suppliers at a distance, viewed purchasing as a lower-level activity, and relied on over-worked engineers to make selection decisions based primarily on a supplier's technical ability. These decisions, which often proved not to be the best as the company moved toward full-scale production, had severe consequences on product reliability and costs.

How did the company achieve its turnaround? Harley-Davidson elevated the reporting level of its chief purchasing officer, pursued longer-term relationships with carefully selected suppliers, adopted just-in-time supplier deliveries, created the position of procurement engineer, and brought together the talents of procurement, engineering, and suppliers in a state-of-the-art design center. Supplier on-site residency programs, extensive communication through the Internet, regular assessments of supplier performance, and active supplier involvement on an executive buyer-supplier council also promoted better working relationships.

While these activities are well and good, can Harley-Davidson show us the money? Without question strategic supply management has delivered the results envisioned by the company's leaders. Material costs are lower, over half of Harley's suppliers perform at a defect level of less than 50 parts per million, early supplier involvement has helped reduce by about half the time and cost it takes to design and build a new motorcycle, and, thanks to cooperative efforts with suppliers, the company now operates with drastically reduced inventory levels. Perhaps most importantly, Harley-Davidson is again one of the world's most admired brands. So, the next time you are riding your Harley and someone calls you a hog, accept the compliment graciously. Thanks in large part to strategic supply management, the hog is back!

Today's competitive environment requires new ways of doing business. This environment is one where capabilities that win business today only qualify for business tomorrow. It is an environment where global pressures to improve are relentless and severe. And it is an environment where speed, flexibility, and innovation now count for more than sheer muscle.

Market success will increasingly require firms to bring a "total package" to the table, a package that must include a set of progressive supply management activities and practices. The supply package can be broad, involving activities such as integrated global sourcing, early supplier involvement, commodity management teams, supplier alliances, and supplier development. A common feature of these activities is they each have the ability to make contributions well beyond the functional level. Supply management can affect *corporate* performance.

This chapter begins our journey through the world of strategic supply management. We thoroughly explore the concept, including a set of principles that underlie strategic supply management and the framework around which this book is structured.

EXPLORING THE CONCEPT

Most firms have worked diligently to improve those parts of the supply chain that are under their direct control. Many managers, in fact, will say they have reached a point of diminishing return as it relates to internal performance. In other words, much of the "low-hanging fruit" has been thoroughly harvested. If this is the case, what will be the next major source of improvements? When 60 percent of total revenue, and sometimes more, passes directly to suppliers as payment for inputs, the source for future cost, quality, delivery, and cycle time improvements becomes obvious. Simply stated, most firms would benefit from a more enlightened approach to managing expenditures and suppliers. And most firms have a long way to go before fully tapping into the competitive advantages that strategic supply management offers.

Not too long ago, placing the terms *strategic* and *supply management* in the same phrase would quickly be dismissed as contradictory by most executive leaders. Consider a comment by Bruce Henderson, a respected purchasing professional. He once observed that most executive managers regard purchasing as a negative function—it can handicap a company if not done well but can make little positive contribution. John Hill, another procurement leader, noted that many executive managers view purchases as simply an inescapable cost of doing business that no one can do much about.

How the times have changed. Extensive outsourcing of major portions of the value chain, constant pressure to improve, and ever-increasing global pressures have combined to create a search for new sources of competitive advantage. For most firms an untapped opportunity surrounds the extensive supply networks they rely on but often take for granted. At progressive firms purchasing is being replaced by strategic supply management, and transactional and arm's-length relationships are being replaced by value-added relationships.

Table 1.1 presents a set of factors that affect how rigorously a company should pursue strategic supply management. Competitive and customer pressure to improve, the rate of change within an industry, the ability of suppliers to impact our competitiveness, and the location of suppliers all affect how seriously a company should endorse strategic supply management. Some companies, such as those in banking or other services, will rightfully not see the potential from strategic supply management the same way as companies in the computer, aerospace, or automotive industries. Today's global model features supply chain against supply chain, and for most firms external suppliers are an increasingly important part of their chain. Strategic supply management is a competitive necessity.

A major item that affects a firm's likelihood of endorsing strategic supply management is the percent of revenue that passes through directly to suppliers. Take a moment and look at Table 1.2. On the income statement of publicly traded companies is a seemingly innocent line item called by various names—*cost of goods sold, cost of revenue,* or *cost of sales.* Whatever its title, this account includes all the costs a company incurs directly to produce its products or services, including material costs to suppliers.

It is not unusual in some industries for suppliers to receive 80 percent or more of the amount that appears in the cost of goods sold account. It does not take a rocket scientist to see how large this amount can be relative to other

Table 1.1 Assessing the Need for Strategic Supply Management

Less Need		Greater Need
Competitors are slow to improve their performance.	⟷	Competitors are rapidly improving their performance.
New product development cycle times are stable.	⟷	New product development cycle times are shortening rapidly.
Our industry features a slower rate of technological change.	⟷	Our industry features a rapid rate of technological change.
Customers exert minimal pressure to improve.	⟷	Customers exert intense pressure to improve.
Competitors are primarily domestic.	⟷	Competitors are primarily global.
Suppliers are primarily domestic.	⟷	Suppliers are primarily global.
Purchases make up a small portion of revenues.	⟷	Purchases make up an extensive portion of revenues.
Suppliers minimally impact our ability to compete.	⟷	Suppliers extensively impact our ability to compete.
We control most of our production requirements internally.	⟷	Outsourcing is a major part of our business model.

financial line items. We must also consider how suppliers affect a firm's capital asset and inventory accounts. Supplier fingerprints are all over their customer's balance sheet and income statement. The importance of making supply management a corporate mandate becomes evident when looking at the numbers.

Defining Strategic Supply Management

Up to this point, the concept of strategic supply management has been mentioned but not defined. First, and perhaps foremost, fundamental differences exist between purchasing and supply management. Purchasing is a functional group (a formal entity on the organizational chart) as well as a functional activity (buying goods and services). The purchasing group traditionally performs many of the activities required to support an organization's operations, including negotiating, buying, contracting, and research.

Table 1.2 Cost of Revenue as a Percentage of Total Sales

Company	Cost of Revenue as a % of Sales
Boeing	83%
Dell	82%
Ford	82%
General Motors	80%
Alcoa	75%
John Deere	75%
Textron	74%
Caterpillar	73%
Procter & Gamble	49%
Colgate-Palmolive	46%
General Electric	45%
Intel	45%
Merck	25%
Bank of America	11%

Source: Recent quarterly and annual income statements, http://finance.yahoo.com.

A problem at many organizations is that purchasing is a legacy term—it's been around for a long time and the legacy is not all that great. Many still view purchasing as a reactive, lower-level activity focused solely on managing prices and transactions. Consider the comment of an engineer at a high-tech company when asked recently to explain the role of purchasing at his company. With a completely straight face he replied, "Someone has to do the paperwork." For many years when someone was transferred to purchasing, the person wondered what he or she did wrong.

Supply management, on the other hand, is a cross-functional, proactive process for obtaining goods and services that features the active management and involvement of suppliers. The supply management process involves identifying a company's total requirements, developing supply strategies, evaluating and selecting suppliers, and then managing and developing those suppliers to realize performance advantages at a level higher than what competitors are realizing. Figure 1.1 presents a broad view of the strategic supply management process.

Keki Bhote, one of the architects of Motorola's Six Sigma quality process, argues that a key part of supply management is its cross-functional nature, meaning it involves purchasing, engineering, supplier quality assurance, the supplier,

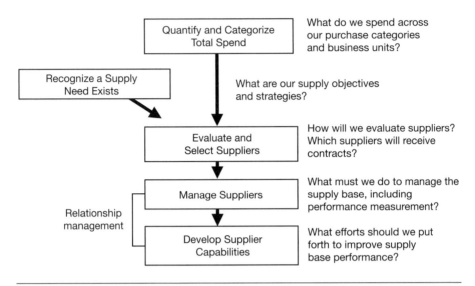

Figure 1.1 The strategic supply management process.

and other related functions working together as one team, early on, to further mutual goals. It is a progressive way of operating, involving internal groups and external suppliers to achieve advantages in cost, product development, technology, cycle time, and quality.

Instead of adversarial relationships, which characterize traditional purchasing, supply management features longer-term win-win relationships between a buying company and *specially* selected suppliers (a later chapter explains the concepts of win-win, win-lose, and lose-lose). Supply management also involves helping to develop supplier performance capabilities in exchange for continuous improvements. Except for ownership, select suppliers become almost an extension of the buying company.

Our discussion so far has only casually mentioned the word *strategic*, a word that is tossed around way too freely. In fact, it's somewhat surprising how often this term is used without ever being clarified or defined. If you had a dollar every time something was called "strategic," you would be independently wealthy.

What, then, makes something strategic? What gives us the right to combine strategic and supply management in the same sentence? One perspective argues that something is strategic if it has great importance within an integrated whole. This means that strategic activities, plans, or decisions have the ability to affect the integrated whole, which for our purposes means they have the ability to affect a firm's overall competitive or market success. *Strategic initiatives can affect market or corporate success.* This perspective excludes day-to-day decisions or routine activities that are part of traditional purchasing and materials management responsibilities.

Several examples will further clarify this concept. Developing a procurement card program to simplify the ordering of lower-value items, while ideal for driving out transactions costs, will not have strategic ramifications. Entering into a supply alliance that provides access to leading-edge technology before competitors even hear about the technology is a different story. Most of the topics presented throughout this book have strategic implications. They can make a difference at the corporate level.

Strategic supply management processes and approaches are remarkably robust as we move across industries. It's surprising how well the language of supply management translates across industry sectors. Every industry evaluates, selects, and measures suppliers; they enter into contracts, many pursue supplier development activities, and most of them source globally. The good new is that laggard industries can learn from those industries that have been at the forefront of supply management. We should not discount the value of someone else's lessons learned, particularly when those lessons are learned the hard way.

No longer a transactional activity, supply management is about creating and sustaining new sources of competitive advantage. These sources could involve better quality, lower costs, faster responsiveness to end customer needs, or incorporating before competitors do the technologies and features that differentiate end products or services. Supply managers should envision the domain of advantages they can bring to the table as being broad.

Contrasting Purchasing and Strategic Supply Management

Table 1.3 provides a more detailed contrast between traditional purchasing and strategic supply management. As this table reveals, major differences exist between the two columns. While it can be risky to overly generalize, traditional purchasing tends to be reactive, functional, measured primarily on price reduction, and placed lower in the organizational hierarchy. Involvement in new product development is also usually quite late in the process. A focus on relationship management is not a priority, and the concept of strategies is somewhat foreign.

The characteristics that describe strategic supply management in this table also help further define this concept. Perhaps most importantly, strategic supply management features strategies that are part of a rigorous development process. The process also involves participants from different functional groups, looks across locations to identify process standardization opportunities, and continuously pursues improvement opportunities with external suppliers. Supply managers and suppliers are also early participants during product development.

Table 1.3 Contrasting Purchasing and Strategic Supply Management

	Traditional Purchasing	**Strategic Supply Management**
Reporting Level	Dispersed throughout lower levels	Report to the executive committee
Supply Base	Large	Optimized
Organization	Functional	Cross-functional, cross-locational, and cross-organizational design features
Skills	Specialized, minimal cross-functional experience	Generalized, draw support and participants from other functional groups
Focus	Task and transaction focus	Proactive process focus, longer term
Contracting	No formal agreements or short-term agreements	Selected longer-term agreements
Supplier Relationships	Adversarial	Cooperative/collaborative relationships with select suppliers
Measurement	Price focus	Lowest total cost, impact on corporate indicators
Product Development	Involved late	Involved early
Planning	Share short-term production schedules	Sharing of information and technology roadmaps with suppliers, longer-term planning horizon
Strategy Development	Strategies are reactive, ad hoc, or nonexistent	A rigorous process guides the development of company-wide strategies
Information Flow	Vertical flow within the purchasing function	Horizontal flow across functional groups and enterprises

Measurement of supply management effectiveness is also dramatically different compared with traditional purchasing measurement.

Does Strategic Supply Management Make a Difference?

Is the transition from purchasing to strategic supply management one that companies should undertake? Case examples, accounts reported in the popular press, and research studies consistently show how supply leaders justify their efforts with tangible performance results. These results move well beyond lower price and better delivery. Research findings supporting the value of strategic supply management are not hard to find. In his classic work *The Competitive Advantage of Nations*, Michael Porter argued the relationships that some companies have with their suppliers is a source not only of competitive advantage but also national advantage. A study of European firms across eight industries by Booz Allen Hamilton found that the best performers practiced a set of sourcing activities described as strategic. These activities included target costing, longer-term contracting, the use of quality certified suppliers, frequent to daily parts deliveries, and supplier-provided design support. This study concluded that any manufacturer that expects to survive long term must fully develop its strategic supply capabilities.

A study reported in Chapter 14 will reveal that firms engaged in integrated global sourcing realize better performance across every performance category evaluated than firms that practice basic and often reactive international purchasing. In other words, there is a strategic value in coordinating and integrating worldwide supply operations. Another study detailed in Chapter 3 will report that teams that make suppliers a part of team activities achieve better performance results than teams that do not involve suppliers. Chapter 13 will reference a study that supports the value of involving suppliers early during product and process design. Chapter 15 presents a compelling case that shows how one firm has developed new technologies through its supplier alliance that have allowed it to grow its market share. And a case in presented in Chapter 8 will illustrate how longer-term contracting has changed the way a business unit operates.

The list of studies and case examples supporting the value of progressive supply management activities could go on and on. And many of the chapters in this book present accounts of highly effective supply management initiatives. When performed correctly, supply managers can take a set of progressive approaches and turn them into a hard-to-beat source of competitive advantage. We know this to be true.

Three Primary Objectives of Strategic Supply Management

The pursuit of strategic supply initiatives should support the achievement of three primary outcomes or objectives. Achieving these objectives at levels higher than the competition will go a long way toward building a competitive advantage. These objectives or outcomes include becoming a preferred customer, receiving relationship-specific investment, and creating a co-destiny with suppliers.

Most suppliers want to be the supplier of choice (the preferred supplier) to their customers. Conversely, most buyers should strive to become the customer of choice (the preferred customer) to their suppliers, especially when these suppliers sell to a variety of different industries. Preferred customers are first in line when a supplier develops new technologies, first in line to receive differentiating ideas that originate from suppliers, and when supply markets are out of synch, first in line when a supplier's limited output is distributed.

Ford and Toyota are both working to be leaders in the production of hybrid vehicles. Ford executives recently complained that Aisin Seiki favored Toyota when supplying scarce hybrid transmission systems.[4] Clearly, a demand for transmissions that exceeds the supply of transmissions prohibited Aisin Seiki from supporting the requirements of both companies. One party here is obviously the preferred customer, while the other is not. Supply managers must take steps to ensure they receive preferential treatment from suppliers.

A second objective is to create a supply base that is willing to commit investment that only benefits the buying company, or what is termed *relationship-specific investment*. Suppliers must invest in their business in order to remain competitive. However, if that investment benefits all customers, what did any one company receive that is different when compared to other customers?

Relationship-specific investment can take a number of forms. It can involve a supplier committing research and development funds to support the buying company's longer-range technology plans, creating a work cell to support a customer's unique production requirements, or assigning engineers to work on a buyer's new product development teams. Relationship-specific investment is an often-sought outcome from longer-term agreements, which Chapter 8 explores.

A third desired outcome is the creation of a co-destiny between the buyer and supplier. Some companies refer to this as a mutual dependency. *Co-destiny* involves a realization that what happens to one firm directly affects the fortunes of another firm. Parties that feel a co-destiny exists between them should be more willing to share information and technology, cooperate on improvement projects, and invest in each other's future. Later chapters will explore how buying companies can develop a sense of co-destiny with important suppliers. These three objectives help us better understand, at a very broad level, what we really want to achieve from our supply management efforts.

13 PRINCIPLES UNDERLYING STRATEGIC SUPPLY MANAGEMENT

A number of principles underlie strategic supply management as it is presented throughout this book. And certainly these principles could be subject to differences of opinion or perspective. The following presents these principle or themes along with a notation of the chapters where each appears in greater detail.

Relationships Matter—Just Not Equally. The prevailing view among most supply managers is that supplier relationships can be a source of competitive advantage. The view here is that supplier relationships are an essential part of strategic supply management. All supplier relationships, however, are not created equally.

It may seem counterintuitive to say, but most supplier relationships are not about win-win opportunities, nor should they be. Even true win-win relationships, such as those featured in longer-term agreements and supply alliances, eventually have a component of win-lose as the parties divide the value from the relationship. Part of the value that supply managers bring is knowing when, where, and how to apply the most appropriate relationship given a supply requirement. Chapters 7 and 11 address supplier relationships and relationship management.

Improvement Is a Never-Ending Journey and Supply Managers Play a Major Role. It is difficult to identify an industry that has not experienced an increase in global competition over the last 15 years, leading to ever-increasing pressure to improve. Even if the number of major competitors in an industry has become smaller, such as in the aerospace industry, sophisticated customers still present their own set of demands. If relentless customer and competitor pressure to improve is a never-ending journey, where will the next major source of improvements come from? For most industrial firms the answer falls within the domain of strategic supply management.

Processes Are Critical. The supply strategies and approaches presented throughout this book can all be presented as processes, whether this involves developing supply strategies, crafting supplier alliances, or evaluating and selecting suppliers. A process is simply *a set of interrelated tasks or activities designed to achieve a specific objective or outcome,* such as the creation of a world-class supply base, the development of supply strategies, or gaining access to technology from suppliers before competitors gain access. Developed processes means that thought has been given to how to perform an interrelated set of activities well. Strategic supply management should be process driven. The topics presented in Chapter 7 to 15 are all process focused.

Measurement Is Essential to Supply Management Success. It is difficult to manage and improve what we do not measure. Measurement motivates behavior while identifying progress and improvement opportunities across the supply chain. We typically apply supply management measurement and measures within four areas—during supplier evaluation and selection, during the normal course of supplier performance, when evaluating the overall effectiveness and efficiency of supply management, and when assessing a supplier's perspectives of the buying company. Interestingly, if measurement is critical to success, then why do so many organizations do such a poor job at it? Chapter 4 explores this question.

Becoming a Strategic Supply Organization Does Not Happen Overnight. Leading organizations work hard to get to the point where strategic supply management becomes a routine contributor to corporate success. One of the dangers of studying leading organizations during performance benchmarking is a tendency to believe that the transformation to strategic supply management is quick and easy. After all, look at how many companies are doing a good job at it! Becoming a strategic contributor on par with other major areas requires patience (but not too much), leadership, and resources. Chapter 2 addresses the supply leadership imperative.

Supply Managers Can Be Creative. Strategic supply management is a place where creativity is welcomed, which is not the case in all organizational areas (consider accounting). And while lawyers think about contingencies, supply managers should think about possibilities. When applied correctly, a creative approach to supply relationships can open up a world of new possibilities.

The slogan for supply managers should be "creativity is spoken here!" The laws covering contract development in the United States are generous about what the parties may enter into as long as they satisfy some basic conditions. Strategic supply management is not about doing business the old way or according to some narrowly defined rules. It is about exploring new possibilities, particularly when working with suppliers, for creating new sources of value. Most of the chapters present topics that will benefit from the creative energy that is bottled up within supply managers.

Strategic Supply Management Is More Than Achieving the Lowest Price. One of the biggest complaints internal customers (and suppliers) have about purchasing is an obsession with price. Actually, a focus on price is easy to understand once we understand that price is the most common metric that supply managers are evaluated against. Price is also an easy measure to capture. The domain of strategic supply management, however, is much broader than price.

If price is a primary focus, then let's understand when and where to apply the most appropriate techniques to achieve the *lowest total cost*. Furthermore, supply managers have the ability to affect many of the factors that make a firm competitive, including delivery, technology, cycle time, responsiveness to end customers, and even contribution to revenues. While price will always be important, it should not be the sole focus of supply managers. Chapter 4 will present a new set of performance metrics that take a different look at how supply managers contribute, while Chapter 12 addresses managing costs strategically.

Do Not Forget about Risk. Risk represents the probability of realizing an unintended or unwanted consequence or outcome. Risk management is one of today's hot topics, particularly when we look at the broader domain of supply chain management. Many of the activities presented throughout this book have the potential to manage or prevent risk. Chapter 8 presents contracting for the longer term, a way to formally address issues related to supply risk. Chapter 10 presents ways to build a world-class supply base that hopefully prevents problems from occurring. Chapter 15 addresses true supply alliances that provide unique advantages that are unavailable to competitors. The reverse is also true. Many of these same topics performed poorly will expose an organization to risk. Risk management must be a key concern to supply managers.

Strategic Supply Management Is Organizational Rather Than Functional. Most supply management initiatives are not possible without the support of executive and other functional leaders. By definition strategic supply management is organizational and cross-functional rather than the exclusive domain of the functional group called purchasing. A lack of respect and support from other functional groups will affect the challenges that supply managers face as they work to create sustainable sources of advantage. And a lack of respect from executive management will affect the resources and visibility afforded the supply management process.

Of course, the best way to get respect is to earn it. Supply managers must step up and demonstrate the value they bring to their organization. And this does not mean simply getting the lowest price for a good or service. It means making a contribution in areas that grab the attention of executive leaders, such as improved return on assets, contribution to economic value-add, improvements to working capital and cash flow, and improved profitability.

Sometimes We Do Not Care How Many Suppliers We Have. While it seems to counter prevailing wisdom, there are times when supply managers should not be overly concerned about the number of suppliers they maintain. Certain items are just not important enough to worry about the actual number of suppliers that provide them, as long as the transaction costs of maintaining those suppliers are not excessive. What we should care about is the number of suppliers that receive the majority of total purchase dollars.

An example will help illustrate this point. Assume a buyer has a requirement to buy 25 standard items. The buyer receives bids from five different suppliers who are all capable of providing the 25 items. Is there a law that says the buyer must use only one supplier? What if the buyer analyzes the bids and identifies where each supplier is the most competitive on price? Unless a single supplier quoted the lowest price for each item, it might make sense to split the contract among the suppliers. Supplier A may provide 8 of the 25 items, Supplier C will provide 10, and Supplier D will provide the remaining 7. While the original intention may have been to single-source the 25 items, splitting the total contract among the three suppliers may work best from a total dollar perspective, even when factoring in any costs associated with maintaining two additional suppliers. Chapter 12 reviews managing costs strategically.

Activity Does Not Necessarily Mean Accomplishment. Selecting suppliers, measuring supplier performance, sourcing globally, forming alliances, and developing longer-term strategies are all *activities*. It is natural to feel positive when pursuing activities that the prevailing wisdom says are good. Activity means nothing, however, unless it translates directly into desired outcomes. What did a longer-term contract provide that traditional contracting did not? What benefits resulted because of a supply alliance? Did a supplier development project deliver a positive return on investment? What are commodity teams doing to justify their expense? In short, what did these activities *accomplish*? We often mistakenly associate activity with accomplishment.

Industries Pursue Strategic Supply Management at Different Rates. Industries pursue supply management at different rates and at different times. Many strategic supply management examples in the popular press involve the electronics and automotive industries simply because these two industries, perhaps more than any other, have been subject to intense global competition and dynamic rates of change. Now we are witnessing industries such as pharmaceutical and aerospace showing a keen interest in strategic supply management. Even the U.S. Postal Service and Internal Revenue Service are taking a more progressive view of supply management. Waves of change seem to affect industries at different times, and it's important for supply managers to understand where their industry is in this wave. It may even be possible to "start the wave" within your industry.

Strategic Supply Management Won't Happen without the Right People. Transitioning toward strategic supply management is not easy. Imagine working at a buying center managing transactions and then being told it is time to take a company-wide view of the supply base. Or imagine being told that you should be a bit more strategic in your outlook. What does this even mean? Will you be strategic from 2:00 to 4:00 p.m. on Wednesdays, assuming there are no crises that must command your attention? Strategic supply management requires a very different skill set that is often in short supply. When push comes to shove, operational activities almost always take precedence over "longer-term" activities. Chapter 3 explains how to create an organization that is responsive to both

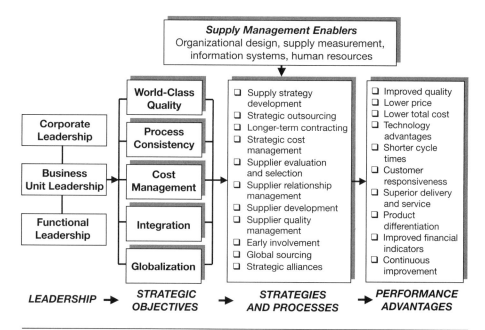

Figure 1.2 Strategic supply management framework. (Adapted from *The Global Electronic Benchmarking Network*, Michigan State University.)

operational and strategic needs, while Chapter 6 presents a set of knowledge and skills that supply organizations should possess.

These 13 principles support our thinking as it relates to strategic supply management. They are embedded as we proceed through this book.

THE STRATEGIC SUPPLY MANAGEMENT FRAMEWORK

Figure 1.2 presents a formal roadmap highlighting what it takes to achieve competitive advantage from strategic supply management. This model also presents the format this book follows. Effective leadership should result in a clear articulation of supply objectives, which drive the development of supply management strategies and practices. Supporting the development of supply strategies and practices are four critical enablers that no supply leader can ignore: organizational design, supply measurement, information systems, and human resources. When all of this comes together, we hopefully achieve a set of performance outcomes that provide a hard-to-beat source of competitive advantage. And, as this figure illustrates, a desired set of performance outcomes includes much more than achieving the lowest price.

Figure 1.2 is not the only way to think about strategic supply management. For example, Ross Reck and Brian Long have detailed four stages that organizations evolve through as they progress toward strategic supply management. These stages include passive, independent, supportive, and integrative. In the 1990s the *Global Electronic Benchmarking Network* at Michigan State University created a similar four-phase supply management model that includes basic beginnings, moderate development, limited integration, and fully integrated supply chains. Each of these models recognizes the importance and contribution of supply management as organizations grow through a series of steps or phases.

CONCLUDING THOUGHTS

For firms that face a future where the only certainty is uncertainty, the pursuit of new sources of competitive advantage becomes a strategic necessity. For most this means endorsing new ways to evaluate, select, manage, and develop their supply base. It is time for supply managers to present a vision, fight for resources that are on par with other major groups, and develop the talent, systems, measures, and processes that will make supply management a hard-to-duplicate source of value creation.

SUMMARY OF KEY CHAPTER POINTS

- Today's competitive environment requires new ways of doing business. Market success requires firms to bring a "total package" to the table, a package that includes set of progressive supply management activities and approaches.
- Extensive outsourcing of major portions of a firm's value chain, constant pressure to improve, and ever-increasing global pressures have combined to create a search for new sources of competitive advantage.
- A range of factors affect the extent to which a firm should endorse strategic supply management.
- Strategic supply management is a cross-functional, progressive approach to obtaining goods and services and managing the supply base. It is about creating and sustaining new sources of competitive advantage in areas that are broad rather than narrow.
- Strategic supply management processes are transferable across industries. Every industry evaluates, selects, and measures suppliers; they enter into longer-term contracts; they pursue supplier development activities; and most of them source globally.

- Examples and research findings supporting the value of strategic supply management are not hard to find.
- While the overall objective of strategic supply management is to gain sustainable advantages over competitors, three specific objectives include becoming a preferred customer, capturing relationship-specific investment, and creating a co-destiny between the buyer and supplier.
- A number of principles underlie strategic supply management—not all relationships matter equally; improvement is a never-ending journey and supply managers play a major role; processes are critical to strategic supply management; measurement is essential to supply management success; becoming a strategic supply organization does not happen overnight; supply managers can be creative; strategic supply management is more than achieving the lowest price; do not forget about risk; strategic supply management is organizational rather than functional; sometimes we do not care how many suppliers we have; activity does not necessarily mean accomplishment; industries pursue strategic supply management at different rates; and strategic supply management won't happen without the right people.

ENDNOTES

1. Adapted from B. Milligan and J. Carbone, "Harley-Davidson Wins by Getting Suppliers on Board," *Purchasing,* 125, no. 5 (September 21, 2000): 52–65.
2. D. Kiley, B. Elgin, M. Arndt, and R. Crockett, "Best Global Brands," *BusinessWeek,* no. 3996 (August 7, 2006): 64.
3. K. R. Bhote, *Strategic Supply Management: A Blueprint for Revitalizing the Manufacturing-Supplier Partnership* (New York: American Management Association, 1989), 13.
4. D. Welch and H. Tashiro, "Japan Takes a New Bite out of Detroit," *BusinessWeek,* no. 3994 (July 24, 2006): 41.

2

RECOGNIZING THE IMPORTANCE OF SUPPLY LEADERSHIP

Gaining sustainable advantages from strategic supply management will never become a reality without leaders who have the vision, will, and determination to create world-class supply organizations. This leadership imperative is vital at all levels of an organization—it includes corporate leaders who recognize the value of supply management; a chief purchasing officer who understands how to produce consistent results; supply managers who know how to coordinate their efforts with other functional groups; and buyers, commodity team members, and team leaders who are able to fulfill their role as important participants within the supply management process.

Perhaps the epitome of a supply management leader is the late Gene Richter. Under his leadership he and his staff won the prestigious *Purchasing* Medal of Professional Excellence award three times at three different companies. Black & Decker (1988), Hewlett Packard (1992), and IBM (1999) each won the coveted prize under Mr. Richter's leadership. This is a feat that is not likely to be repeated soon.

What did Gene Richter do to earn these awards? While at IBM he put together a procurement organization staffed with the best people he could find, centralized and controlled the $45 billion of expenditures that were previously uncoordinated across the company's business units, worked hard to improve supplier relationships, and focused on selecting the world's best suppliers. A sample of his team's achievements over a six-year period includes $9 billion in material and service cost savings, improved satisfaction ratings from internal clients from 43 percent to 89 percent, increased annual purchases over the Internet from zero to $13 billion, an improvement from near last in supplier surveys of industrial customers to first, reduced contract lengths from over 40 pages to six, and earning the IBM Chairman's Award for Excellence.[1] Wherever Mr. Richter went good things seemed to happen.

Since leadership is perhaps the most widely presented management topic in the world, this chapter will not be a general discussion of leadership. Instead, it explores the importance of supply leadership from several perspectives. The first considers the importance of individuals as supply leaders. Organizations do not become supply leaders without individuals who demonstrate leadership. The second perspective looks at organizations as supply leaders. The chapter concludes with a profile of a supply leader whose efforts have helped a struggling company to survive.

THE SUPPLY LEADERSHIP IMPERATIVE

According to the late Gene Richter, a major challenge facing organizations is how to develop a generation of leaders who understand how to make supply management their company's most critical core competency. In his view failure to do so minimizes the chances of winning in the marketplace, particularly as companies rely on their suppliers for an ever-increasing amount of value-add. Effective leadership is a necessary prerequisite for creating an effective supply management organization. This is why leadership appears so early in this book.

Anyone can be a supply leader if we view being a leader as a *formally* assigned role. Congratulations—you have been selected to be your company's chief procurement officer. With a title like that, few will question your legitimacy as a formal leader. What we do not yet know is how well you will demonstrate *leadership*.

So, what do we mean by leadership? A leader who demonstrates leadership is any person who influences individuals and groups within an organization, helps them in the establishment of goals, and guides them toward the achievement of those goals, thereby allowing them to be effective.[2] Given the magnitude of change a company faces as it endorses strategic supply management, it should become evident why the profession needs supply managers who are capable of being supply leaders, and supply leaders who are capable of demonstrating leadership.

Throughout this book the terms *manager* and *leader* will be used somewhat interchangeably. Technically, there are differences between the two that should be brought forth. Managers tend to focus on the present while maintaining stability and the status quo. They also use their positional power to implement policies and procedures in an objective rather than emotional manner. Leaders, on the other hand, focus on the future as they strive to create change. Instead of positional power, leaders use their personal power to create a culture based on shared values. Leaders also work to create an emotional rather than impersonal link with their followers.[3]

Different Levels of Supply Leadership

Leadership is not is not the exclusive domain of executive management. As the opening of this chapter noted, supply leadership must permeate the entire organization. An argument can reasonably be made that four levels of supply leadership exist. The first three levels are supply executives as leaders, supply managers as leaders, and buyers and team members as leaders. If these three levels of leadership are present, it's a safe bet that the fourth level—the supply organization as a leader—will become a reality. Later sections identify the characteristics of leading supply organizations and identify those companies that have earned *Purchasing* magazine's Medal of Professional Excellence award. Chapter 6 presents strategies for ensuring a steady pipeline of future supply leaders.

The ways that individuals working within the different supply levels demonstrate leadership are varied. At the highest executive levels, Chapter 3 will reveal that the presence of a chief procurement officer is essential to supply management success. But what is the chief procurement officer supposed to do to demonstrate leadership? Perhaps one of the most visible indicators of executive supply leadership is leading an executive supply council or committee that establishes a supply management vision. In addition to senior supply leaders, this committee often includes other functional and business unit executives.

Figure 2.1 outlines the responsibilities of the executive leadership council at a leading supply organization. Clearly, as this figure reveals, this committee engages in some real work. One of the most important objectives of an executive leadership council is to create consistency across the supply organization. This means developing supply processes and systems that eliminate redundancy, build in best practices, and move the entire supply organization toward a higher level of professionalism. Furthermore, it is important for supply executives to report performance results regularly to the executive committee, and, on occasion, to the board of directors. Chapter 4 presents a set of performance metrics that should be part of every executive supply leader's tool kit.

Besides establishing an organization's supply vision, executive supply leaders should engage in two other important activities. The first involves leadership development and succession planning, areas where too many companies fall short. The second involves obtaining the necessary resources that allow supply management to be a strategic contributor on par with other major groups.

Perhaps the most tangible evidence of supply leadership is the development of strategies and approaches that produce consistent results. The development of

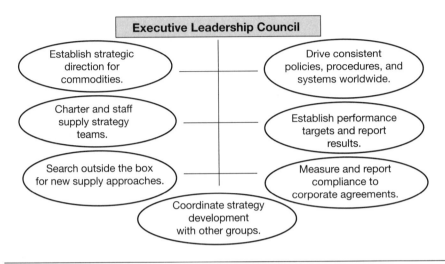

Figure 2.1 Executive supply leadership council responsibilities.

specific commodity strategies is often the responsibility of supply managers, who represent the second level of supply leadership. For companies that take a strong commodity management focus, this is a critical leadership level.

While the importance of this second leadership level appears obvious, developing future executive leaders from these ranks is often a challenge. Fully one-third of companies surveyed by ClearRock, an executive coaching and outplacement firm, said their middle managers were unqualified for promotion to higher-level positions. As one managing partner at ClearRock commented, "At best, most companies rate their middle managers as being in the middle of the pack and sorely in need of the strategic thinking and leadership skills that will help raise them to the next level."[4] Strategic thinking and leadership skills rank as the top two skills that senior executives believe middle managers need to develop. These skills are followed by communication, developing direct reports, and motivating people.

The third leadership level involves buyers and other procurement personnel who should demonstrate leadership in a number of visible ways. They can be active members of product development or global sourcing teams, or active members of any other team to which they are assigned. When team activities address areas that relate to supply issues, the procurement representative should step up and assume a leadership role. These individuals can also develop their knowledge and skill sets to the point where other organizational members view them as a valuable resource. At some point these individual can begin to assume demanding team leadership roles.

Increasingly, some companies have created a position called "lead buyer." This individual assumes responsibility for managing items that do not qualify for company-wide contracts yet have some commonality across locations or buying centers. The buyer who assumes a lead role is expected to demonstrate leadership as he or she manages these items. The lead buyer and team leadership positions are excellent proving grounds before moving on to greater responsibilities.

UNDERSTANDING SUPPLY MANAGEMENT TRENDS AND CHANGES

Over the last 15 years we have witnessed some major changes related to purchasing and supply management. While a discussion of these changes and their impact could fill an entire book, it is worthwhile to at least briefly identify some of the more important changes. A quality that separates effective from less effective supply leaders is their ability to understand the trends and changes that have occurred and are occurring. While it is one thing to say a trend is occurring, it is something entirely different to understand why it's occurring, its effect on the supply organization, and how to take advantage of that trend.

Starting in the early 1990s, data were collected annually from mainly U.S. supply leaders attending Michigan State University's Executive Supply Chain Management seminar. Analysis of this data has revealed a set of trends and changes that have affected most industries over the last 15 years:

- Supply organizations have assumed responsibility for strategic and externally focused supply activities.
- Purchasing and supply management's scope has expanded.
- Companies have drastically reduced the number of tier one suppliers they maintain.
- The use of longer-term contracting has increased dramatically.
- Companies are more willing to commit resources to develop supplier performance capabilities.
- Executive management's perception of supply management has increased.
- Higher-level outsourcing is moving suppliers up the value creation stream.
- Early supplier involvement, while increasing, still must become more commonplace.
- External suppliers have become an important source of product and process technology.
- The measurement of supplier and supply management performance has increased.
- Supply management has become a globally coordinated activity.

- Shorter cycle time times and supply chain flexibility have become competitive necessities.

While later chapters discuss many of these items in greater detail, a presentation of four of these changes will illustrate the kind of thinking that supply leaders should apply.

Supply Organizations Have Assumed Responsibility for Strategic and Externally Focused Supply Activities. Supply management organizations are increasingly getting out of the business of managing day-to-day operational and tactical transactions. Over the last 15 years a shift toward strategic and externally focused supply activities and away from operational duties has become quite clear.

At many organizations transaction management is now the responsibility of individual site buyers, internal customers, or materials management groups. During the 1990s we began to witness a fairly dramatic reduction in the activities that were considered part of the purchasing or supply management domain. Activities such as inventory control, receiving and shipping, distribution planning, production control, and material releasing all saw noticeable responsibility shifts away from the purchasing group.

By getting out of the materials management and low-value procurement business, supply organizations should be able to focus attention on those areas that will lead to more significant paybacks. Most supply groups are divesting themselves of the 20 percent of expenditures that have consumed 80 percent of their time and effort and instead focusing on the 20 percent of suppliers that provide 80 percent of total requirements. Making this shift requires an entirely different set of supply activities and skill sets.

What does this shift mean for supply leaders? First, supply leaders must recognize that getting out of the transaction business is not as easy as it sounds. It is usually supply management's responsibility to develop and then manage the systems and tools that allow internal users to obtain low-value goods and services. These approaches may include procurement card programs, local purchase orders systems, and online ordering tools. Second, and this may be the biggest challenge related to this change, supply leaders must work hard to obtain or develop the human resources that can transition from transaction management to supply management. These are two different worlds, requiring very different roles and responsibilities. Finally, supply leaders must have a vision of where they want to go once they are no longer burdened with day-to-day transactions.

Purchasing and Supply Management's Scope Has Expanded. The scope or reach of supply management has expanded dramatically over the last 15 years. As a concept, scope has several dimensions. The first refers to how purchasing groups see themselves. Very few purchasing groups referred to themselves as supply organizations 15 years ago. Now this term, as defined in Chapter 1, means something specific and is used by many leading companies. Purchasing has evolved from a functional activity into a cross-functional and even cross-organizational process.

Supply groups have also taken on more responsibility for managing purchase categories than was previously the case, further expanding their scope. Compared with 15 years ago, supply groups are more involved in managing all kinds of purchases besides direct materials, including inbound and outbound transportation, travel, health care, indirect purchases, construction and capital equipment, and other miscellaneous service categories. As an example of this expanded scope, in the mid-1990s the purchasing group at UPS controlled only 15 percent of the company's total expenditures. Today that figure is almost 80 percent.

The third dimension involves the responsibilities that have become part of the supply management domain. International supply management, involvement with new product development, commodity management, inbound and outbound transportation management, and strategic purchase planning are increasingly part of supply management's area of operation. Almost 12 percent of supply organizations in 1990 said they had responsibility for international supply management, for example, while over 50 percent said they had responsibility in 2000. This figure has surely continued its climb.

What does an expanded scope mean for supply leaders? An expanded scope requires that supply leaders develop the human and systems capabilities to manage a wide range of purchase requirements. While we may be good at buying widgets, are we as good at sourcing supplier-engineered systems, worldwide service contracts, or even the corporate jet? Also, do supply leaders have the vision, organizational visibility, and resources to expand the scope of purchasing and supply management?

Companies Have Drastically Reduced the Number of Tier One Suppliers They Maintain. One of the most critical prerequisites for pursuing advanced supply strategies is reducing the supply base to a reasonable size. For most U.S. firms this has meant a drastic reduction in the number of tier one suppliers they maintain. It is simply not feasible to develop close working relationships with 5,000 suppliers. The best a buyer can hope for is to efficiently manage the thousands of transactions that move across the supply chain daily. The need to eliminate supply chain variability and gain pricing advantages from larger volumes are also strong motivators for reducing the size of the supply base. Many U.S. supply organizations have drastically adjusted the size of their supply base over the last 15 years, some by as much as 90 percent.

What does a drastically reduced number of tier one suppliers mean for supply leaders? First, it means they must be able to lead a process that guarantees a massive amount of change. Next, they must work to develop measurement systems that accurately quantify supplier performance. It would be a shame to keep suppliers in the supply base that are not the best performers. Third, they must develop strategies for working closer with the remaining suppliers. And finally, they must be willing to commit the time and resources to bring even better suppliers into the supply base. Supply base reduction does not have to mean staying the course with a smaller group of current suppliers. And if new suppliers are brought into the fold, then supply leaders must be comfortable with managing the supplier switching process.

The Use of Longer-Term Contracting Has Grown Dramatically. During the early 1990s few supply organizations engaged in longer-term contracting with suppliers. The supply model of the day featured adversarial relationships, frequent supplier switching, and short-term agreements. This began to change as supply organizations reduced their supply base to a manageable level with less year-to-year supplier switching. Remaining suppliers often received longer-term supply agreements. Today, an important metric is the percent of total purchases under longer-term agreements.

What does an increased willingness to enter into longer-term supply agreements mean for supply leaders? First, supply leaders must develop the negotiating skills of their people, since longer-term agreements are almost always negotiated. Longer-term agreements address a range of topics that must be articulated well during the negotiating process. Supply leaders must also develop the means to quantify the value obtained from these agreements, since longer-term agreements are no guarantee of better performance. Next, supply leaders must be able to transition their organization away from purchase order and transaction management and toward contract and relationship management. And finally, supply leaders must understand how to involve different sites and locations during the contracting process, since longer-term agreements often represent company-wide interests.

If the reader agrees that the changes and trends presented here are reasonable, then a constructive exercise would be to assemble your supply team to evaluate these or whatever changes and trends your group feels are important. Part of the supply leadership imperative is understanding and then taking advantage of the changes and trends that are affecting supply management.

CHARACTERISTICS OF LEADING SUPPLY ORGANIZATIONS

What are the characteristics of companies that truly operate at the top of their supply management game? What do leading companies do to separate themselves from the pack? Table 2.1 summarizes a set of characteristics that define strategic supply management leadership. These characteristics are not the result of an overactive imagination. They have been identified through executive focus groups, quantitative research projects, interviews with supply executives, extensive visits to companies, and reliable reports in the public domain. The items in this table consistently emerge as characteristics of leading supply organizations. Organizations that relate highly to the items in Table 2.1 will be hard to beat.

One advantage of this table is that supply leaders can compare their organization against these characteristics. These items can be evaluated against a five- or seven-point scale where one endpoint is "highly disagree" while the other endpoint is "highly agree." Even though these endpoints are not too objective (what one person "agrees" to may not be the same as what another person perceives) this exercise is often valuable because it encourages discussion across a broad range of topics. Individual items can also be weighted to reflect their relative importance.

Table 2.1 Characteristics of Leading Supply Management Organizations

- Supply leaders promote teamwork, risk taking, and innovation.
- Supply leaders demand ethical treatment of suppliers.
- Suppliers are involved early in new product and process development.
- Strategic alliances with critical supply chain members are fully developed.
- Supplier development activities lead to continuous supply chain improvements.
- An effective supplier evaluation and selection process is in place.
- Centrally coordinated commodity teams manage a major portion of total purchases.
- Future supply leaders are identified and targeted for development early in their career.
- Total expenditures are calculated and segmented into commodities or purchase groups.
- Supply strategies are developed that match the strategy to the requirement.
- Global sourcing strategies are in place that coordinate common requirements, processes, designs, technologies, and suppliers across worldwide locations.
- Executive-to-executive interaction routinely occurs with key suppliers.
- Supply leaders measure the impact of supply initiatives on corporate indicators.
- Major supply decisions are based on total cost rather than unit price.
- External benchmarking is pursued, with findings shared across the supply organization.
- Electronic systems are in place to streamline the procurement process and to remove transactions cost.
- A quantified set of supply goals directly support business goals.
- Longer-term agreements are negotiated with select suppliers to provide value that shorter-term contracts do not provide.
- The procurement organization is on par with other functional groups in terms of professionalism, training, compensation, resources, organizational reporting, and career opportunities.
- Supply personnel are colocated as necessary with internal customers.
- A central data warehouse provides critical supply information to all buying centers.
- A chief procurement officer reports regularly to the executive leadership team.
- A set of supply practices and policies is in place that reduces redundancy and promotes best practices.
- An executive steering committee establishes a company-wide supply management vision.
- Supplier relationships are actively managed at the appropriate organizational level.

These characteristics can also help supply organizations perform a gap analysis. A gap represents the difference between where we currently operate compared to where we would like to operate. For example, let's say supply managers are evaluating how well their organization identifies future supply leaders for development early in their careers. On a seven-point scale where 1 = *not very well* and 7 = *extremely well* at identifying future leaders, the consensus across the supply group is that the organization currently scores a 3 out of 7. Furthermore, let's say the group feels the importance of this item is a 6 out of 7 where 1 = *not important* and 7 = *extremely important*. The gap across the two scales is 6 − 3, or 3. These items can be ranked according to the magnitude of their gaps. Supply leaders can then develop plans to close any gaps.

IDENTIFYING THE SUPPLY LEADERS

Have you ever wondered what companies are strategic supply management leaders? Wonder no more. Each year *Purchasing* magazine selects a company to receive its prestigious Medal of Professional Excellence award. The article that accompanies the award provides excellent detail about what these winners are doing to earn this recognition. Table 2.2 provides a history of the Medal of Professional Excellence winners since the inception of the award.

An evaluation of the winners leads to several conclusions. Except for one company, all the winners are from manufacturing. This should not come as a surprise, since Chapter 1 revealed that manufacturing companies usually commit a higher percentage of revenue to external suppliers. The companies on this list are also generally larger in terms of sales. These companies not only have a need for supply management, they also have the resources to support their efforts. An analysis of the write-ups for each winner also reveals they have focused on the four supply management enablers presented in Chapters 3 to 6. Leading companies understand the importance of building the foundation that supports the development of supply management strategies. Next, it is noteworthy how similar the winners are, even though they come from different industries, in their approaches to strategic supply management. This supports a point made in the first chapter that supply management approaches are often transferable across industries. Finally, the winners can point to tangible improvements from their efforts. Supply leaders at these companies know that activity must lead to accomplishment.

One of the best sources of public domain information about supply management leaders is *Purchasing* magazine's Web site (www.purchasing.com). This user-friendly site contains a wealth of best practices, company examples, and the ability to search *Purchasing* magazine's extensive archives. Many online articles also contain links to other related topics or information about particular companies or by

Table 2.2 Purchasing Magazine Medal of Professional Excellence Winners

Year	Winner
1984	General Electric
1985	Xerox
1986	Alcoa
1987	Chrysler
1988	Black & Decker
1989	NCR
1990	Ford
1991	Motorola
1992	Hewlett-Packard
1993	Intel
1994	Tennant
1995	Honda
1996	Sun Microsystems
1997	AlliedSignal
1998	AMR
1999	IBM
2000	Harley-Davidson
2001	Deere
2002	Lucent
2003	Cessna
2004	Hewlett-Packard
2005	Rockwell Collins
2006	United Technologies

Source: *Purchasing* magazine

a certain author. It is well worth the supply manager's time to become familiar with this site. For the broader domain of supply chain management, *Inbound Logistics* and *Supply Chain Management Review* are highly recommended resources.

A second source when identifying possible supply leaders is *IndustryWeek's* Best Plant winners. While this competition does not focus exclusively on supply management, the companies that win are often good benchmark candidates. Some of the metrics that *IndustryWeek* uses are supply related, and many of the initiatives these companies have put in place would not be possible without a supportive supply base. Try pursuing on-site supplier-managed inventory or just-in-time deliveries with suppliers that do not particularly enjoy working with your company. Achieving parts-per-million defect levels in the single digits or consistently meeting customer delivery dates is also a stretch if upstream suppliers are not performing anywhere near those levels.

A third source of information is the *Institute for Supply Management* Web site (www.ism.ws). The ISM publishes its *Practix* series that highlights innovative supply management approaches. The site also includes links to *CAPS Research* and its vast array of focused studies. And recently the institute created the R. Gene Richter Awards for Leadership and Innovation in Supply Management. Awards will be given annually to companies within four categories:

- *Process.* Company submissions relate to leadership and innovation in transforming a supply-related process (recent winners are Johnson & Johnson and KLA-Tencor).
- *Technology.* Company submissions relate to an innovation where technology was the key driver and source of substantial contribution to organizational success (recent winners are Fluor Hanford and Rockwell Collins)
- *People.* Company submissions relate to an innovation in attracting, retaining, developing, or managing human capital to make a substantial improvement in supply's contribution to organizational success (recent winner is BP).
- *Organization.* Company submissions relate to the structure and organization of the supply process and function (recent winner is DaimlerChrysler).

A characteristic of an effective supply leader is a recognition that many good ideas reside outside of his or her firm. And today there is simply no excuse for not knowing how leading companies are pursuing strategic supply management. Those companies that believe they have nothing to learn or think they are the best at everything are destined for decline. The landscape is littered with arrogant companies and civilizations that felt they had nothing to learn or believed they would always be at the top. A willingness to humbly learn and reinvent oneself is very different from believing we have cornered the market on wisdom.

PROFILE OF A SUPPLY LEADER

Imagine being part of a company that experienced one of the sharpest and quickest declines in U.S. industrial history. Imagine further that financial analysts were betting against your company's very survival. For Lucent Technologies (now part of Alcatel-Lucent), some poor technology decisions, a severe market downturn after Y2K, and a worldwide telecommunications slump combined to make this scenario painfully real. For Lucent, survival demanded some radical changes.

An area ripe for change involved Lucent's vast worldwide supply chain.[5] The company's global supply model featured different buying centers acting with minimal coordination. The company practiced decentralized manufacturing, purchasing, and inventory management. Six different organizations, for example, purchased comparable integrated circuits. In a company where every dollar counts, changing the way the supply network was managed became a competitive necessity.

Enter Jose Mejia, then president of Supply Chain Networks at Lucent Technologies. Under his vision and leadership, Lucent implemented an array of progressive initiatives and changes. Moving procurement from a junior role, Mejia became one of the four key operational leaders of Lucent's business. The company's chief operating officer goes as far to say that the focal point for driving improvement at the company has been the supply chain organization.

Under Mejia's leadership, the supply chain organization put in place an impressive set of changes that have helped the company weather some tough times. One of Meija's first steps was to drastically reduce the size of Lucent's supply base, a common step at most U.S. firms as they make their transition toward strategic supply management. Previously, more than 1,000 suppliers accounted for less than 40 percent of Lucent's total purchase expenditures. Around 60 suppliers now account for 80 percent of total expenditures.

Mejia also created centrally coordinated commodity teams and charged them with developing strategies for about 70 purchase categories. Cross-functional teams are responsible for identifying the best suppliers and strategies for their commodity groups. Besides the benefits achieved through leveraged contracts, these coordinated strategies have allowed Lucent to enter the marketplace as a single entity rather than as separate buying centers.

Perhaps the crown jewel of Lucent's supply chain organization is its profit margin forecasting model. This model forecasts profit margins for products one year out. The tool considers demand, future material costs, labor costs, and other cost categories that impact margins. This model is so valuable that when Lucent's CEO needs to know the profit margins on a product, she calls the supply chain group.

Relationship management is also a critical part of Lucent's supply model. The company has created the position of global supplier relationship manager to represent suppliers inside Lucent and represent Lucent to the suppliers. Meija formally defined the responsibilities of this role, including serving as the "owner" of a supplier relationship, managing relationships using a performance improvement plan, compiling and monitoring supplier scorecards, working with cross-company teams to improve performance, working with suppliers to set the direction of technology, and writing and managing alliance agreements.

What else have the supply leaders at Lucent done to demonstrate supply leadership? The company relies extensively on supplier scorecards to manage performance, looking at supply continuity, the quality of the relationship, technology leadership, total cost, and quality improvement. Lucent also conducts supplier suggestion workshops that follow a seven-step process; shares information with suppliers, including technology roadmaps; and involves suppliers early in product design. The latter allows suppliers to influence final product design, help manage product costs, and invest in technology that supports Lucent's requirement.

The results from these efforts have been impressive. Lucent's supply chain networks group has helped the company increase its margins from the low teens to almost 25 percent, reduce inventory levels by over 65 percent, and reduce component costs by about half. Some attribute Lucent's very survival to the success of the supply chain organization.

None of these changes would have been possible without a strong centralized supply organization headed by a leader who understands how to create value where very little existed previously. And while skeptics could point to the company's overall difficulties as a reason not to recognize it as a supply leader, others will note that the company might not exist today if it weren't for its progressive supply leadership, a leadership that will be further tested as it integrates its supply chain operations within a new corporate structure called Alcatel-Lucent and experiences the inevitable changing of personnel that accompanies mergers and acquisitions.

CONCLUDING THOUGHTS

Succeeding as a supply leader requires strategic thinking, tactical execution, business knowledge, and the ability to communicate with, motivate, and lead people.[6] And since strategic supply management is about new ways of doing business, managing the change process is also essential. As we progress through this book, it is critical to understand that underlying any successful supply management initiative will be supply leaders who are capable of demonstrating supply leadership.

SUMMARY OF KEY CHAPTER POINTS

- Strategic supply management is not possible without leaders who have the vision, will, and determination to create world-class supply organizations. A major challenge is developing a generation of leaders who understand how to make supply management their company's most critical core competency.
- Succeeding as a supply leader requires strategic thinking, tactical execution, business knowledge, and the ability to motivate and lead people.
- A supply leader who demonstrates leadership is any person who influences individuals and groups within an organization, helps them in the establishment of goals, and guides them toward the achievement of those goals, thereby allowing them to be effective.

- Multiple levels of supply leadership exist—an organization as a supply leader, supply executives as leaders, supply manager as leaders, and buyers and team members as leaders.
- Perhaps the most tangible evidence of supply leadership is the development of strategies and approaches that produce consistent results.
- Over the last 15 years we have witnessed some major changes as they relate to purchasing and supply management. It is critical for supply managers to understand why a change or trend is occurring, determine its effect on the supply organization, and identify how to take advantage of that trend.
- A characteristic of an effective leader is a recognition that many good ideas reside outside his or her company. Those companies that believe they have nothing new to learn from others or believe they are the best at everything are destined for decline.
- Not all organizations should endorse strategic supply management at a comparable level. Part of being an effective supply leader is recognizing the supply management model that best fits a company's needs.

ENDNOTES

1. As reported in the foreword to R. D. Nelson, P. E. Moody, and J. Stegner, *The Purchasing Machine: How the Top Ten Companies Use Best Practices to Manage their Supply Chain* (New York: The Free Press, 2001); by and from a personal conversation with Gene Richter.
2. A. Nahavandi, *The Art and Science of Leadership* (Upper Saddle River, NJ: Prentice-Hall, 2003), 4.
3. Nahavandi, 15.
4. As reported in *The Express-Times*, Easton, PA, December 3, 2006, D6.
5. As reported by J. Carbone, "Lucent's Supply Chain Focus Fattens Margins," *Purchasing* 135, no. 15 (September 19, 2002): 21–29.
6. W. Fello, "Today's Leadership Needs," *Inside Supply Management* 17, no. 5 (May 2006): 10.

CREATING THE RIGHT SUPPLY ORGANIZATION

Several years ago the executive leaders at a household furnishings company hired a consultant to help them understand why the team they had assembled to improve supply chain performance failed to achieve much. As the consultant worked with the team members, he could not recall seeing a team so demoralized. Isn't teamwork supposed to energize employees? Aren't teams the foundation around which future organizations will be built? What had gone so wrong here?

It quickly became evident what went wrong. Some members admitted they were unable to view supply chain issues beyond their limited functional perspectives. Others said they did not understand how to work on a cross-functional team, having received no special training about how to work collectively. Still others complained that functional managers challenged the team's authority to address issues that "encroached" on their functional turfs. Certain members noted, somewhat discreetly, that executive management was not all that supportive after the team was formed. A few choice comments were even directed at the team leader when he was not in the room. So, what went wrong? Well, just about everything. To make matters worse, these members now have a well-formed view of using cross-functional teams: We tried teams—and they don't work!

When thinking about the many ways that companies achieve competitive advantage from their supply management efforts, we often hear about exciting initiatives involving real-time information systems, early involvement of suppliers, and the development of global sourcing strategies. Rarely mentioned, and often not thought about all that much, is how the more mundane topic of organizational design promotes or interferes with supply management performance.

This chapter explores a number of topics related to creating the right supply organization. We first present the design features that companies put in place as they attempt to achieve their supply objectives. Given their widespread use, the second section examines the use of teams. Next, some broad observations are made about designing an effective supply organization. The chapter concludes with an examination of how one company uses organizational design to support its global purchasing and engineering process.

DESIGNING A SUPPLY ORGANIZATION

As the opening example illustrates, neglecting how supply organizations are designed to conduct work can have serious consequences. *Organizational design* refers to the process of assessing and selecting the structure and formal system of communication, division of labor, coordination, control, authority, and responsibility required to achieve organizational goals.[1] An organization's design, including the specific features put in place to support that design, is much more than what an organizational chart can ever depict. Its early placement in this book reflects the importance of organizational design as a critical supply management enabler.

There are several ways to think about how to design an effective supply organization. The first considers the features that firms currently and expect to emphasize. While this is insightful, it does not necessarily tell us that the design features in place are effective. An assumption is made that a feature is used because it is the result of a well-thought-out analysis. A second way considers those features that correlate with the attainment of supply objectives. The following sections look at both ways. The conclusions presented here are based on research involving over 160 firms.[2]

Most Widely Used Design Features

Table 3.1 presents the most widely used organizational design features that medium and larger firms rely on as they pursue their supply management objectives. While smaller firms also have in place various features, they do so at a much lower level of emphasis. Medium and larger firms differ from smaller firms in terms of scope, complexity, and available resources. They are much more likely to have operations that are worldwide rather than local or regional, have more organizational levels covering a wider array of businesses, and have broader and more diverse product lines. Larger firms emphasize some design features simply to coordinate a globally complex organization. These firms are also more likely to have greater access to the human and financial resources that allow them to pursue certain features.

Table 3.1 Top 10 Organizational Design Features

Medium Firms	Larger Firms
Specific individuals assigned responsibility for managing supplier relationships (4.77)	Specific individuals assigned responsibility for managing supplier relationships (5.09)
Physical colocation between procurement and internal customers (4.30)	Centrally coordinated commodity teams that develop and implement company-wide supply strategies (4.89)
Centrally coordinated commodity teams that develop and implement company-wide supply strategies (4.22)	Cross-functional teams that manage the procurement and supply process (4.75)
Lead buyers to manage non-centrally coordinated items (4.18)	Lead buyers to manage non-centrally coordinated items (4.68)
Regular strategy/performance presentations by the CPO to the president or CEO (4.18)	A higher-level CPO who has a procurement- and supply-related title (4.56)
Physical colocation between procurement and technical personnel (4.05)	Physical colocation between procurement personnel and internal customers (4.55)
New product teams that include procurement and supply representatives (4.02)	New product teams that formally include procurement and supply representatives (4.47)
A higher-level chief procurement officer who has a procurement and supply-related title (4.02)	Regular strategy/performance review presentations by the CPO to the president or CEO (4.45)
A corporate level steering committee that oversees company-wide supply initiatives (3.89)	A shared services model that coordinates common activities or processes across locations (4.38)
Formal strategy coordination and review sessions between functional groups (3.71)	Physical colocation between procurement and technical personnel (4.35)

1= Do not use, 4 = Use somewhat, 7 = Use extensively
Source: Robert J. Trent, *Organizational Design Research Study*, 2004.

Physical colocation, the widespread use of teams, a higher-level chief procurement officer (CPO) who makes regular strategy presentations to the president or CEO, and specific individuals assigned to manage supplier relationships are all features that medium and larger firms have in common. Larger firms, in an effort to overcome inefficiencies and duplication, also rely more highly on a shared services model that coordinates common needs across locations.

Features that are expected to become a more important part of the formal design over the next several years include *project teams that work on specific supply tasks* and *new product development teams that include suppliers as members.*

Table 3.2 Correlation between Design Features and Design Effectiveness

Medium Firms		Larger Firms	
Regular strategy/performance presentations by the CPO to the president or CEO	.661	Regular strategy/performance presentations by the CPO to the president or CEO	.561
Physical colocation between procurement and internal customers	.604	Centrally coordinated commodity teams that develop and implement company-wide supply strategies	.498
Cross-functional teams that manage the procurement and supply process	.515	An executive position responsible for coordinating supply chain activities	.493
Lead buyers to manage non-centrally coordinated items	.485	Cross-functional teams that manage the procurement and supply process	.491
Regular strategy/performance review presentations by the CPO to the board of directors	.483	Formal supply strategy coordination and review sessions between units or divisions	.481
Formal supply strategy coordination and review sessions between units or divisions	.479	An executive buyer-supplier council or committee that coordinates supply chain activities with suppliers	.418
N = 46 firms		**N = 65 firms**	

Source: Robert J. Trent, *Organizational Design Research Study*, 2004.

Larger firms also expect *formal strategy coordination and review sessions between supply units and with other functional groups* and the *formal separation of strategic and tactical supply responsibilities* to be more emphasized.

Features That Correlate with Supply Effectiveness

A second (and perhaps better) way to look at organizational design is to correlate the design features with design effectiveness. In other words, if a supply manager says her company's organizational design is effective, what are the features that are used?

Table 3.2 presents the features for medium and larger firms that correlate the highest with designs that help achieve our supply objectives. Although not shown, smaller firms view regular strategy and performance reviews by the CPO to the CEO and board of directors as an important part of design effectiveness, although the correlation is much lower than what appears in this table. Physical colocation between procurement and marketing personnel is also important to smaller firms that say their current design is effective.

Interestingly, the most used design feature from Table 3.1, assigning responsibility for managing supplier relationships to specific individuals, is not part of the features that correlate highly with design effectiveness. Chapter 11 will explore

Table 3.3 Creating the Right Supply Organization

- A corporate-level steering committee guides global procurement and supply initiatives.
- Regular strategy coordination and review sessions occur between business units and functional groups.
- Centrally coordinated commodity teams have responsibility for developing supply strategies.
- A chief procurement officer regularly makes strategy presentations to the executive committee and board of directors.
- IPOs have been established to support supply efforts across different regions.
- Specific individuals are assigned responsibility for managing key supplier relationships, including strategic supplier alliances.
- Cross-functional teams work directly with suppliers to develop performance capabilities.
- Lead buyers or site-based experts are designated to manage noncommodity team items.
- Supply personnel are colocated with internal customers as required, including operations, engineering, and marketing.
- Supply managers and suppliers are actively involved with new product development teams.
- On-site suppliers manage routine inventory requirements, including ordering, replenishment, and inventory control.
- A formal group is responsible for demand and supply planning.
- A shared services model is used to coordinate and manage common activities across business units.
- Procurement and supply personnel are separated according to operational and strategic responsibilities.
- An executive position is responsible for coordinating and integrating key supply chain activities from suppliers through customers.
- Global matrix organizational structures are used to achieve full integration across global locations and product lines.
- An executive buyer-supplier council meets regularly with suppliers to coordinate strategies and long-range plans.

how to manage supplier relationships effectively. Table 3.3 summarizes in words instead of data the profile of what a leading supply management organization should look like. All three of these tables provide insight into the kinds of design features that supply organizations rely on.

TEAMS AND STRATEGIC SUPPLY MANAGEMENT

U.S. companies have become enamored with teams, often for good reason, and the use of teams to support supply management is widespread. Take a look again at Tables 3.1 and 3.2 to appreciate how many design features relate to groups or teams. Table 3.4 provides additional examples where teams and groups are used to support strategic supply management.

Table 3.4 Examples of Groups and Teams That Support Supply Management Objectives

Group or Team	Description
Customer advisory boards	An executive-level group that brings suppliers, customers, and the OEM/producer together to share information such as end customer requirements and expectations
Buyer-supplier councils	An executive-level group that brings together the OEM/producer and a rotating group of suppliers to share information such as product forecasts and product development plans
Executive steering committees	A cross-functional, executive-level group that has responsibility for overseeing centrally led supply initiatives and objectives
Commodity management teams	Cross-functional teams that develop commodity strategies with responsibility for supplier selection decisions and relationship management
Buyer-seller improvement teams	Cross-organizational teams that focus on improvement opportunities and projects between the buyer and seller
Value analysis/value engineering teams	Cross-functional teams that have responsibility for systematically analyzing the relationship between product/service function and cost
New product teams with purchasing and supplier involvement	Cross-functional teams that have responsibility for developing new products and services with purchasing and supplier support
Supplier development teams	Cross-functional teams that have responsibility for managing supplier performance improvement opportunities

Anyone who says the use of teams guarantees better results should venture into the real world more often. High-performing teams, in theory, should deliver benefits that outweigh their cost. Conversely, poorly designed and managed teams can waste the time and energy of members, enforce lower rather than higher performance norms, engage in destructive conflict, and make notoriously bad decisions. Teams can also exploit, stress, and frustrate members—often at the same time.[3] Supply management teams are not immune from team dysfunctions.

Companies often face some serious barriers when using teams, and it's important for supply managers to understand these barriers. Organizations can create barriers to teaming simply by how they structure their use. While a few organizations have created supply teams staffed by full-time members, teams with part-time members are still the most prevalent way teams are structured. Members who provide a part-time commitment maintain their existing functional responsibilities while taking on additional team-related duties. This often leads to time conflicts.

A second hurdle is a failure to recognize and reward the effort that teams put forth toward their assignments. Outdated reward structures that focus on traditional or functional activities while ignoring the time a member commits to a team are still a common reason why teams fail. The results of various surveys reveal that many companies have yet to revamp their compensation programs to increase the emphasis given to team participation and performance. Members often express frustration at their organization's inability to evaluate and reward individual and team performance.

A third hurdle relates to the U.S. national culture. By nature, the United States is not a group-oriented society, particularly compared with a country such as Japan. While some cultures place group needs above individual needs, this is generally not the case within the United States. Team members may perceive assignments to be a drain on their time or feel that working on a team stifles their individual creativity and personal recognition. Some team members find that a shift away from individualism is uncomfortable and threatening.

While these three hurdles are important, they certainly do not represent an exhaustive list of what can affect a supply management team. In fact, a host of barriers may adversely affect any specific team that pursues a supply chain objective. The successful use of teams requires identifying potential barriers and then acting to minimize their effect.

The use of teams has become so widespread that supply managers must have an understanding of the nuances surrounding their use. While the issues related to using teams are not unique to supply management, their extensive use to support supply objectives demands thoughtful answers to some important questions. Asking and answering the right questions should increase the probability of using teams successfully, which the following sections address.

Have We Considered Team Planning Issues?

Effective planning requires the careful consideration of many issues at the organizational level. Figure 3.1 summarizes the more important planning topics that supply managers should consider when using teams. Effective planning correlates directly with effective teaming.

Selecting the Right Task. Even though teams will remain a popular design option, it is not the case that all supply tasks will benefit from the use of teams. In fact, teams are cost-prohibitive and should be used selectively. While no rules exist

	YES	NO

Identify Appropriate Team Assignments

Do assignments justify the use of teams? ☐ ☐

Has the proper team model been identified (part-time vs. full-time and project vs. continuous)? ☐ ☐

Does executive and functional management support the use of a team for the assignment? ☐ ☐

Form Work Team and Select Qualified Members and Leader

Have core versus as-needed members been identified? ☐ ☐

Do selected members have the proper skills, time, and commitment to support the work team? ☐ ☐

Have team sponsors identified and selected a qualified team leader? ☐ ☐

Are customers or suppliers part of the team if required? ☐ ☐

Do members understand their formal team roles? ☐ ☐

Determine Member Training Requirements

Have team member training requirements been assessed? ☐ ☐

Is required training available on a timely basis? ☐ ☐

Identify Resource Requirements

Are resources provided or available to support the team's task? ☐ ☐

Determine Team Authority Levels

Have team authority levels for the team been determined? ☐ ☐

Have team authority levels been communicated across the organization? ☐ ☐

Establish Team Performance Goals

Has the team established performance goals that align with the team's mission? ☐ ☐

Determine How to Measure and Reward Participation and Performance

Are approaches and systems in place that objectively assess team performance and member contribution? ☐ ☐

Do reporting linkages exist to team or executive sponsors? ☐ ☐

Is team performance effectively linked to performance reward systems? ☐ ☐

Develop Team Charters

Has a formal charter been developed that details team mission, tasks, broad objectives, etc.? ☐ ☐

Has the charter been communicated across the organization? ☐ ☐

Figure 3.1 Supply management team planning guide.

to tell us if teams are the right design option, teams are logical when an assignment, project, or task directly supports the attainment of higher-level objectives. Teams are also suitable when decisions require buy-in from different groups or locations or when organizations face complex or large-scale assignments that no single individual, function, or location can manage effectively. A team may also be appropriate if the value-add from a collective effort exceeds the expense of that effort.

Selecting the Right Team Members. Individuals for team membership should satisfy certain criteria. Unfortunately, member selection is often by convenience rather than objective assessment, increasing the probability that a group is unqualified or incompatible. Perhaps most importantly, members should have knowledge and experience that is relevant to the task at hand. They should also have the time to commit to team assignment—something that can be a challenge when using part-time teams with members drawn from different functional groups. Members should also demonstrate a level of interpersonal skill that enables them to work with other individuals on a team.

Members should also be able to take a broader rather than a narrower view of the supply organization. This is critical for supply teams that must assume a worldwide rather than local or regional perspective. Members should also have no personal agenda that conflicts with team agendas. While it is often difficult to determine if members have ulterior motives or agendas, these agendas, when present, quickly undermine team morale and effectiveness.

Providing Training. It is a misconception to believe that members naturally know how to operate on a team or have the skill set to be effective in a group. Supply leaders should assess whether employees have the skills to work collectively. Few organizations, however, evaluate the skills that team members have or will require. Training, when offered, is usually generic and applied to a larger group. While training can occur at any time during the teaming process, proactive organizations assess training and development needs early. Possible training areas include managing conflict, managing projects, setting goals, providing feedback, and using creative and critical thinking skills.

Making Resources Available. A set of important but often overlooked variables includes the resources that help translate team member abilities and motivation into performance. A study of cross-functional sourcing teams found the availability of resources to be the second most important predictor of team success behind effective leadership. The resources required by a team are a function of its assignment. Supplier evaluation teams will find that budget and time are critical for supporting site visits while teams that are responsible for developing global contracts will rely heavily on data. Access to the right resources reduces the likelihood that team performance will suffer because of inattention to this important issue.

Addressing Team Authority Levels. A potential area of conflict when not addressed early concerns a team's decision-making authority. Whether explicitly stated or not, teams usually have varying degrees of authority across four dimensions. The first dimension, *scheduling authority*, is a lower level of authority that allows a team to schedule meetings without others approving the decision. The second dimension, *selection authority*, allows a team some latitude to select members as required. Internal *process authority*, a third dimension, allows teams to manage internal activities, including their budget and goal setting, without direct management approval. Finally, *external decision-making authority* allows a team to bind an organization through its decisions. Many teams do not understand the limits placed on their authority because we ignore this issue.

Research suggests that supply teams with higher levels of internal process authority often realize the outcomes sought from their use. Qualified teams should also have external decision-making authority when a task requires decisions rather than recommendations. If the reason to use a team is to improve decision making, then a competent group should have clearly defined internal and external decision-making authority.

Other Planning Issues. Supply leaders should also create a formal team charter. This conveys a team's mission and responsibilities, identifies appropriate authority levels, and identifies as-needed members who will support the core team. Perhaps most importantly, a charter provides organizational authority for a team to operate—something that is critical when addressing supply chain issues that cross functional boundaries (refer back to the opening story to this chapter). Planning is also the time to articulate executive performance expectations and identify linkages to the performance measurement and reward systems.

Are the Right Individuals Selected as Team Leaders?

While asking if the right individuals are positioned as team leaders could certainly be addressed in the previous question, this issue is so important that it warrants special attention. Researchers have studied group leaders for many years and have reached consensus that leaders disproportionately affect group effort, cohesion, goal selection, and goal attainment. Furthermore, the formal leader is in a position to see to it that team responsibilities are important, challenging, recognized, and rewarded. Only a formal team leader can perform many of the responsibilities associated with leadership.

Research with over 100 supply management teams revealed that the relationship between leader effectiveness and team effectiveness to be the strongest of any variable studied.[5] This study also found, unfortunately, that few individuals have the qualifications, experience, or training to assume team leadership responsibilities. Failing to staff this position with qualified individuals will, more often than not, undermine team success. Ensuring that teams have qualified leaders must become a priority for supply management executives.

Should Suppliers Be Part of Our Supply Teams?

An objective of any supply organization should be to develop closer working relationships with key suppliers. When we think about the many ways that integration across the supply chain can occur, supplier involvement on teams may be one of the better options. Most organizations have at least an implicit appreciation of the potential benefits that supplier involvement on teams offer.

Certain research findings about supplier involvement on teams should cause supply managers to investigate this idea further. Teams that involve suppliers, for example, put forth greater effort and are more effective on average than teams that do not involve suppliers. Furthermore, teams with supplier involvement are more satisfied with the quality of information exchanged with suppliers and report fewer problems coordinating work activity between the two organizations. These same teams also report a higher reliance on suppliers to support directly the team's goals—the supplier becomes an additional resource. Finally, teams with external involvement report a higher level of supplier support across many performance areas, including cost, quality, and delivery improvements, new technology suggestions, and ways to reduce cycle times. The relationship between supplier involvement and positive team outcomes is compelling. Chapter 13 will explore the topic of early supplier involvement in more detail.

While external involvement on teams sounds attractive, and perhaps even easy, implementation can be anything but. The protection of proprietary information consistently remains an issue. A second issue is that many firms are inexperienced and uncomfortable with involving third parties in their activities. Some organizations simply are not proficient at using cross-functional teams, particularly those with external members. External involvement is probably too much to expect until they better manage their own teaming activities.

Do Our Supply Teams Establish Goals?

An important factor characterizing effective from less effective teams is the presence of objective goals. While executive managers often establish broad objectives (for example, reduce the time it takes to evaluate and select a supplier), teams should be responsible for establishing specific targets, goals, and milestones. Chapter 7 will describe the differences between objectives and goals.

Supply leaders must convey clearly the many reasons why their teams must establish goals. Strong evidence suggests that effort and performance are greater when teams develop and accept challenging goals. It is also desirable for teams to develop their own goals because they often establish more challenging goals than individuals who are external to the team. And teams with goals usually perform better than teams requested to perform their best without explicit end goals.

There are other good reasons for establishing goals. Goal setting enables feedback (and eventually rewards) as others external to the team compare progress against stated targets. The positive effect of feedback on individual and group performance is widely accepted in social psychology. Goal-directed effort is greater in teams that receive feedback about how well they are progressing. And the quality of a team's productivity increases as the feedback becomes more complete.

Supply leaders should assume ownership for developing a goal-setting process that is consistent across teams and locations. They should also require teams to report regularly about their progress to executive leaders, an activity that links goal setting and accountability. Leading organizations also post team goals and progress on an intranet so team activities and milestones are highly visible.

Do We Reward Member Participation and Team Performance?

As mentioned earlier, a hurdle to using teams is a failure to recognize and reward the effort that team members put forth toward their assignments. Positive work ceases when organizations fail to reinforce, recognize, or reward work, particularly work that is in addition to regular responsibilities or involves activities outside a team member's functional area.

Teams usually perform better when management rewards the entire team rather than providing only individual rewards. In fact, the negative effects of rewarding individual rather than team performance can be considerable. Although members surmount challenges as a group, providing only individual rewards and recognition often increases tension and competition between members.

While many types of team rewards are available, most cluster into four categories. This includes merit increases to a member's base salary, one-time monetary bonuses, organizational recognition, and nonmonetary rewards, such as tickets to events and gift certificates. Some organizations tailor rewards to specific teams or members, since individuals and teams are often motivated differently. Furthermore, the most effective rewards tend to occur at random rather than expected intervals.

Research findings are clear that group-based incentive systems positively affect team performance. Creating a strong linkage in each member's mind between effort, performance, accountability, and rewards, particularly when participation is in addition to regular job responsibilities, must be a priority for supply managers. The challenge when providing rewards is to stress the collective nature of teams while still promoting the importance of the individual members.

Using teams comes with no guarantee of better supply management performance compared with traditional work methods. If supply leaders ignore the issues that affect team success, more often than not they will wonder why the reality of using teams does not match the hype surrounding their use. But make no mistake about it—teams are not going away anytime soon.

OBSERVATIONS ABOUT ORGANIZATIONAL DESIGN

Organizational designs must evolve as firms continue their transition from traditional purchasing to strategic supply management. A number of broad observations can be made as they relate to designing an effective supply organization.

1. **A higher-level procurement officer is critical to supply management effectiveness.** While this conclusion seems intuitive, the importance of a higher-level CPO who has access to the highest executive levels is essential when pursuing strategic supply management. Furthermore, regular presentations by the CPO to the president, CEO, or board of directors also characterize an effective design.

   It's not the formal executive position per se that makes this feature important. Rather, the visibility and resources that come with having a position that is on par with other functional executives is critical. Strategic supply management will not become a reality without an executive champion who has the authority and resources to put in place a supportive organizational design. Companies that expect advantages from their organizational design must consider the importance of a higher-level supply officer as well as the reporting level of that position.

2. **Organizational size affects the type and intensity of the design features that are put in place.** Smaller, medium, and larger firms differ in terms of their scope, complexity, and available resources. As a result, they view the need for organizational design features differently. Some features that larger firms emphasize simply are not applicable to smaller firms. While some design features are common regardless of firm size, organizations also emphasize features that support their unique requirements. For medium and larger firms, this means relying on features that support coordination and inte-

gration across the supply chain. Larger firms use their organizational design to manage the complexity that comes from supporting worldwide operations.

3. **A shift toward centrally coordinated or centrally led supply management will continue.** Throughout purchasing history, we have witnessed movement between centralized and decentralized placement of authority. We are now witnessing a shift toward central control or coordination that is not likely to reverse soon, at least for some important decisions and activities. What separates this period from others is the intense cost pressure brought about by global competition. An inability to easily raise prices demands the coordination of worldwide supply activities and the consolidation of purchase volumes in an effort to minimize total supply costs.

    Supply managers should think about organizational design as a way to coordinate their activities without necessarily having to group purchasing personnel in a central location or sacrificing responsiveness to individual locations. In fact, some purchasing activities should remain at a decentralized level, particularly those involved with day-to-day materials and supply management.

    Firms should consider putting in place features that support an expected movement toward centrally led or centrally coordinated purchasing. This includes the use of centrally coordinated commodity teams, formal positions that separate strategic and tactical supply responsibilities, lead buyers to manage non-centrally coordinated items, strategy review and coordination sessions between functional groups and locations, and a higher-level CPO. These features should enable organizations to capture the benefits of a centrally led organization while avoiding the poor perception that internal users or sites often associate with central control.

4. **The use of teams will remain a popular and even growing design option.** As discussed earlier in the chapter, the use of teams is a popular and growing organizational design option. The design features that supply organizations rely on when pursuing their objectives continue to stress the use of cross-functional and cross-locational teams. However, we need to be careful here. Few studies have established a clear connection between teaming and better performance except in the area of new product development.

5. **Organizational design features may be a large part of the answer if coordination and integration across the supply chain remains a challenge.** We often think of information systems as the enabler

that promotes coordination across supply chains. If supply managers hope to achieve increased coordination and integration within and across the supply chain, then a closer look at certain design features may yield some pleasant results. Organizational design supports three kinds of integration—cross-functional, cross-locational, and cross-organizational.

Coordination across functions and organizations is becoming an increasingly important supply objective. The focus in purchasing and supply management will shift from functional coordination to managing the interfaces that purchasing and supply management has with other functional units, thus leading to "management of the white space" that is present on the organizational chart. Purchasing and supply managers will increasingly rely on organizational design features to help manage the strategic connections with other functional groups as well as across enterprise boundaries.

6. **Colocation of procurement personnel will become an increasingly important part of the organizational design.** Research reveals that physically colocating supply personnel with their internal customers will increase in use as an organizational design feature. There are some good outcomes that result when colocation works as intended:

   - Increased interaction with other functional groups
   - Enhanced role clarity and understanding
   - Development of positive internal relationships and trust
   - Faster decision making and problem solving
   - Enhanced creative thinking from working together physically
   - Early insight into internal customer needs and requirements

Supply people should gain first-hand insight into supplier performance, internal customer requirements, and capacity, material, and service needs when colocated with operating personnel. When colocated with engineering, we expect to gain insight into material specifications and new product, process, and technology requirements. When colocated with marketing, we should gain insight into demand requirements, new product ideas, and promotions and other planned shifts in demand. Colocation is not about simply working in the physical presence of other groups. Rather, it is about embedding the purchasing professional into the planning and operating systems of the colocated group.

Supply managers must consider a number of issues when considering a colocation model. One involves the amount of time to commit to colocation. Will supply professionals be colocated full-time or part-time with the other functional groups? Another issue is determining what reporting relationship best supports colocation. In a typical colocation model, the purchasing professional maintains a dotted-line relationship to the colocation group with a solid-line relationship to the purchasing or supply group.

7. **Supply organizations will shift gradually from a vertical to a horizontal perspective.** A horizontal perspective features an organization designed around supply processes, such as supplier evaluation and selection, supplier development, and new product development. The extensive use of cross-functional teams, particularly teams that feature full-time members, is one indication of this shift toward a process orientation. When organizing around processes, cross-functional participants work concurrently in an environment featuring the horizontal (i.e., cross-functional) flow of information across the supply chain.

    When shifting from a functional to a process orientation, the process rather than the functional group becomes the focal point of the organizational design. It is unlikely that firms will ever move totally away from functional groups. The disbursement of functional personnel into full-time teams would dilute the expertise and knowledge required to operate a business. The need to maintain a critical mass of functional knowledge ensures that some functional structure, albeit a diminished one, will remain. Furthermore, the dramatic changes surrounding a shift from a functional to a process perspective, also called a shift from a vertical to a horizontal design, ensure that any changes will be gradual.

8. **Separating strategic and operational activities will support the attainment of supply objectives.** Strategic and operational thinking involve two very different mind-sets and time frames. It is a challenge, if not impossible, for an individual or department to practice both types of thinking well. Given this challenge, we should expect to see a formal separation within the organizational design between strategic and operational responsibilities. An emphasis on strategic tasks and objectives is a clear indication of the growing importance of supply management. Furthermore, those responsible for taking a strategic view of supply management will increasingly take a global rather than a regional view.

    Examples of strategic activities include managing critical supply relationships, developing company-wide electronic systems, developing company-wide sourcing strategies and contracts, managing strategic supply alliances, and establishing a common supply vision. Operational or tactical activities include managing day-to-day transactions and performance issues with suppliers, sourcing items that are unique to an operating unit, generating material releases, managing accounts payable, and controlling the flow of material across the supply chain.

LINKING ORGANIZATIONAL DESIGN TO GLOBAL OBJECTIVES

Air Products and Chemicals, Inc., a U.S.-based company that designs and operates industrial gas and chemical facilities worldwide, was surprised when an internal study concluded the company must lower operating costs dramatically to remain competitive. This was due to the emergence of low-cost competitors in Asia-Pacific along with industrial buyers viewing the company's products as commodity items, both of which created extensive downward pricing pressures.

An executive review concluded that using regional design and procurement centers resulted in duplication of effort and a lack of coordination between the company's North American and European procurement and design units. A major action taken by the company was the development of a global engineering and procurement process.

In an effort to capture benefits from a global approach to design and procurement, each newly designed facility undergoes an extensive analysis between U.S. and European centers to identify areas of design commonality, standardization, and synergy. Project teams, with members from the United States and Europe working jointly, develop common specifications and global contracts that satisfy each center's needs while supporting future spare part and maintenance requirements. This process involves agreeing on a worldwide common design and then agreeing on a common supplier.

Perhaps the major reason Air Products has enjoyed success from its global process is due to the organizational design features it has put in place. This includes two steering committees to oversee the process, reliance on a globalization manager, and extensive use on teams to manage global engineering and procurement projects.

Steering Committees. Air Products has created two steering committees to support its global process: an executive steering committee and an operating steering committee. The executive steering committee consists of senior managers from engineering, procurement, and operations with finance participation as required. The committee provides the budget that supports a globalization manager's staff, along with the travel and living expenses that team members incur during meetings and supplier site visits.

The core operating committee is composed of a globalization manager, a project procurement manager, and the director of Asian sourcing. Besides meeting regularly on its own, this group also participates in a weekly teleconference meeting with the capital equipment and control system supervisors from the United States, a capital equipment supervisor from Europe, and the globalization manager's counterpart in Europe.

The operating steering committee is responsible for identifying the items to assign to global engineering and procurement teams. Furthermore, the process of identifying opportunities is continuous. The committee regularly asks for ideas regarding future projects. An operating steering committee member maintains these ideas in an online spreadsheet that can be accessed through the company's intranet. While engineering design centers and global sourcing project teams are responsible for achieving cost savings, the steering committee is responsible for tracking the savings from the global process.

Globalization Manager and Staff. Consensus exists at Air Products concerning the importance of the globalization manager, a position created specifically to oversee the global engineering and procurement process. This position reports to the vice presidents of engineering in Europe and the United States. This is an important consideration, since the two design centers must work together during global projects. The globalization manager has located his office within the procurement group at U.S. headquarters, which helps develop teamwork and trust between engineering and procurement.

The globalization manager commits a full-time effort to supporting the global process. His duties include working with the operating steering committee to identify future projects, monitoring the status and progress of projects, determining where to spend budgeted funds, approving all operating steering committee expenditures, identifying and recruiting team members for project teams, and working with teams to establish project goals and milestones. This manager's staff includes four support people.

Cross-Functional/Cross-Locational Teams. Air Products relies extensively on teams to support its global engineering and procurement process. Teams are formed and then chartered by the operating steering committee to develop global strategies. Each team has representatives from the United States and Europe participating, with two engineers and at least two buyers. The teams meet face-to-face on a regular basis. The engineers assigned to these teams work full-time to develop common specifications between design centers. The buyers generally commit a part-time effort.

Has the development of a global process supported by these design features been worthwhile? With over 100 global design and sourcing agreements in place, Air Products is averaging 20 percent in cost savings compared with regional agreements. Furthermore, worldwide design and procurement centers have better aligned their philosophies and strategies between themselves and with the company's business strategy. This process adds even additional value as supply managers work with marketing to include expected savings from in-process projects when responding to proposals from customers. Global engineering and procurement, supported by a responsive organizational design, is creating a new source of competitive advantage for a company that operates in a mature industry.

CONCLUDING THOUGHTS

The Corporate Executive Board issued a report in 2001 that concluded supply management executives must think about how their organizational structure can enable substantial improvements in performance and operational excellence. While other supply management topics certainly generate more excitement than organizational design, we should not overlook the role that an effective design plays in enhancing supply management performance. And in today's globally competitive environment, overlooking any area that has the potential to affect performance can be a serious mistake.

SUMMARY OF KEY CHAPTER POINTS

- Rarely mentioned within supply management is how organizational design promotes or interferes with performance.
- Organizational design refers to the process of assessing and selecting the structure and formal system of communication, division of labor, coordination, control, authority, and responsibility required to achieve organizational goals.
- Larger firms emphasize certain design features simply to coordinate and integrate a globally complex organization. These firms are much more likely to have operations that are worldwide, more organizational levels covering a wider array of businesses, and broader and more diverse product lines.
- U.S. managers have become enamored with teams, and the use of teams to support supply management is widespread. However, firms often face some serious barriers when using teams, and it is important for supply managers to understand these barriers.
- Using teams effectively requires evaluating a set of team planning issues, selecting the right team leader, making suppliers a part of supply teams, establishing team goals, and rewarding member participation and team performance.

- A number of broad observations can be made as they relate to the design of effective supply organizations—a higher-level procurement officer is critical to the effectiveness of strategic supply management; organizational size affects the type and intensity of the design features that are put in place; a shift toward centrally coordinated or centrally led supply management will continue to occur; the use of teams will remain a popular and even growing design option; organizational design features may be a large part of the answer if coordination and integration across the supply chain remains a challenge; colocation of procurement personnel with internal customers will become an increasingly important part of the organizational design; supply organizations will continue to shift gradually from a vertical to a horizontal perspective; and separating strategic and operational activities and authority will support the attainment of supply objectives.

ENDNOTES

1. G. Hamel and C. K. Pralahad, *Competing for the Future* (Cambridge, MA: Harvard Business School Press, 1994), as referenced in D. Hellriegel, J. W. Slocum, and R. W. Woodman, *Organizational Behavior* (Cincinnati: South-Western College Publishing, 2001), 474.
2. Material in this section is adapted from R. J. Trent, "The Use of Organizational Design Features in Purchasing and Supply Management," *The Journal of Supply Chain Management* 40, no. 3 (August 2004): 4–18.
3. J. R. Hackman, "The Design of Work Teams," Chapter 20 in *Handbook of Organizational Behavior* (Englewood Cliffs, NJ: Prentice Hall, 1987), 315–342.
4. L. H. Peters and E. J. O'Connors, "Situational Constraints and Work Outcomes: The Influences of a Frequently Overlooked Construct," *Academy of Management Review* 5, no. 3 (March 1980): 391–397.
5. R. M. Monczka, and R. J. Trent, *Cross-Functional Sourcing Team Effectiveness* (Tempe, AZ: CAPS Research, 1993).
6. R. D. Pritchard, S. D. Jones, P. L. Roth, K. K. Stuebing, and S. Ekeberg, "Effects of Group Feedback: Goal Setting, and Incentives on Organizational Productivity," *Journal of Applied Psychology* 73, no. 2 (May 1988): 337–358.
7. J. R. Carter and R. Narasimhan, "Purchasing and Supply Management: Future Directions and Trends," *International Journal of Purchasing and Materials Management* 32, no. 4 (Fall 1996): 2–12.

Web Added Value™

This book has free material available for download from the Web Added Value™ resource center at *www.jrosspub.com*

4

MEASURING ACROSS THE SUPPLY NETWORK

The customer service manager at a large Midwestern company could barely conceal his anger. During a meeting with a transportation buyer, he pointed to a report that showed his group was consistently falling short on its most important measure—the "order to cash" cycle time. He looked across the table and accused the buyer of being the reason for his group's shortcoming. The buyer, by now feeling a bit defensive, responded that he was doing quite well on his performance metrics, which focused largely on transportation cost reductions. He even thought he should be congratulated! Frankly, the buyer wasn't seeing the problem here.

This sad but true story is an example of a performance measurement system that results in conflicting behavior. The transportation buyer will logically take action to drive costs to their lowest possible level. He might aggregate shipments for volume discounts, even if this means holding orders for a few days as he searches for the lowest price but perhaps not the most consistent carriers. The customer service group, on the other hand, must achieve measures that focus primarily on speed. That group's goal is to get orders to the customer as quickly as possible so payment can be received. Unfortunately, in the transportation world, speed usually means higher costs, and that directly counters the buyer's performance measures. In the buyer's mind, why would he opt for speed when doing so will cause him some real *personal* pain at his performance review time?

To the customer service manager, the transportation buyer is not acting rationally. When something appears irrational, a common explanation is that a performance measurement system is driving behavior in ways that seem counter to the goals of other groups or even to the organization. A young buyer at a major logistics company was surprised to see procurement personnel still being

55

measured on "purchase orders written." What surprised the young buyer even more was watching his colleagues divide orders into smaller quantities so they could write more orders to the same supplier, a non-value-added activity that made the buyers look better on that performance measure. Performance measurement, which is our second critical enabler of strategic supply management, can be your best friend or your worst enemy. Take your pick.

This chapter first presents an overview of supply management measurement, including the reasons for measuring performance and the characteristics of an effective measurement system. The next sections discuss the four primary areas of supply measurement and address the important role that benchmarking plays during the measurement process. We conclude with the lessons learned from a seemingly state-of-the-art but deceptive supplier scorecard system.

SUPPLY MANAGEMENT MEASUREMENT

While measurement is a critical supply management enabler, it is certainly not unique to supply management. In fact, a strong argument can be made that measurement systems are not nearly as well developed within supply management as they are for other groups, particularly marketing and finance. When supply professionals are asked in a group setting who is very satisfied with how their firm measures supplier performance, for example, few hands are ever raised. This includes supply managers from smaller as well as larger firms. For many firms the development of supply measurement systems is still on their "to do" list. Organizations that are effective at supply management will likely have a well-defined set of performance measures backed by an information technology system.

Why Measure Supply Performance?

The reasons for measuring any kind of performance are simple. Without question, performance measurement, as the opening example illustrated, motivates us to act in certain ways. It's important we act in ways that support organizational goals rather than narrow and sometimes conflicting goals. Develop the right set of measures and the chances are very good that the right kind of behaviors will result. Measurement also helps identify areas that are most in need of improvement. Measurement can also identify internal areas that might benefit from performance benchmarking.

Another reason to measure performance is to identify rates of change. Measurement provides a picture of performance over time that supply managers can use to project into the future. These trends can relate to supplier performance or internal indicators such as budget compliance. Performance measurement also conveys what is important within an organization. This includes the set of performance measures and targets that suppliers must exceed.

Performance measurement supports some important principles of total quality management. Supply measurement, particularly supplier performance measurement, is an ideal way to convey a buying organization's (i.e., customer) requirements and expectations. Measurement also helps supply managers base decisions on objective rather than subjective analysis, another important quality principle. The measurement process is also an ideal way to drive continuous improvement. Once a performance target is reached, it is a good bet that a new, more challenging target will be established.

The last reason to measure supply management performance is somewhat self-serving. Supply leaders can use the right set of measures to report to executive leaders the value of strategic supply management. Without measures that show the impact that supply initiatives have on corporate indicators, including bottom-line performance, the supply management story will often remain untold.

Characteristics of Effective Supply Measurement Systems

How do we know if we have an effective supply measurement system? Fortunately, a set of principles exists that will help identify, at a fairly broad level, whether a measurement system is meeting the criteria that define effective measurement. Table 4.1 summarizes these principles in the form of a guideline that supply managers can use when creating or reviewing their systems. Disagreeing with one or more of these guidelines may indicate a problem with the system.

FOUR AREAS OF SUPPLY MEASUREMENT

This discussion about supply measurement has been somewhat broad to this point. What exactly do we mean by supply management measurement? Perhaps the best way to address this question is by identifying the areas where supply measurement primarily occurs.

Supply management measurement happens primarily, but not exclusively, in four areas: during supplier evaluation and selection, during the ongoing assessment of supplier performance, during the evaluation of the performance of the supply management organization, and during the evaluation of suppliers' perception of the buying company as a customer. Additional measurement areas could include the individual performance reviews that supply professionals receive or when certifying supplier quality performance (such as during ISO 9000 certification), although these areas will not be discussed here. The following addresses the four major areas of supply measurement.

Table 4.1 Characteristics of Effective Supply Measurement Systems

Characteristic	Agree	Disagree
Measures use data from sources visible throughout the supply organization.		
Performance objectives are reviewed regularly and adjusted as required.		
Measurement targets are based on world-class performance, ideally through performance benchmarking.		
Performance measures link to and support corporate strategies and objectives.		
Performance measures link to and support performance strategies and objectives of other functional groups.		
Individuals or groups are held accountable for achieving performance measures.		
Supply measures do not encourage unintended consequences or behavior.		
Supply measures promote teamwork, continuous improvement, and cross-functional cooperation.		
Key supply performance results are reported to executive leaders.		
Performance measures focus primarily on accomplishments rather than activities.		
Performance measures include well-defined action plans regarding how to achieve each measure.		

Supplier Evaluation and Selection

Site visits to suppliers, including formal assessments of a supplier's financial health, should be performed objectively before awarding a purchase contract. Leading supply organizations should develop a set of tools and templates that support the formal assessment of supplier capabilities. Chapter 10 presents supplier evaluation and selection, including the use of measurement, in detail.

Supplier Performance

Supplier performance measurement includes the methods and systems to collect and provide information to measure, rate, or rank suppliers on a continuous basis.[1] Many companies use the term "scorecards" to describe the report or system that conveys supplier performance data.

The type of scorecard a supply organization uses typically falls into one of three categories: categorical, weighted point, or cost based. Categorical measurement systems require simple check-offs to items that describe a supplier's performance across different categories. For relatively unimportant items this may be an acceptable way to evaluate supplier performance. As it relates to supplier scorecards, most firms use a weighted point system that includes a variety of performance categories, weights for each category, and scales to determine a supplier's score within each category. The third type, cost-based systems, is the least used of the three when measuring supplier performance. This approach attempts to quantify the total cost of doing business with a supplier. Supply organizations can also rely on hybrid systems that blend total cost elements with weighted-point assessments. For example, is it realistic to expect supply managers to calculate the total cost of supplier responsiveness (or unresponsiveness)? Some measurement areas are better suited to a weighted-point scheme. Chapter 12 will address supplier measurement from a total cost perspective.

There is no such thing as a standardized supplier scorecard across industries, although a supply organization should attempt to apply internally a standardized measurement approach. It does not make sense to have every business unit or location reinvent how they will measure supplier performance. The challenge is to develop a scorecard system that offers flexibility to internal locations. Providing a system that allows users to adjust the performance categories and their weights for the items they are responsible for sourcing is an example of scorecard flexibility.

At times it might be better if supply organizations did not even use supplier scorecards (or at least the ones they have developed). Some scorecards are so ill designed that the measurement process fails to be of any value. When a supplier challenges the legitimacy of a buyer's scores or discounts the process altogether, which has been known to happen, the supply organization must reconsider the supplier measurement process. Scorecards have also created unhealthy conflict with suppliers. Does this mean that measuring supplier measurement is wrong? Absolutely not!

What are the shortcomings of too many supplier scorecard systems? Perhaps the most obvious shortcoming is that many scorecards *measure suppliers the same way*. Chapter 7 will go to great lengths to convey that not all supply strategies, requirements, or suppliers are equal. If all suppliers are not created equal, then why apply equivalent measures? Many systems also *rely extensively on data collected manually* for their input. This can affect the timeliness and quality of data. Some systems are also *populated with too many subjective assessments* of supplier performance.

Chrysler has changed the way it evaluates suppliers by involving more personnel in the process and giving them the power to adjust the weights used to evaluate suppliers.[2] Previously, a buyer weighed the importance of each category

Table 4.2 Creating the Perfect Supplier Scorecard System

- Scorecard system allows adjustments to performance categories and weights to reflect the realities of different supply requirements.
- The system uses real-time data drawn from other systems such as accounts payable, quality control, and inbound transportation to determine supplier conformance.
- The system minimizes subjective measurement and the need for manual data input.
- The system quickly alerts the proper personnel to supplier performance problems, such as a late delivery.
- Internal customers or sites have the ability to evaluate supplier performance through Web-based input.
- Suppliers have the ability to view their scorecards online and compare their scorecard performance to other suppliers.
- Scorecards are reviewed by executive supplier management with acknowledgement required.
- Scorecard database allows user flexibility in retrieving and displaying data.
- Scorecards are updated as transactions occur to present a real-time picture of supplier performance.
- Each supplier site receives a separate scorecard.

on a supplier's scorecard. Chrysler now relies on 240 internal boards, one for each of its product segments, with at least four employees on each board to determine annually the weights of four performance categories that suppliers are evaluated against—cost, quality, technology, and delivery. Each board consists of specialists in cost, technology, quality, and logistics. Supplier data are posted monthly on the DaimlerChrysler Global Supplier Portal. Suppliers are even able to see the names and performance of their competitors, although the product boards have the authority to withhold names within their product groups.

A worthwhile exercise at most companies would be to put together a team to design, at least conceptually, the features of a "perfect" supplier scorecard system and then compare those features against the current system. What might the perfect scorecard system look like? Table 4.2 includes a list of features a perfect scorecard system would likely include. This table can be used as a benchmark when evaluating a scorecard system.

Supplier Assessment of the Buying Company

Do suppliers like working with your company? Do they bring new ideas before they approach your competitors? Or would they quickly drop you as a customer if given the chance? The least practiced area of supply measurement involves supplier assessments of the buying company. For a variety of reasons, most buying companies do not systematically measure how their suppliers feel about doing business with them. In an era where capacity is often tight and the importance of supplier relationships is growing, failing to tap into supplier sentiment might not be the smartest thing to do.

Some firms will say they don't ask their suppliers what they think about them because the buyer is the customer, and the customer is the king or queen. It is up to suppliers to satisfy the buyer, not the other way around. Others will say these assessments are too much work. And still others will grudgingly admit they might not like what their suppliers have to say.

Companies that are serious about strategic supply management regularly assess how their suppliers feel about doing business with them. Formal surveys, usually sent on an annual basis, are forwarded by a third-party to suppliers the buying company feels are critical to supply chain performance. A third-party administers the survey to ensure confidentiality and objective responses. What a buying company does not want are biased answers from suppliers that reflect a fear of retribution if something is said that the buyer might not like to hear. The survey administrator also works to ensure a high response rate.

What areas should a buying company ask questions about? A supplier survey should capture information about the buying company's[3]

- Ability to articulate its quality and performance requirements
- Quotation, negotiation, and contracting practices
- Effectiveness of performance feedback provided to suppliers
- Procurement knowledge and skills
- E-procurement and transaction systems
- Responsiveness to supplier concerns or questions
- Business opportunities and payment terms
- Buyer-supplier relationships
- Ethics and business conduct
- Cross-organizational communication and information sharing
- Supply chain planning and execution
- Relative comparisons to other companies with which the supplier does business

The survey should also capture demographic information such as supplier size, total sales to the buyer, type of good or service provided, country of origin, and so on. Demographic information is valuable when segmenting data at a more detailed level and when making comparisons.

Supply Management Performance

An important set of measures are those that formally report on supply management performance. Developing measures that encourage the desired behavior and then collecting data and information that accurately report actual performance is not easy. Too often measures result in unintended consequences that have longer-term detrimental effects. For example, the need for continuous cost reductions will always be a major supply management focus. However, there are instances where suppliers have been so pressured for price reductions that they eventually stopped selling to a buyer, or at the extreme, went out of business. Putting a supplier out of business is likely not in the business plan of most supply managers. This chapter could be extended by many pages if we listed the bizarre behavior that sometimes results in order to "make the numbers."

A general observation when one is looking at supply management measurement systems is that lower-level supply management performance measures tend to be tactically focused, while higher-level measures should be strategic in scope. Another way to look at supply management measurement is that lower-level supply groups tend to emphasize efficiency indicators, while higher-level supply groups tend to emphasize effectiveness. A simple way to differentiate between efficiency and effectiveness is that efficiency is *doing things right*, while effectiveness is *doing the right things*. This is an important point, as a transition occurs from traditional purchasing to strategic supply management. Major change requires a serious review of the performance measures that are in place.

An effective supply measure has four distinct parts. The first part relates to what the measure addresses—it should be very clear to the supply organization what is actually being evaluated. The second part includes the performance target or objective for that measure. A later section discusses the importance of looking externally when establishing targets. The third part of a supply measure is the actual performance. The fourth component is one that is too often absent in measurement systems. This includes the action plans that will be put in place to achieve the performance target. Along with these plans is a clear identification of the individual or group that has eventual accountability for success or failure.

For many supply organizations it is time to perform a serious review of their supply management measures. Like many other supply areas, performance measurement has its own legacy—a legacy that reflects the past quite well but does not necessarily align with future directions. It is time for supply managers to think outside the measurement box.

A new set of performance metrics must focus on accomplishments that reflect the objectives of a strategic supply organization. This does not mean that some of the new metrics will not be activity focused. The percent of total dollars under longer-term agreement, for example, reflects activity more than accomplishment. Recall, however, that measures should promote desired behaviors. An organization that wants to pursue longer-term agreements as part of its supply model might want to have a measure that promotes the development of longer-term agreements. This measure does not tell us if the agreements are providing

Table 4.3 A New Set of Supply Management Metrics

Measurement Area—Corporate Performance

- Supply management's impact on return on invested capital (ROIC), return of net assets (RONA), earnings per share (EPS), or economic value add (EVA)
- Working capital and cash flow improvements resulting from supply initiatives
- Revenue gained due to supply initiatives
- Improvements to gross margins resulting from supply initiatives

Measurement Area—Supply Base Management

- Churn or turnover rate for key suppliers
- Percent of a supplier's business the buyer represents
- Percent of dollars provided by the top 100 suppliers
- Percent of suppliers that represent 80 percent of total expenditures
- Percent of purchase dollars under longer-term agreements

Measurement Area—Supplier Performance

- Average supplier performance index (SPI) by supplier and commodity
- Parts-per-million quality performance by supplier and commodity

Measurement Area—Supply Management Performance

- Price performance compared to market indexes
- Price performance compared to baseline prices
- Average ratio of actual price to theoretical price
- Internal customer satisfaction with supply management
- Supply management overhead as a percent of total revenue
- Supplier score of the buying company as a customer
- Return on investment (ROI) for supplier development projects
- New product development cycle time improvements due to early supplier involvement
- Savings achieved through a supplier suggestion program

the return that is expected of them. Presumably, a set of accomplishment measures will reflect any new value that results from these agreements.

Table 4.3 presents examples of performance measures that begin to reflect what a strategic supply management organization should be about. This table includes measurement categories that reflect supply management's impact on *corporate performance*; measures that report on *supplier performance*; measures that focus on *supply management performance*, and measures that promote the appropriate kinds of *supply base management* behavior. The reader should notice that these measures are not at all typical. And for many supply managers they may

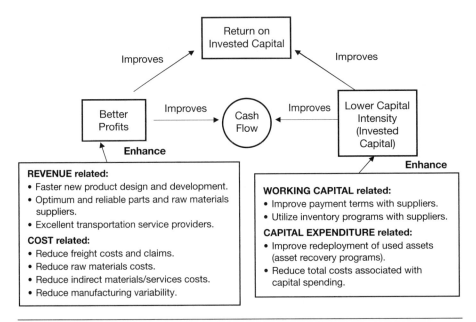

Figure 4.1 Strategic supply management can improve financial performance in many ways. (Copyright 2004, Greybeard Advisors, All rights reserved, reprinted with permission)

deviate far from their comfort level. These measures are not about reporting "purchase orders written" or "changes in unit price." Corporate and supply leaders can use these metrics to assess supply management's performance contribution or to promote behaviors that are associated with strategic supply management.

Let's take a closer look at a potential new metric—supply management's contribution to return on invested capital (ROIC). Figure 4.1 shows how supply management can potentially affect the four main components of ROIC—revenue, capital assets, working capital, and costs. Aside from supply management, not too many groups have the ability to affect each of these areas. We need to partition and then measure supply management's contribution across each of the four areas. This will begin to demonstrate the impact that the supply organization has on an important corporate performance indicator. (Chapter 8 will illustrate how to partition another major corporate performance indicator called return on net assets.)

With any performance measure the hard part is capturing the data that accurately reflect performance or compliance. Finance involvement will be critical for validating these higher-level numbers, particularly when calculating supply management's effect on corporate indicators, determining the return on investment (ROI) from supplier development projects, or calculating the total cost of doing business with a supplier.

USING BENCHMARKING TO SUPPORT MEASUREMENT

Performance benchmarking should play an important role during supply management measurement. The benchmarking process can help identify best practices, compare strategies, uncover new and innovative ways to work, provide objective ways to measure against the best performers, and provide valuable insights when establishing world-class performance targets. Formally defined, *benchmarking* is the continuous process of evaluating a firm's strategies, products, processes, practices, and services against competitors or other companies recognized as industry leaders.[4] This evaluation can be through direct visits to companies, participation in benchmarking consortiums, extensive surveys of public documents and research, or the use of third parties to collect benchmark data. The Hackett Group is an example of a third party that collects benchmark data within supply management.

Every supply organization can benefit from benchmarking, even industry leaders. No organization can possibly be the best in all conceivable areas. Furthermore, a company that is a leader today does not have a guarantee it will be a leader tomorrow. Continuous benchmarking should help prevent complacency, arrogance, and unwelcome surprises.

The benefits of benchmarking can be profound. This practice helps uncover best practices from any industry. The opportunity might present itself to introduce an innovative supply approach that while practiced in one industry may not be practiced in another. This process also breaks down ingrained resistance to change. Oftentimes those responsible for managing a change are better able to implement or accept a change once they see how it worked elsewhere. Benchmarking also offers the opportunity to develop a network of professional contacts that can be called upon in the future. It is an essential process for any company that is striving to evolve from purchasing to strategic supply management.

There is no shortage of areas that supply managers can benchmark. The most obvious ones are those areas where the supply organization has a performance gap between where it is operating and where it should operate. Perhaps the most desirable outcome from benchmarking is that the process can help create a culture that is externally focused and receptive to change. Every chapter in this book offers possible areas that might benefit from benchmarking. A company could even benchmark how to benchmark!

THE CASE OF THE DECEPTIVE SCORECARDS

Almost every supply organization has at least thought about developing a supplier scorecard system. And the ones that are serious about measuring supplier performance have committed a significant amount of time, budget, and technology resources toward system development. One such company is a major logistics company located in the United States. On the surface this company's system is one that most can only dream about. Do you want to know which suppliers improved in performance during the last quarter and which declined? Do you want a ranking of supplier performance reported by commodity group? Do you want a listing of the company's most elite suppliers? This, and much more, is available "at the push of a button."

Sometimes everything is not what it seems. During a training session at this company, a third-party facilitator asked a buyer in attendance to name one of his best-performing suppliers, or what this company called an elite supplier. The facilitator planned to use actual suppliers to demonstrate the data features of the scorecard system. Without hesitation, the buyer provided a supplier's name. Across the room another participant responded quite vocally, saying that "out back" in operations this was one of the worst suppliers they dealt with on a day-to-day basis. Something was definitely wrong here. How can one person say this is an elite supplier worthy of all the benefits this status bestows while another would like to see this supplier go away? And what are the dangers of a system that awards high scores to a poorly performing supplier? The training session quickly took an unexpected turn.

These differences of opinion led to an interesting discussion that resulted in some conclusions the group as a whole could agree upon. The group agreed that although the supplier scorecard system was supported by an extensive database that allowed all kinds of fancy analyses, the data to support that system was still collected manually. Furthermore, many items in the scorecard were subjective. Also, most buyers had responsibility for inputting data quarterly for about 25 suppliers. Most agreed this was a heavy burden in addition to their normal workload. In addition, most buyers acknowledged that management used supplier scores as an indicator of a buyer's job performance. Next, the group agreed that material suppliers were all held to the same set of criteria and weights, even though all suppliers were not of equal importance. Finally, the group agreed that internal customers or stakeholders really had no formal way to be part of the supplier measurement process.

What are the lessons to take away from this situation? An effective scorecard system requires much more than a database that can cut and dice data in many ways. And scorecards should not ignore the voice of internal customers. After all, when was the last time a truck backed up and unloaded material into a supply manager's office or cubicle? On a day-to-day basis, operating sites are positioned well to evaluate supplier performance, at least in delivery, quality, and responsiveness. How to involve these individuals efficiently in the measurement process should be part of the measurement discussion. In today's electronic age, internal stakeholders should have the ability to provide comments and ratings about a supplier's performance directly into the scorecard system. Furthermore, suppliers should be able to see those comments through a Web-based portal.

Another lesson is that scorecards often place a heavy work burden on the supply organization. Here a buyer is responsible for managing about 25 fairly complex quarterly scorecards that require a significant amount of manual input. The burden of collecting and inputting manual data often results in scorecards that are late or input at the last minute. A concern must also surround the integrity of the data. Have scorecards placed an undue burden on supply personnel, particularly when they require the collection of large amounts of data? And is a reliance on manually collected and often subjective evaluations affecting the integrity of the supplier scores? In a perfect world, scorecard data would flow automatically from other databases.

A further learning is that scorecard systems can result in excessive averaging of data for suppliers that have more than one location. One supplier to this company, for example, provided goods from 15 locations around the world. Should this be one scorecard or 15? If this supplier were pursuing ISO 9000 certification, the certification would apply to individual sites, not to the entire company. So why does the scorecard apply to the entire company? The number of suppliers and the number of shipping points are often very different figures. A possible solution is to evaluate each supplier's shipping locations across a basic set of operational metrics, while the supplier as a corporate entity is evaluated by some higher-level metrics.

A fifth lesson is to be careful that scorecard systems do not drive the wrong behavior. Here a buyer's annual performance evaluation is based partly on the performance of the buyer's suppliers. And that performance is determined by scorecards these same buyers are responsible for completing! This invites the possibility of inflated supplier performance. It also presents a possible conflict of interest that could work to the detriment of the entire organization. The old saying about the fox watching the chicken coop may aptly apply here. To summarize, this case provides the following lessons learned:

- An effective scorecard system is much more than a database.
- The supplier measurement process should not ignore the voice of internal customers.
- Scorecards that require the manual collection of data by buyers may suffer from incomplete, inaccurate, or untimely inputs.
- Scorecards can result in excessive averaging of data for suppliers that have more than one location, making the data hard to attribute to a specific location.
- Be careful that the scorecard measurement process does not drive the wrong behavior or create conflicts of interest.

No one at this company believes that measuring supplier performance is not a worthwhile endeavor. What this company is beginning to realize is that measurement involves more than creating a database that resides on a dedicated server. And like any process, supplier measurement must be actively reviewed and improved.

CONCLUDING THOUGHTS

Performance measurement is not free and is certainly not a substitute for good management. A well-designed system will enable supply managers to pursue the kinds of activities that fall under the strategic supply management umbrella, while a poorly designed system could very well cause more harm than good. Supply leaders are urged to give this subject the attention it deserves. At too many companies it has not received all that much attention.

SUMMARY OF KEY CHAPTER POINTS

- When behavior appears irrational within the supply chain, a common explanation is often a performance measurement system is driving individuals or groups to act in ways that seem counter to the goals of other groups or even to the organization.
- While measurement is a critical strategic supply management enabler, measurement is certainly not unique to supply management. A strong argument could be made that measurement is not nearly as well developed within supply management as it is for other groups, particularly marketing and finance.
- The reasons for measuring performance are straightforward. Performance measurement motivates people to act in certain ways, helps identify areas that are most in need of improvement, helps identify rates of change, conveys what is important within an organization and to suppliers, supports some important principles of total quality management, and allows supply managers to report the value of strategic supply management to executive leaders.
- There is no single measure that captures how well a supply organization or its suppliers are performing. Like a balanced scorecard, a variety of measures are needed to portray how well a supply organization is performing.
- Supply management measurement happens primarily in four areas: during supplier evaluation and selection, during the ongoing assessment of supplier performance, during the evaluation of the perform-

ance of the supply management organization, and during the evaluation of suppliers' perception of the buyer as a customer.

- Supplier performance measurement includes the methods and systems to collect and provide information to measure, rate, or rank suppliers on a continuous basis. The type of supplier scorecard a supply organization uses typically falls into one of three categories: categorical, weighted point, or cost based.
- An effective supply management measure has four distinct parts: what the measure addresses, the target or objective for that measure, actual performance, and the action plans (with accountability) that will be put in place to achieve the performance target.
- For many supply organizations, it is time to perform a serious review of the performance measures they use to evaluate performance. Like many other supply areas, performance measurement has a legacy that reflects the past quite well but does not always align well with future directions.
- Companies that are serious about strategic supply management regularly assess how well their suppliers feel about conducting business with them.
- Performance benchmarking should play an important role during supply measurement. Benchmarking is the continuous process of measuring a firm's strategies, products, processes, practices, and services against competitors or other companies recognized as industry leaders.

ENDNOTES

1. R. M. Monczka, R. J. Trent, and R. B. Handfield, *Purchasing and Supply Chain Management* (Mason, OH: Thomson Southwestern, 2005), 269.
2. This example is adapted from J. Armstrong, "Chrysler Changes Scorecard," *Automotive News*, www.AutomotiveNews.com, November 8, 2004.
3. This list of categories is adapted from J. Schildhouse and R. M. Monczka, "Do You Measure Up?" *Inside Supply Management* 17, no. 8 (August 2006): 22.
4. R. C. Camp, "Benchmarking: The Search for Best Practices That Lead to Superior Performance—Part I." *Quality Progress* 22, no. 1 (January 1989): 66.

USING INFORMATION TECHNOLOGY TO SUPPORT SUPPLY OBJECTIVES

Leveraging volumes across business units or buying locations, once considered to be innovative, is now an expected part of strategic supply management. For some companies, the task of combining volumes has not been as simple as it sounds. Consider the case of a global energy company that has dozens of facilities and buying centers around the world. It did not take a rocket scientist to figure out that the company's uncoordinated buying practices were leaving a great deal of value unrealized.

If it were simply a matter of getting people together in a room and combining their requirements into leveraged contracts, the advantages of volume leveraging would be quickly realized. However, this company has grown, in part, through mergers and acquisitions. And everyone knows that when separate companies come together, the transition is smooth and easy. The combined companies bring with them the same set of suppliers, information systems, part coding schemes, procedures, and practices. Well, perhaps not. And the "perhaps not" part was what was affecting this company.

The toughest hurdle facing supply managers was a lack of data. The process of collecting data about a purchase requirement across different locations, a process that should have taken days or weeks, was taking six months or longer. Obtaining accurate data became so time-consuming that suppliers were finally asked to provide information about what they had sold to the energy company. More than one supply manager lamented about the lack of a common information system and material classification scheme.

It would be easy to say that the use of information technology (IT) within supply management has a long and impressive history. Saying that, however, would be wrong. It is only recently, perhaps within the last decade or so, that software solutions have become available that enable supply leaders to explore the creative possibilities offered by IT tools and applications. This chapter focuses on a third enabler of strategic supply management—the use of IT to support an organization's supply objectives. This chapter first presents some IT applications that most supply managers will find to be relevant. We next identify examples of how leading supply organizations use IT to their advantage. The chapter concludes with a case example about a company that has developed a home grown IT system packed with functionality.

SO MANY TOOLS AND APPLICATIONS—WHERE DO WE START?

Hardly anyone would argue against the notion that IT has made our lives easier. Whether we bank online or use ATM machines to get some quick cash, check in for flights from home, shop online, or search for information on the Internet using powerful search engines, the uses of IT grow daily. Using IT to support our supply chain needs also seems to grow daily. Whether we want to manage transactions or gain visibility to expenditures across an entire company, someone is offering software that just might do the trick.

Dozens of applications and hundreds of software suppliers make a discussion of IT a difficult topic to get our hands around. With so many choices, it is not surprising to find a confusing array of applications and acronyms. Throw any three letters together randomly and there is a decent chance they apply to some IT application. *Inbound Logistics* magazine recently featured its list of the 100 top supply chain and logistics IT companies, which was narrowed down from a list of more than 300 companies![1] The supply chain domain features many areas where IT solutions are offered, and each of these areas will have its own set of sub-applications. This analysis also considered whether the IT product includes radio-frequency identification (RFID) capability, if it is wireless-enabled, and whether it supports global supply chain and logistics management. The following are the areas the editors at *Inbound Logistics* magazine included in their assessment of the top 100 software suppliers:

- Cross-enterprise collaboration
- Customer relationship management
- Network modeling
- Optimization

- Demand management
- Distribution requirements planning
- Enterprise resource planning
- Freight payment
- Freight auditing
- Inventory control
- Logistics
- Load planning
- Materials requirements planning
- Procurement
- Reverse logistics
- Routing and scheduling
- Security
- Supplier relationship management
- Trade compliance
- Transportation management system
- Vendor management
- Warehouse management system

In the procurement and supply arena, the number of software providers and applications is also large. One software company has developed a suite of tools and applications that gives us some perspective about what makes up at least part of the IT domain supporting procurement and supply management.[2] These tools and applications include spend analysis, e-RFX, e-auction, e-contract management, vendor management, project management, e-procurement, catalog management, print procurement, and supplier performance management. It would take an entire book to address all the tools and applications that are available to support our supply management efforts. We will focus instead on a selected set of tools and applications that are most relevant to supply managers.

E-procurement through the Internet

E-procurement is a broad term that relates to the application of Internet technology to the buying and selling of goods and services. An e-procurement network provides a secure marketplace, sales platform, and transaction tracking system to buyers and sellers.[3] Electronic procurement systems generally consist of four components: content management, requisition management, transaction management, and connectivity management.[4] A variety of applications reside within the e-procurement domain, including auctions, trading exchanges, e-RFX, and online catalogs.

Internet Auctions. This application consists of auctions and reverse Internet auctions. The Internet is an efficient way to dispose of excess and obsolete equipment and inventory by allowing a seller to efficiently reach thousands of potential buyers, including through auctions. Reverse Internet auctions have received most of the attention as a platform for conducting auctions, and they will receive our attention here.

Not too long ago reverse auctions were touted by many as the best way to reduce purchase prices. Reverse auctions differ from regular auctions in two ways. First, the buyer initiates the auction rather than the seller. Second, the objective of the auction is to drive a price lower rather than higher. For many supply managers the use of IT tools to conduct reverse auctions became the quickest and easiest way to reduce prices across a wide range of purchase categories. And there is no doubt that reverse auctions became somewhat fashionable among supply organizations.

For some firms just about everything they purchased became a candidate for a reverse auction. A company with operations around the world mandated that its regional buying centers conduct reverse auctions even though many third-world suppliers didn't have a clue about how to participate. The misapplication of reverse auctions can also harm any semblance of a supplier relationship. Get a better deal and the switch is on.

It is important to know when and where to use reverse auctions. This approach is best suited for standardized items that can be readily specified and that have known volume requirements, and where supplier switching costs are low. When using reverse auctions, a cynical supplier will say that a buyer's three most important selection criteria are price, price, and then price. Relationships do not seem all that important.

Consider the case of Toro, a landscape equipment manufacturer. The company endorsed the use of online auctions until half its suppliers stopped participating in the auctions. As the director of sourcing and supply management for Toro explained, "Even when their business depended on reverse auctions, they wouldn't go for it. These suppliers wanted to be treated in a different manner. They wanted us to look at total cost and their purchase value, not just purchase price."[5] Toro's philosophy now is to work with suppliers on managing total cost rather judging them only on price reductions.

We do not hear quite as much about reverse auctions today. This may be due partly to the novelty of this approach wearing off. It may also be due to a more enlightened view that not all items are candidates for reverse auctions. While reverse auctions are a tool that Hewlett-Packard uses to reduce its costs, the company is also very careful about where it uses them. A senior supply executive maintains HP is not going to e-source microprocessors or operating system software. Reverse auctions are appropriate at HP when there are a large number of suppliers to choose from. The company uses reverse auctions for indirect materials, transportation services, packaging, plastic resins, power cords, and batteries.[6]

Another reason we do not hear so much about reverse auctions is a tightening of supply markets. Reverse auctions work best when suppliers are hungry for a buyer's business. During a seller's market (capacity is tight), suppliers are not going to be quite as anxious to participate in an auction. Why would a supplier reduce its price if it can readily sell its available capacity at a preferred price?

An obsession with price during reverse auctions increases the risk of overlooking other important variables such as quality, capacity, delivery, and financial stability. Just because a supplier participates in a reverse auction and quotes a marvelously low price does not necessarily mean it is a qualified performer. Supply managers are strongly encouraged to prequalify any suppliers that participate in an auction. Do not let the use of this tool overwhelm your good judgment.

Any concern about this approach does not mean reverse auctions should not be part of a supply manager's toolbox. When conditions are right, reverse auctions can be an efficient way to create a competitive marketplace that results in double-digit price reductions. The process often identifies new suppliers that are more efficient than current ones. Even incumbent suppliers that have been complacent about lowering prices but that have been diligent about raising prices are often able to dig deep and come up with reductions. Just make sure the suppliers that are invited to a reverse auction are capable of meeting your requirements in areas besides price. Quality and delivery performance should never be taken for granted.

Trading Exchanges. Another major part of e-procurement involves trading exchanges, or what some call e-marketplaces. These exchanges or marketplaces provide an electronic forum where buyers and sellers meet online to exchange information and bids, greatly expanding sales opportunities for sellers and often reducing prices for buyers.[7] Like reverse auctions, trading exchanges grew rapidly after their introduction. An estimate in 2000 pegged the number of exchanges that were operational or planned as close to 1,500. One source boldly went where no one had gone before and predicted that 20,000 exchanges would soon be in operation![8] While precise figures are hard to come by, the number of trading exchanges in operation today is likely in the hundreds.

In an attempt to catalog the different types of exchanges, AMR Research in Boston has constructed a classification of exchanges:[9]

- **Independent trading exchanges.** These exchanges, which are usually targeted to a specific industry, are owned by third parties rather than by industry buyers or sellers.
- **Vendor-managed trading exchanges.** These exchanges, which are a subgroup of independent exchanges, are created by software vendors that include trading exchange operations in their product offering.
- **Consortia trading exchanges.** These exchanges are formed by a group of industry buyers and sellers coming together to create an exchange for themselves or an entire industry.
- **Private trading exchanges.** These exchanges are established by one large buyer or seller exclusively for its own set of customers or suppliers

AMR recommends using independent trading exchanges for commodity-like, nonstrategic direct and indirect manufacturing goods and services; using private trading exchanges for non-commodity, low-volume strategic direct materials and services; and using private exchanges supplemented by traditional EDI for strategic, high-volume direct materials and services.

A major consortia exchange for the automotive and health care industries is Covisint, which is now part of Compuware. The following is how Covisint describes its exchange for the automotive industry.[10] This also provides a broad description of a trading exchange.

> *Covisint's Collaborative Platform for Automotive is a web-based, services oriented exchange delivering flexible, secure access to information and applications regardless of where they reside. Extending existing IT investments while mitigating the cost and complexity of changing system requirements, Covisint shortens time to value by providing a hosted environment where trading partners can share common infrastructure, security, content, and process management tools.*

E-RFX. This application is designed to streamline the paper, transactions, time, and decisions associated with managing requests for information (RFIs), quotes (RFQs), and proposals (RFPs). Global eProcure, a supply chain consulting firm, describes its e-RFX application as a way to simplify and automate the process of creating bid documents by multiple team members, forward requests to suppliers, collect responses, and score responses. The primary benefits of this application are that it removes time and cost from the request process.

E-catalogs. E-catalogs are electronic representations of information on the products and services a company offers, and they are a means for buyers to view and interact with a supplier's information.[11] E-catalogs are more current and less cumbersome than manual catalogs, quicker to reference, and with the help of third-party software, offer the opportunity to compare supplier prices for like items.

There are three approaches to dealing with electronic catalogs: supplier-managed catalogs, buyer-managed catalogs, and third-party-managed catalogs.[12] With supplier-managed catalogs, the suppliers host the content and its presentation. With the buyer-managed model, data must be applied, or massaged, into the exact format required to load correctly into the buyer's target application. Third-party catalogs consist of aggregated catalogs containing data from multiple suppliers. The data are then made available on a commercial basis, often by the same people that manage trading exchanges. With the buyer and third-party-managed models, purchasing companies and e-marketplaces or exchanges play the role of catalog aggregators. Suppliers and distributors play the role of catalog providers in the supplier-managed model.

While e-procurement through the Internet is revolutionary for those of us who are more "mature," college graduates who are now entering the profession will know nothing but an IT-based approach to supply management. And they are totally at home within a virtual world. This new breed of professional will simply not know what it was like, as our parents used to say, to "walk to school 10 miles a day, barefoot, uphill both ways."

Electronic Data Interchange

A popular approach for using IT to manage transactions involves electronic data interchange (EDI). EDI is a communications standard that supports the electronic exchange of common business documents and information across businesses. While a discussion of EDI could take place within the e-procurement discussion, early versions of EDI were not Internet based. The importance of this topic warrants a somewhat broader presentation. Traditional EDI is composed of at least three parts.[13] The first is a set of EDI standards and forms that include the rules for formatting and syntax agreed to by the users in the EDI network. The American National Standards Institute ACS X12 EDI standards is a common format. The second part is translation software that translates the company-specific database information into EDI standard format for transmission and receipt. The final part is a third-party network provider that is responsible for transmitting documents through a value-added network, or VAN. This network, which is operated by a third-party provider on a subscription basis, serves as an intermediary between the EDI parties.

The promise of EDI during the 1990s never matched the hype surrounding its use.[14] During that time, EDI's perceived importance prompted one observer to write a paper titled "EDI or Die." While this is a clever title, it was perhaps a bit overstated. So, what happened? Many small suppliers balked at the costs associated with a full-blown EDI system. Early cost estimates of $5,000 to get up and running were grossly underestimated. And many of these suppliers had difficulty adopting the different EDI systems that their trading partners were using. Some of these smaller suppliers ended up adopting smaller-scale systems like autofax. We have also come to realize that forwarding documents electronically, while essential for driving out waste and transactions costs, is not what defines strategic supply management. EDI does not offer an opportunity to interact and reach decisions through two-way communication.[15] With EDI, a decision is reached unilaterally and then that decision is forwarded in the form of an electronic document to another supply chain member. EDI is really best suited for managing documents and transactions.

The technology underlying EDI systems has changed dramatically since its early days, making it easier for firms to adopt EDI. The new version of EDI is called EDI XML, which is a standardized framework in which EDI-based business documents and messages are described using XML (extensible markup language) syntax. This form of EDI relies on virtual private networks (VPNs) supported by the Internet. This format is quickly replacing the use of third-party VANs because it is less expensive and presents fewer standards issues. As an example, VANs add document transmission fees that range from 10 cents to 50 cents per kilocharacter, while a basic Internet-based, private exchange service may charge 5 cents to 7 cents per kilocharacter.[16]

There at least three ways to look at the state of your company's EDI implementation: the percent of suppliers that are EDI capable, the percent of total transactions moving through an EDI system, and the percent of total dollars moving through an EDI system. While EDI is not considered leading-edge today, it's hard to imagine a progressive supply organization not endorsing some sort of technology to reduce the transactions costs of moving information across the supply chain.

Supplier Relationship Management Software

Given the importance of supplier relationships, we knew it would not be long before software companies bundled a set of applications and called that bundle supplier relationship management (SRM). After all, the downstream side of the business has customer relationship management (CRM) software. It only seems fair that the supply side should have its own important-sounding acronym and software.

According to a provider that installs mySAP SRM solutions, SRM software encompasses a broad suite of capabilities that facilitate collaboration, sourcing, transaction execution, and performance monitoring between an organization and its trading partners.[17] What are some of the more interesting capabilities housed within an SRM package? Table 5.1 presents some of the features that one provider offers with its SRM product. One feature that should set all SRM software apart from other applications is the ability to engage in some sort of collaboration with suppliers. Without this feature, the product starts to resemble a host of other applications that are available within the procurement and supply domain.

Sourcing Data Warehouses and Databases

A data warehouse is a collection of integrated, subject-oriented databases designed to support a specific function. A database is a large collection of data organized especially for rapid search and retrieval. In a data warehouse, each unit of data is relevant to some moment in time and contains atomic data and lightly summarized data. Atomic data represent the lowest level of process analysis data stored in a data warehouse.[18]

Let's illustrate this in a way that makes more sense. Assume you have been assigned to a team that is charged with the task of developing a company-wide supply contract for a commodity. Consider some of the information that would

Table 5.1 Sample of Supplier Relationship Management Software Features

Feature	Description
Automated RFX	Automates requests for information, quotes, and proposals.
Weighted attributes and scoring	Applies complex algorithms for quantitative scoring of supplier responses with side-by-side comparisons.
Event scoreboard	Provides side-by-side comparisons of supplier responses to promote faster, better-informed decisions based on total costs.
Real-time bid graph	Visually graphs bids from all suppliers in a dynamic, real-time display, including during auctions.
Supplier report cards	Allows the configurable development of supplier report cards based on user-defined parameters.
Collaboration	Allows online information sharing, collaboration, and negotiation with suppliers.
Event mechanisms	Supports various events, including English auctions, Dutch auctions, sealed bids, and dynamic ascending and descending events.
Alerts	Provides notification of upcoming events.
Search filters	Search capabilities allow buyers and suppliers to find events, items, and partners that meet their objectives.
Procurement	Allows end users to create their own requisitions 24/7 using established contracts with appropriate controls.

Source: www.epicor.com

be valuable to your work—a listing of existing contracts and suppliers, pricing data by location, supplier capability and performance data, projected worldwide volumes by commodity or category, information about new suppliers, internal customer requirements, part numbers that are part of the commodity, and volume requirements across buying units. As the opening to this chapter illustrated, searching for the data to perform a decent strategy analysis can be time-consuming and frustrating. Databases and data warehouse are designed to overcome the inherent problems associated with trying to collect data, often manually, from many diverse sources. The case at the end of this chapter will show the time required to collect the data for a printed circuit board analysis before and after development of a data warehouse. The productivity improvements are staggering.

Data warehouses are an important part of spend management systems. Spend management is about gaining visibility, through the use of IT, of company-wide expenditures so they can be grouped and managed more effectively. The objective of a spend management system is to cleanse and feed data that have been correctly classified according to some scheme, such as the United Nations Standard Products and Services Code (UNSPSC), into a data warehouse. Classifying the data is critical—this is what supports future retrieval and analysis.

Dozens of companies offer spend management software solutions. Ariba, a recognized leader in the spend management arena, now offers its suite of spend management solutions in an on-demand delivery model through the Internet. This is different from buying, installing, and maintaining software on your company's own system. Pricing is based on a "pay as you go" model.

Procurement Cards

Procurement cards may not be the first thing that comes to mind when we think of IT or electronic tools and applications. Since their use has become so common, at a personal and professional level, we take it for granted that credit cards will work each and every time. Procurement cards can be an effective way for obtaining low-dollar goods and services that are not part of a corporate contract. Some companies even use their cards as a releasing mechanism for items that are covered by contracts. These companies say they like the control and reporting features that their card provider offers. The use of procurement cards, while important, is no longer considered innovative. Like EDI, however, progressive firms know they need systems to manage transactions and "nuisance" items.

Most organizations provide procurement cards to internal users so supply personnel can focus on tasks that are more important than chasing around low dollar requirements. What we sometimes overlook is that a card program also requires many administrative duties. A CAPS Research study that investigated how organizations reduce the transactions costs of purchasing low-value goods and services revealed that procurement is responsible almost two-thirds of the time for administering a card program.[19] Finance or accounting is responsible for the program only a third of the time.

Responsibilities associated with administering a card program include selecting a card provider, controlling access and distribution of the cards, training for new card holders, compiling usage and spending reports, performing card audits, developing program guidelines and a user manual, convincing suppliers to participate, establishing spending limits, and working with the card provider to continuously improve the program. Failing to recognize the importance of the card administrator jeopardizes the success of the program.

Most firms that have put in place a card program have successfully captured the benefits they wanted from their use. The top five benefits of a card program, which statistically stand out from other possible benefits from using procurement cards, include faster response to user needs, reduced transactions costs, reduced total transaction time, improved accounts payable process, and streamlined payments made on a monthly consolidated statement. Nonindustrial organizations say the card has also allowed more effective decentralized purchasing and improved user perception of purchasing's responsiveness.

Companies that have experience with procurement cards are able to offer some good advice. While it is tempting to restrict suppliers, most organizations ultimately realize the program benefits from opening up the number of suppliers that can participate. Card administrators also caution against setting transaction limits too low, since this restricts card usage. And while it is tempting, do not track too much data. Excessive data begins to undermine the objectives of the card program.

When establishing a pilot program, cardholders should be placed throughout the organization rather than in a single location. It may also become necessary to eliminate other low dollar procurement systems to force card usage. Finally, do not discount the important role that accounts payable and finance play in a card program.

HOW SUPPLY LEADERS USE INFORMATION TECHNOLOGY

Table 5.2 summarizes how recent winners of *Purchasing* magazine's Medal of Professional Excellence Winners use IT to support their efforts. Several examples appear after each company describing how that company uses IT to support its procurement or supply chain efforts.[20] This table is the result of an analysis of the articles in *Purchasing* magazine that accompany the Medal of Professional Excellence Award. After reviewing this table, you can easily see that leading firms are quite clever in how they use IT to support their supply objectives. A visit to any leading supply organization will quickly reveal the importance these organizations place on IT as a critical supply management enabler.

USING INFORMATION TECHNOLOGY TO SUPPORT STRATEGIC SOURCING

This case reports on the efforts of a $4 billion U.S. company to develop an IT-enabled system to supports its centrally led strategic sourcing initiatives, particularly during contract development. This company provides power, control, and information solutions to a wide range of customers and industries.[21] The challenges faced by this company are similar to other producers with business units located around the world. With over 40 production sites, the company must contend with a diverse set of procurement processes and contracts, product lines, business models, supply chain relationships, information systems, and language, currencies, and culture.

Table 5.2 Examples of How Leading Supply Organizations Use Information Technology

Feature	Description
Harley-Davidson	• Launched an Internet-based information link (SiL'K) that supports EDI through the Internet and allows suppliers to link to vital business transaction information via an electronic portal.
John Deere	• Created a Web-enabled supplier suggestion system program called JDCROP. • Processes most orders through an EDI system. • Uses reverse Internet auctions. • Uses an Ariba B2B platform to support indirect purchasing.
Hewlett-Packard	• Developed internally a software tool that uses sophisticated statistical techniques to predict future demand and material requirements. • Developed internally a spend analysis and management system. • Worked with Ariba to develop a single worldwide buying channel for indirect purchases. • Uses electronic sourcing, contracting, e-RFX, and e-auction tools.
Rockwell Collins	• Uses an online tool called Impact that provides engineers with a catalog of parts offered by preferred suppliers. • Employs online booking for travel. • Forwards supplier scorecards monthly via e-mail and also lets supplier access scorecards online. • Developed an e-strategy that covers requirement identification to supplier payment. • Uses both an e-RFQ and automated purchase order process. • Suppliers have access to designs and forecasts through a supplier portal based on the SAP platform.
United Technologies	• Conducts reverse Internet auctions through Ariba. • Uses tools from Open Rating to manage supplier risk. • Relies on IBM to manage its procure-to-pay process. • Created UTC Mall to leverage the Internet and offer one-stop shopping for online supplier services.
Cessna	• Uses software from ESIS that allows suppliers to receive production forecasts 18-24 months out, automate processes for purchasing transactions, access blueprints and performance ratings, and print bar code shipping labels for paperless receipt at Cessna.

Early efforts at developing leveraged supply agreements relied on manual data collection and analysis. This process, while still yielding some positive results, was labor-intensive and costly. Supply leaders quickly realized that a better way to access data company-wide was critical for developing coordinated supply strategies. This realization led to the internal development of a system designed to support the operating needs of this company's central sourcing organization.

The resulting system is called the Spend Analysis & Vendor Evaluation System (SAVES). SAVES is a complete system and interface solution that provides the information required by the strategic sourcing organization and other groups that support the company's supply chain management efforts. Figure 5.1 identifies the suite of applications possible through SAVES as well as through the company's intranet and extranet. The components of the SAVES system include a relational database and server, a file staging server, a Web and application server, a document server, an authentication server, and application source code.

Perhaps the most important capability of this system is its ability to capture all expenditures for direct items. (Indirect items and locations outside the United States will soon be part of this system.) After capturing a transaction, the system compares the price paid at a location against a baseline price. The baseline price is defined as the last price paid from the previous year. All transactions over a 12-month period are captured, compared against the baseline prices, aggregated across commodities, and reported to executive management. And most importantly, the finance group has signed off on the validity of the figures reported through SAVES.

SAVES also serves as a contract repository. This allows easy access to the company's formal agreements and details the language, terms and conditions, and clauses that are part of these agreements. Previously, supply managers would store physical documents in their department, a process that severely limited visibility. To overcome this limitation, the SAVES system allows uploading and viewing of electronic copies of contract documents.

Initiating a database search for a part number, supplier, or contract will yield a list of matches with links to other information, a feature that expands the amount of information available to users. A detail page displays as much relevant supplier and part information as possible without cluttering the screen. Users across the company use this system as a resource when completing their supply reports. This information is also valuable during different phases of the contract development process.

One might think that a drawback to a system likes SAVES is the amount of money required for development. In this case, one would be wrong. The internal development of this system was $300,000, a relatively small sum compared to the cost of some third-party IT applications. These costs were allocated across four categories: planning and administration (11 percent), application development

Intranet	**SAVES**	**Extranet**
Provides access to . . .	Provides access to . . .	Suppliers have access to . . .
• Preferred supplier lists	• Data gathering	• Supplier metrics
• Contract templates	• Data warehouse	• Sourcing review support
• Commodity news	• Data mining	• Supplier registration
• Organizational charts	• Web application	• Order management
• Project status	• Analytical tools	• Order promising
• Industry reports	• Meta data management	• Print room
• Part transfer	• Document management	
	• Spend reporting	
	• Savings reporting	
	• Contract compliance	
	• Trend monitoring	
	• Knowledge management	
	• Contract repository	

SAVES—Spend Analysis and Vendor Evaluation System

Figure 5.1 Information technology applications.

and testing (54 percent), developing the savings reporting feature (22 percent), and additional enhancements (13 percent). Hardware costs were insignificant, since excess server capacity was available. To appreciate the payback from this system, consider a before-and-after comparison when developing a supply strategy for printed circuit boards:

	1999	**Current**	**Change**
Data collection time (workdays)	40 days	1 day	–39 days
Data cleansing time (workdays)	20 days	7 days	–13 days
Total team members	20	6	–14
Analysts required	60	5	–5.5
Data accuracy	85%	99%	+14%
Strategy development costs	$384K	$15K	–369K

As with most major projects, managers are able to look back and identify a set of factors that were critical to the successful development of the system. These factors include the following:

- An internally designed and developed system, which was cost-effective and flexible according to user requirements

- Supply personnel who understood the objectives of strategic sourcing and the features required of the system
- Senior management's resource support during system development
- Availability of clean data to be incorporated into the system
- Designing the system to include user needs beyond strategic sourcing, such as incorporating the needs of various supply chain functions
- System design independence that did not require major changes to other systems
- System friendliness and usability
- A phased approach to system launch
- A dedicated IT team using project management tools during development

How does this company plan to extend this system's capabilities? Planned enhancements include moving beyond direct expenditures to capturing indirect spend, a topic that is on the minds of most supply managers. A new SAVES feature will also allow the tracking of total spend with diverse and disadvantaged suppliers, as well as tracking the tooling and dies required to produce a part. The system will also begin to capture spend data from the company's European and Asia-Pacific facilities. This company understands that while strategic sourcing is good, strategic sourcing backed up by a system like SAVES is even better.

CONCLUDING THOUGHTS

Even though this chapter focused on a variety of specific IT tools and applications, the chapter's overall message should not be ignored: IT is a critical enabler of strategic supply management. Managing even the most mundane supply activities will be a cumbersome process if we ignore the value of IT tools and applications. A supply organization that is bogged down with transactions, paperwork, and low-dollar items will never have the freedom to pursue the activities that can make supply management a strategic pursuit.

SUMMARY OF KEY CHAPTER POINTS

- A full set of IT applications to support supply management should include spend analysis, e-RFX, e-auction, e-contract management, vendor management, project management, e-procurement, catalog management, and supplier performance management.
- E-procurement is a broad term that relates to the application of Internet technology to the buying and selling of goods and services.
- Reverse auctions are best suited for standardized items that can be readily specified and have known volume requirements, and where supplier switching costs are low.

- Trading exchanges or marketplaces provide an electronic forum where buyers and sellers can meet online to exchange information and bids, greatly expanding sales opportunities for sellers and often reducing prices for buyers.
- E-RFX tools are designed to streamline the paper, transactions, time, and decisions associated with managing requests for information, quotes, and proposals.
- E-catalogs are electronic representations of information on the products and services a company offers, and they are a means for buyers to view and interact with a supplier's information.
- The technology underlying EDI systems has changed dramatically. Increasingly, firms are using a standardized framework in which EDI-based business documents and messages are described using XML syntax.
- SRM software encompasses a broad suite of capabilities that facilitate collaboration, sourcing, transaction execution, and performance monitoring between an organization and its trading partners.
- Data warehouses are an important part of spend management systems. A data warehouse is a collection of integrated subject-oriented databases designed to support a specific function.
- Most organizations provide procurement cards to internal users so supply personnel can focus on more important tasks. Procurement is responsible almost two-thirds of the time for administering the card program.

ENDNOTES

1. "The Top 100 Logistics IT Companies," *Inbound Logistics* 26, no. 4 (April 2006): 55–65.
2. From www.globaleprocure.com.
3. M. P. Papazoglou and P. Ribbers, *e-Business: Organizational and Technical Foundations* (West Sussex, UK: John Wiley & Sons, 2006) 227.
4. Papazoglou and Ribbers, p. 241, citing Pettinga, 1998.
5. "Toro Moves from e-Auctions to SRM Strategy," www.purchasing.com, April 6, 2006.
6. J. Carbone, "Hewlett-Packard Wins for the Second Time," *Purchasing*, (September 2, 2004), www.purchasing.com.
7. D. Neef, *e-Procurement* (Upper Saddle River, NJ: Prentice Hall, 2001), 9.
8. Neef, 9.

9. As cited in T. Stevens, "Exchange for the Better?" *IndustryWeek* 249, no. 8 (August 21, 2000): 39.

10. From www.covisint.com. Accessed on January 24, 2007.

11. M. P. Papazoglou and P. Ribbers, 243.

12. The information presented on e-catalogs is adapted from M. P. Papazoglou and P. Ribbers, 242–245.

13. R. M. Monczka, R. J. Trent, and R. B. Handfield, *Purchasing and Supply Chain Management* (Mason, OH: Thomson Southwestern, 2005), 603.

14. R. M. Monczka and R. J. Trent, "Purchasing and Supply Management: Key Trends and Changes throughout the 1990s," *International Journal of Purchasing and Materials Management* 34, no. 4 (Fall 1998): 2–11.

15. Monczka, Trent, and Handfield, 605.

16. D. Drickhamer, "EDI Is Dead! Long Live EDI!" *IndustryWeek* 252, no. 4 (April 2004): 31–38.

17. From an industry white paper titled "Accenture Builds High Performance in Supplier Relationship Management with mySAP SRM Solutions," www.accenture.com.

18. W. H. Inmon, J. D. Welch, and K. L. Glassey, *Managing the Data Warehouse* (New York: John Wiley & Sons), 365–366.

19. The material in this section is adapted from R. J. Trent and M. G. Kolchin, *Reducing the Transactions Costs of Purchasing Low Value Goods and Services*, CAPS Research (Tempe, AZ: CAPS Research, 1999), 72–86.

20. S. Avery, "Lean, but Not Mean: Rockwell Collins Excels," Purchasing 134, no. 14 (September 1, 2005): 26–32; J. Carbone, "Hewlett-Packard Wins for the Second Time," (September 2, 2004): www.purchasing.com; S. Avery, "Cessna Soars," *Purchasing* 132, no. 13 (September 4, 2003): 25–35; S. Avery, "Supply Management Is Core of Success at UTC," *Purchasing* 135, no. 12 (September 7, 2006): 36; B. Milligan, "Harley-Davidson Wins by Getting Suppliers on Board," *Purchasing* 129, no. 5, 52–65; D. Smock, "Deere Takes a Giant Leap," Purchasing 130, no. 17 (September 6, 2001): 26–35.

21. This case was developed as part of a global sourcing research project conducted by Robert M. Monczka, Robert J. Trent, and Kenneth Petersen. The published results of this study, titled "Effective Global Sourcing and Supply for Superior Results," includes an expanded version of this case and can be found at CAPS Research, www.ism.ws.

6

MANAGING THE HUMAN SIDE OF SUPPLY MANAGEMENT

When a North American and a European producer of transportation equipment merged during the 1990s, one of the merger's selling points to financial analysts was the savings that would result from leveraging the combined purchase volumes of the two companies. Within months of the merger, executives had assembled global sourcing teams composed of engineering and procurement representatives from across the two companies. The teams were charged with developing a common set of engineering specifications for their commodities and then reaching agreement on a single source that could satisfy the requirements of both regions. The twenty-something-year-old analysts on Wall Street rejoiced with glee in anticipation of the savings!

As John Steinbeck once wrote, "The best laid plans of mice and men often go astray." And the best laid plans here did go astray as the teams failed to achieve the kinds of savings envisioned at their conception. It's not because the "local" members who were assigned to the sourcing teams were incompetent. They were simply placed in a setting that was far removed from their normal frame of reference. Traveling long distances and working side by side or virtually with strangers from another continent were not something the team members had ever experienced. Some team members were not even all that familiar working with another functional group from within their own company.

Cost reduction was the primary driver behind this process. Talking about cost reductions of more than 5 percent was pushing the boundaries of these members' experience. In a good year most of the local procurement groups achieved a 2 to 3 percent cost improvement, if they achieved any improvement at all. Expecting these teams to deliver 15 or 20 percent cost savings, which was the stated target for these global initiatives, was pushing the bounds of reality.

It also became evident that team members suffered from a condition called "home market bias." During the analysis phase of strategy development, team members favored the suppliers with which they were most familiar. Objective analysis and decision making were, unfortunately, in short supply. Other than these minor problems, Wall Street analysts were probably told that everything was going quite well.

This chapter addresses perhaps the most important enabler of strategic supply management: the human resource element. First presented is a set of knowledge and skill areas that every supply management organization should possess. The next section identifies a variety of approaches for recruiting and developing future supply leaders. The chapter concludes with a presentation of one company's innovative approach for developing its human assets.

SUPPLY MANAGEMENT KNOWLEDGE AND SKILL REQUIREMENTS

It would be difficult to argue that the relationship between effective human resources and effective strategic supply management is not important. A major study found that having the right people as participants when pursuing global supply initiatives was the most important predictor of success. This study also found that a lack of access to people with the right knowledge and skills was the most serious problem affecting global sourcing success.[1] We can safely conclude, as most supply managers would, that having the right people is critical for attaining our supply objectives.

Many organizations that have transitioned from traditional purchasing to a strategic supply model have had to undergo a major turnover of personnel. The knowledge and skill set required to succeed in supply management is quite different from the knowledge and skill set required to succeed in a transactional purchasing environment. The challenge today becomes one of identifying a set of knowledge and skills that supply organizations require now and in the future.

Depending on how finite we become we could literally identify hundreds of skills that could be part of the supply management skill set. Some skill areas have been mentioned so often that their importance is taken for granted. Who wants to argue against the need for supply managers to demonstrate leadership, communicate and listen well, solve problems, manage change, and plan effectively?

A CAPS Research report by Larry Giunipero and Robert Handfield is one of the most recent and in-depth projects addressing human resource requirements within supply management. During the quantitative (i.e., survey) portion of their research these researchers formally evaluated and ranked 51 skills and 64 knowledge areas. While it is out of our scope to drill down into the specific areas evaluated during that study, Giunipero and Handfield also clustered the top knowledge and skill areas required of supply managers as identified through focus groups. The following identifies these areas listed in order of their frequency of mention:[2]

- *Team-related skills.* Leadership, decision making, influencing, and compromising
- *Strategic planning skills.* Project scoping, goal setting, and execution
- *Communication skills.* Presentation, public speaking, listening, and writing
- *Technical skills.* Web-enabled research and sourcing analysis
- *Broad financial skills.* Cost accounting and the ability to "make the business case"
- *Relationship management skills.* Ethics, facilitation, conflict resolution, and creative problem solving
- *Legal issues, contract writing, and risk mitigation in a global environment.* Protecting the organization against supplier and supply chain uncertainties

Our interest here is more on the knowledge that a supply organization should have rather than any one individual. The following presents a set of broader knowledge and skill areas identified through many discussions with supply leaders.

Ability to Understand the Competitive Business Model

A business model describes how an organization competes. A number of years ago, Treacy and Wiersema identified three broad ways that companies primarily compete: through a focus on operational excellence, through product leadership (which today must be modified to include innovation), and/or through customer intimacy.[3] Dell Computer, for example, has historically focused on operational excellence through its build-to-order, direct-ship model. Apple has focused primarily on product leadership and innovation, although the company is highly capable across the other two dimensions. Federal Express and UPS stress operational excellence to achieve their much publicized service levels. As a support function, supply management has an obligation to understand and support a company's competitive business model.

Best-in-class companies, almost by definition, should have clearly articulated the model they must put in place to succeed. Imagine the problems that will result when a company's business model features speed to market with niche product offerings while supply managers focus on selecting suppliers that are excellent at providing lower costs through high volume runs and long lead times. Material costs will be low, but is that really a good thing in a model that stresses responsiveness, speed, and flexibility? Supply managers must develop strategies that align directly with their firm's competitive business model. And to be effective, this means they must clearly understand that model.

Ability to Assume a Holistic Perspective

According to the WordNet Lexical Database, *holistic* means "emphasizing the organic or functional relation between the parts and the whole."[4] For supply managers, a holistic perspective means evolving from a narrow, functional perspective to one that understands how the different elements of a value chain interact to create value. Holistic thinking is about understanding how seemingly diverse pieces of a puzzle fit together. It requires the development of supply strategies that support not only corporate objectives but also the objectives of supply management's internal customers, particularly operations and engineering.

Ability to Support Nontraditional Supply Areas

Some readers might recall the good old days when the world of purchasing involved the buying of components according to internally derived specifications. Instead of just buying components, today supply managers are sourcing assemblies, systems, and even finished goods. And instead of just sourcing direct materials, today's supply manager becomes involved with buying, well, just about everything. This includes services of all kinds, capital equipment, and even employee benefits. At a major automotive original equipment manufacturer (OEM), the supply management group has negotiated a contract with a hospital covering employee heart bypass surgeries (hopefully based on more than price). At another company the CEO tapped the CPO to develop a proposal and then negotiate the purchase of a corporate jet. In the words of the CEO, "You're the expert in buying things—now go buy a jet." When the CPO was asked later what he knows about corporate jets, he responded, "A heck of a lot more than I did a few months ago!"

A note from a supply chain graduate to his former professor sums up well the scope of even this young buyer's expanding involvement into many different supply areas:[5]

I am working at National Steel and Shipbuilding Company (NASSCO), which is wholly owned by General Dynamics. I've been here since graduating in 2004. I started my career in spares purchasing, helping to outfit the

Navy ships we are building with everything from engine spares to toilet paper to gun holsters. Everything that isn't bolted down I have purchased. I've moved on to bigger things now. I'm in charge of several specs, including the rudder, hull castings, anchor, and anchor chain. I'm also the buyer for all labor subcontracts, whether it is for temporary welders or engineering consulting work. I also have all weld rods and some spare parts responsibility. Needless to say, they keep me busy here.

How the times have changed. Even the free lunch with suppliers isn't what it used to be.

Knowledge of Process Management

As defined in Chapter 1, an organizational process consists of a set of interrelated tasks or activities designed to achieve a desired outcome or objective. Examples of objectives include the selection of world-class suppliers, the timely fulfillment of customer orders, or the development of innovative new products or services. And because they don't know better, organizational processes almost always cross functional boundaries. The ability to take a holistic view will come in handy when focusing on organizational processes.

Because processes create the output that leads to desired outcomes, it is important to understand those processes that create value, both within and outside of supply management. Supply managers must be able to visualize these processes, articulate their objectives, and understand the role, either leading or supportive, that they play in making sure the process leads to desired results. Assuming a process view also helps manage the conflict and trade-offs that inevitably occur across a supply chain.

Assuming a process perspective also will help geographically diverse locations and units adhere to a single approach rather than developing, and probably suboptimizing, local processes. Developing supply personnel with strong process design and management skills supports nicely the goals of strategic supply management.

Ability to Manage Supplier Relationships

A theme that has become prevalent across most industries is the increasing importance of supplier relationships. As Chapter 3 reported, the most common organizational design feature that medium and larger firms have put in place is assigning specific individuals to manage supplier relationships. It was also a design feature that did not correlate highly with design effectiveness. The need to manage relationships effectively remains an ongoing challenge. Most firms would benefit from a more enlightened approach to managing their relationships.

Supplier relationship management is a broad-based management methodology and set of practices describing how a firm manages its supply base. It is also a philosophy promoted by supply leaders across a company that recognizes the importance of relationships. Chapter 11 addresses relationship management in detail, including a discussion of why relationships matter, what suppliers want from the buyer-seller relationship, and specific actions that supply managers can take to promote better supplier relationships.

Understanding of Electronic Business

Perhaps one of the most important reasons for developing electronic systems is to relieve supply managers of mundane duties such as generating and sending material releases. Chapter 5 revealed that electronic systems development is critical for creating an information-enabled supply organization. Many of these systems support the separation of strategic and operational responsibilities, allowing supply managers to focus their efforts in areas that should provide the greatest return. Supply managers must understand their role in developing and using ERP, SRM, EDI, contract management, reverse Internet auction, and e-procurement systems.

An undergraduate supply chain management program in the eastern United States recently required all supply chain majors to take an e-business systems course before they could graduate, reflecting industry feedback about the importance of electronic business competency. E-business competency has become an essential knowledge and skill area for supply managers.

Ability to Perform Statistical Analyses and Make Fact-Based Decisions

The ability to perform statistical analyses and make fact-based decisions means that strategic supply management processes are supported by objective data. It also implies that measurement systems are in place to provide timely and objective information. As Chapter 4 noted, this may not always be the case. What are some supply management areas that will benefit from statistical analyses and fact-based decisions? The following is a partial list:

- Selecting suppliers
- Identifying candidates for supply based reduction
- Identifying expected paybacks from supplier development efforts
- Calculating the impact of supplier nonconformances
- Ranking supplier suggestions in terms of importance and feasibility
- Identifying which suppliers to offer longer-term agreements

- Identifying the impact of price concession strategies during negotiation planning
- Identifying the benefits of leveraging purchase volumes with suppliers
- Calculating bankruptcy probabilities based on supplier financial health
- Making outsourcing decisions

Strong Knowledge of Cost and Quality Management

As Chapter 12 will explain, very important differences exist between price and cost management. Knowing when and where to apply each type of analysis is an important part of strategic supply management. Cost analytic techniques focus primarily on the individual costs that are aggregated to create a price. While a price is technically a cost, it is a macro cost composed of various elements that are added together. Traditional purchasing has been largely price focused regardless of the item or service being considered for purchase.

A primary difference between price and cost analysis is that cost analysis requires a more technical and detailed understanding of costs. Cost analytic techniques require the management of costs elements and cost drivers. Cost analysis also requires greater cooperation with a seller to develop strategies to improve cost performance. Cost management and relationship management are closely related—it is hard to do one (cooperative cost management) without the other (SRM).

The ability to understand and manage supplier quality is also an essential part of supply management. Never before have so many companies relied on suppliers for such a large portion of value-add. As Chapter 11 will point out, supply managers should never assume that suppliers will always perform as required or that supplier performance is not vital to supply chain success. Supply management is not the "field of dreams," where if we build it they will come. The supply management version of this fantasy is "source it and they will perform."

Ability to Span Boundaries

While supply management by definition is a boundary spanning process, the degree of boundary spanning is increasing. Figure 6.1 provides a perspective about the changing nature of boundary spanning across the supply chain. Supply managers must increasingly work across a mix of boundaries:

- *Functional boundaries.* This relates to the growth in cross-functional interaction, especially through teams.
- *Organizational or enterprise boundaries.* This relates to the need to work with suppliers and customers to manage product development,

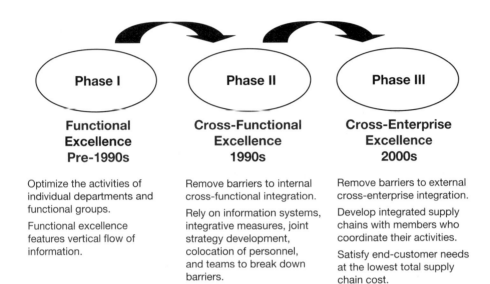

Phase I	Phase II	Phase III
Functional Excellence Pre-1990s	**Cross-Functional Excellence 1990s**	**Cross-Enterprise Excellence 2000s**
Optimize the activities of individual departments and functional groups.	Remove barriers to internal cross-functional integration.	Remove barriers to external cross-enterprise integration.
Functional excellence features vertical flow of information.	Rely on information systems, integrative measures, joint strategy development, colocation of personnel, and teams to break down barriers.	Develop integrated supply chains with members who coordinate their activities.
		Satisfy end-customer needs at the lowest total supply chain cost.

Figure 6.1 Phases of supply chain development.

demand and supply planning, sourcing, customer order fulfillment, and continuous supply chain improvement

- *Geographic boundaries.* This relates to the growth in working with units or divisions within a company or with suppliers that are geographically dispersed, such as during the development of company-wide purchase agreements.

- *Cultural boundaries.* This relates to working internally and externally with people from different cultures. Many supply managers know more about Chinese culture than they ever thought was possible. An extension of cultural boundaries is language boundaries. Supply managers increasingly work in a virtual and globally dispersed world.

No single individual will be completely competent in all the knowledge and skill areas presented here. However, it is not unreasonable to expect to have core capabilities across the supply organization, rather than with any one individual, within each area.

STRATEGIES FOR ACQUIRING AND DEVELOPING FUTURE SUPPLY LEADERS

A company should not only be concerned where its supply leaders will come from over the next several years but also 10 years now. There are many creative ways for ensuring access to future supply leaders. While a shortage of talented individuals may have been an excuse a few years ago for not pursuing strategic supply management, this excuse needs to be replaced with a proactive approach to acquiring and developing future leaders. Excuses just won't cut it anymore.

Approaches for Acquiring Human Resources

A variety of approached exist for obtaining the human resources required for supporting strategic supply management. The objective of all these approaches is to gain access to leaders that will guide the future supply organization.

Develop Close Relationship with a Select Group of Colleges. Some companies develop close relationships with a select group of colleges and universities. These companies extensively recruit interns, co-op students, and recent college graduates from these institutions. Merck, for example, uses its supply management internship program as a means to evaluate potential job candidates before their senior year. Soon after the fall semester begins, Merck makes full-time job offers to the most promising interns from the previous summer. Those that accept Merck's offer are placed into a supply management rotation program after they graduate. As an example of how aggressive recruiting has become in general, the Central Intelligence Agency recruits prospective employees as early as high school through its Undergraduate Scholarship Program.[6]

Hire the Talent from Outside. Like many professional sports teams, some companies go to the marketplace and "buy" the talent they need. This approach requires a willingness to make attractive offers that will entice supply managers to join a company. It is often worthwhile to team up with a first-rate executive search firm to coordinate recruiting efforts if this is a preferred strategy for obtaining talent.

Recruit Management Consultants. Another possibility for identifying future supply leaders involves recruiting management consultants who are leaving the consulting industry. Consulting firms hire some exceptional individuals who quickly take on demanding supply management projects for their clients. And while consulting may appear to be an exciting career, many consultants find the travel demands placed on them to be burdensome, particularly if they have a family. After a few years, some of these very qualified individuals are looking for a different work environment.

Recruit from Other Functional Groups. Many supply organizations recruit talent from other functional groups. It is increasingly common to see individuals with engineering or finance backgrounds working in supply management. At many companies supply management is now viewed as a promising career path offering exciting opportunities. John Deere, for example, has developed a career path model so buyers and managers, including those from other functional groups, can visualize their career progression. Keep in mind, however, that when one group recruits from other functional groups, it is important to not be perceived as "poaching" talent, particularly when those groups are needed to support supply management objectives.

Recruit Honorably Discharged Military Personnel. Some companies regularly tap into one of the best leadership pipelines available—and they do not want you to know about it. This pipeline includes individuals who are honorably leaving the military. Consider the maturity and skills that a Navy petty officer, lieutenant, commander, or captain bring to the workplace. The same is true for the other military branches. Besides receiving training that is highly technical, these individuals have often worked under stressful conditions that require teamwork and commitment. This is a human resource pipeline that many supply organizations should pursue more aggressively.

Approaches for Developing Human Resources

It's surprising how many ways exist for developing personnel who are currently part of the supply organization. The following summarizes some of these ways.

Assign Promising Personnel to Team Leadership Assignments. Team leadership assignments offer one of the best training grounds for developing future supply leaders. Besides the challenge of managing people from different functional disciplines, the team leadership role is one of the most important in organizations today. As noted in Chapter 3, most firms rely extensively on teams to develop supply management strategies. In some respects, team leadership roles are like the minor leagues before entering the major leagues. Effective team leaders are prime candidates for future supply leadership positions.

Create a Mentoring Program. Many companies have created mentoring programs to develop promising supply leaders. With these programs a senior supply leader works directly with junior personnel to provide guidance and to share knowledge and experiences. The mentors meet with the junior personnel on a regular basis, introduce him or her to other executives, and include these individuals in any experiences that would further develop these prospective leaders, such as participating in a buyer-supplier executive council meeting.

Not all mentoring occurs at the executive level. Given the importance of teams, it makes sense for team leaders to mentor team members who will eventually assume formal leadership roles. It also makes sense to assign a mentor to new college hires. This approach assumes the mentors are qualified to assume that role and will be diligent in their responsibilities.

Develop Leadership Rotation Programs. Leadership or management rotation programs can also be an effective approach for developing future supply leaders. Progressive firms identify early on their most promising recruits, perhaps during the college recruiting process, and then place them in a leadership development or rotation program. These programs, which generally last from one to two years, rotate new hires across different assignments. At the end of the development program, these individuals have a solid understanding regarding how the supply management process works. These individuals are also highly visible as they move through their rotation assignments. Over 30 of the top 50 companies and organizations that *BusinessWeek* identified as the best places for college graduates to work offer formal management training programs.[7]

Provide Continuous Training and Leadership Development Programs. As companies shift toward strategic supply management, they usually find they need to retool or further develop their existing workforce. This retooling or development often takes the form of continuous training programs and leadership development training. The case at the end of this chapter profiles Boeing's efforts at exposing thousands of employees to a set of supply management best practices. Boeing understands that supply management is now as important as program and product management.

A word of caution is in order here. Some companies have experienced a disappointing attrition rate after their participants have completed a leadership development program. Many young managers, whose higher potential was a major factor in being nominated for a development program in the first place, often find they are attractive to other companies after completing the development program. A company headquartered in Pennsylvania is concerned because over half of the managers that have completed its advanced management program have left the company. This rate is much higher than managers who have not participated in the program. This company needs to better understand the root cause of why so many talented managers are leaving.

Make Training Courses Available on a Just-in-Time Basis. Another approach for developing the workforce includes offering shorter courses related to various aspects of supply management. These courses, developed internally or by third parties, usually cover a wide range of topics such as quality management, lean thinking, team building, and negotiation. Most companies develop a generic menu of courses and then offer them to employees on a regular basis. Best practice companies carefully assess the knowledge and skill needs of their future supply leaders and then craft training programs that are customized to that employee's unique development needs. For example, an employee that is assuming the role of commodity team leader might benefit from team leadership training modules. Another employee that is being assigned to a supplier development team would likely benefit from a course on lean supply or Six Sigma quality improvement. Increasingly these training modules should be available for on-demand viewing asynchronously through Web-based systems.

Reward Personnel for Skill Advancement. Another development approach focuses on rewarding personnel for advancing their skills and knowledge through formal education. This includes earning degrees or certificates in supply management. Each year the Institute for Supply Management (ISM) publishes a list of colleges and universities that offer degree and certificate programs related to procurement and supply management. Even many colleges and universities that do not have formal supply programs offer courses related to supply management. Supporting continuing education through tuition reimbursements should further encourage the development of a firm's human resource capabilities.

SUPPLIER MANAGEMENT UNIVERSITY AT BOEING

Like many other industries, the aerospace industry is undergoing changes that are radically affecting the role that supply managers play. Consider the case of Boeing. The company is working hard to solidify its position as the preeminent builder of commercial aircraft with its new 787 Dreamliner, its extensively redesigned 747, its new longer-range versions of the 777, and a wide range of improvements to its Next-Generation 737. And on the defense side, Boeing is transforming itself from a company that offers a diverse portfolio of defense products and services into one that also integrates these multiple products, platforms, and services into networked systems.

Boeing's new business model relies on suppliers like never before. Let's consider one of Boeing's boldest initiatives ever—the 787 Dreamliner. Boeing's assembly plant near Seattle will receive cockpits that a supplier in Kansas has fully "stuffed" with avionics. The plane's fuselage will be made of a single-piece advanced composite developed by a supplier named Toray. Fully assembled wings will be built by a Japanese supplier and delivered just-in-time by specially modi-fied 747s. Rockwell Collins will take the lead in designing and producing some of the most advanced avionics and flight management systems ever developed. To make things even more interesting, some of Boeing's supply markets, particularly for metals like titanium, are facing capacity constraints. The list of suppliers that are integral to Boeing's success could go on and on.

What do you do if supply management is becoming as important as program and product management? And what do you do if your company has historically downplayed the importance of suppliers only to endorse a new business model that demands a total commitment to supplier management? If your company is Boeing, you respond with an innovative approach to human resource develop-ment called Supplier Management University.

The Supplier Management University program resulted from internal and external customer feedback that suggested that perhaps Boeing could do a better job managing its supply base. The vision behind this program was to develop a single, best-in-class process for managing suppliers that is used across all of Boeing's business units. The program's stated objective is to improve the skills, competencies, and effectiveness of those who work with major suppliers. While certainly not the only supply management program offered at Boeing, Supplier Management University has become the most visible and effective. The program has been featured in Boeing's *Frontiers*, the company-published magazine for its employees.

In 2001 two executive vice presidents, one from the commercial and one from the defense side of the business, formed a team with representatives from each business unit to develop the new training program. Boeing rolled out its enter-prise-wide supplier management program by offering its initial eight-hour overview course in October 2001 and its first one-week Practices course in April 2002. Executive management created the position of Supplier Management University program director and provided him with budget and staff support. One of the director's responsibilities involves putting together class rosters that include participants from different business units, locations, and backgrounds.

Boeing set out to create a learning environment that allows participants to become familiar with a set of best practices related to supplier management, develop an understanding of how to use these approaches, share experiences with others from around the company, and assume leadership responsibility for improvement projects. As Scott Amelung, the program director, explains, "We need to know how to work with our suppliers. If all Boeing people are using com-mon processes and techniques in their relationships, it makes our jobs easier and the job easier for suppliers."[9] Since Boeing is made up of many diverse units, the company recognizes the value of developing a more consistent "one voice" approach when interacting with suppliers.

Supplier Management University is a series of programs that progress in sequence from a one-day overview through two weeklong sessions to eventually assuming responsibility for a two- to three-month project. While the programs must be taken in sequence, not all participants complete all four offerings. Table 6.1 summarizes the four major components that make up this program. About 40 percent of the attendees are non-supplier management personnel, including engineers, quality, and finance personnel. And in 2006 external suppliers, for the first time, participated in the one-week Practices course.

Courses are taught primarily by Boeing's own subject matter experts, with course locations rotating between Boeing's Leadership Development Center in St. Louis, the commercial aircraft headquarters building near Seattle, and a central location in Southern California. The final day of the Practices course features a capstone presentation by a third-party about the overall changes and trends affecting supplier management. The Applications course features a supplier panel discussion. Boeing has even developed an Australian version of Supplier Management University that it offers annually.

Leading companies understand that competition is not only for the hearts and minds of customers but also for the hearts and minds of suppliers. As Steve Winkler, director of F-15 Production Programs, noted, "Three-fourths of our total expenditures on the F-15 program are with suppliers. Suppliers are the name of the game. The times are changing, and the Boeing story is changing with it."[10]

Working with suppliers offers an opportunity to become a preferred customer, receive relationship-specific investment that is not necessarily available to others, and create a co-destiny that further strengthens supplier relationships. Boeing employees will tell you that gaining these hard-to-beat advantages requires the right people who know how to work with suppliers. To make sure it has the right people, Boeing has made a major investment in Supplier Management University.

CONCLUDING THOUGHTS

Table 6.2 summarizes a set of best-practice characteristics pertaining to the acquisition, retention, and development of human resources within supply management. It is hard to imagine a world-class supply management organization that has not addressed its human resource needs. Several years ago a printed ad featured a concert hall with a stage, chairs, music, and instruments but no musicians. The message was quite clear: Nothing happens without the right people to make it happen. Strategic supply management is no different than the orchestra.

Table 6.1 Summary of Boeing Corporation's Supplier Management University

Course	Course Objectives	Target Audience	Frequency	Graduates
Overview (Open enrollment via Boeing's intranet)	• Identify supplier management best practices. • Match best practices as they apply to pre-award, award, and post-award phases of a contract cycle. • Identify the benefits of best practices through the use of a supplier management plan.	• All supply managers. • Those involved directly in supplier management and procurement. • Managers and senior-level specialists outside of supply. • Team leaders, program managers, equipment engineers, and other team members.	• Offered 50 times per year. • Length: One 8-hour session.	4,500
Practices (Nomination by supervisors required)	• Explain the relationship between supplier management best practices and program management best practices. • Demonstrate an understanding of best practices during pre-award, award, and post-award phases. • Identify how to enhance supplier relationships and performance.	• Similar to Overview. • Must have completed Overview.	• Offered nine times per year. • 28 attendees per session. • Length: One-week residence.	900
Application Strategies (Nomination by senior managers required)	• Create an environment for teamwork and trust with suppliers. • Identify appropriate source selection criteria and weighting. • Refine all aspects of supplier management, including proposal review, risk management, communication, and metrics.	• Similar to Overview. • Must have completed Overview and Practices.	• Offered three times per year. • 24 attendees per session. • Length: One-week residence.	300
Learning Project (Nomination by directors required)	• Address current supplier management challenges. • Develop leadership competencies. • Promote individual and team skill development through applied learning.	• Nominated by directors. • Must have completed Overview, Practices, and Application Strategies.	• Length: Two-to three-month directed project.	15

Table 6.2 Human Resource Acquisition and Development—Best Practice Characteristics

• Training is targeted to individual knowledge and skill needs rather than generic needs.	• An extensive profile of employee skill and knowledge sets is accessible through a database.
• Benchmarking takes place to ensure that human resource strategies are current.	• A process exists to identify high-potential candidates for leadership development early in their career.
• Tactical/operational development programs are separate from strategic supply development programs.	• Potential supply personnel are targeted, recruited, and supported early in their academic career through co-ops and internships.
• A mix of internal and external experts are used to develop and deliver training programs.	• Executive leadership supports development programs with budget support and public recognition.
• Measurement is used to validate the efficacy of human resource management policies and programs.	• An objective assessment of employee satisfaction with compensation, benefits, career path planning, and human resource policies is conducted regularly.
• Professional development options include on-the-job training, external and in-house classes and seminars, and Web-based modules and instruction.	• The employee appraisal process recognizes the individual attainment of new knowledge and skills and requires joint agreement on employee development plans.
• Qualified nonprocurement and external candidates are actively recruited for supply assignments.	• Promising new hires have access to mentors, career path guidance, and job rotation opportunities.
• An executive leadership team is responsible for developing human resource policies, plans, strategies, and approaches.	
• A variety of strategies are in place to acquire the necessary supply management human resources.	

Leading companies understand that developing their human resources is a key enabler of strategic supply management, if not the key enabler. They view training and development as an investment rather than an expense. And they have well-developed strategies in place to recruit and develop future supply leaders.

SUMMARY OF KEY CHAPTER POINTS

• The relationship between effective human resources and effective strategic supply management is critical. Many organizations that have transitioned from traditional purchasing to a strategic supply model have had to undergo a near-total turnover of personnel.

• The knowledge and skill set required to succeed in supply management is quite different from the knowledge and skill set required to succeed in a transactional purchasing environment.

- A set of knowledge and skill areas that supply management organizations should have includes understanding the competitive business model, assuming a holistic perspective, supporting nontraditional supply areas, knowledge of process management, managing critical supply chain relationships, electronic business competency, performing statistical analyses and making fact-based decisions, a knowledge of cost and quality management, and the ability to span boundaries.
- The ability to span boundaries includes functional boundaries, organizational or enterprise boundaries, geographic boundaries, and cultural and language boundaries.
- There are many creative ways for recruiting and developing future supply management leaders.
- Leading companies understand the need to develop their human resources. They view training and development as an investment rather than an expense.

ENDNOTES

1. R. M. Monczka and R. J. Trent, "The Global Sourcing Research Project," 2000.
2. L. Giunipero and R. B. Handfield, *Purchasing Education and Training II* (Tempe, AZ: CAPS Research, 2004), 49.
3. M. Treacy and F. Wiersema, "The Discipline of Market Leaders" (Reading, MA: Perseus Books, 1995), 45.
4. Available at http://wordnet.princeton.edu.
5. The author appreciates Brandon Duncan's sharing of his comments.
6. L. Gerdes, "The Best Places to Launch a Career," *BusinessWeek*, no. 4001 (September 18, 2006): 81.
7. Gerdes, 78.
8. The author would like to thank Boeing for permission to feature the Supplier Management University program in this book and, in particular, program director Scott Amelung for his generous sharing of insights.
9. D. Arkell, "School's In Session," *Frontiers V*, no. VII (November 2006): 42.
10. Arkell, 43.

MATCHING
SUPPLY STRATEGIES
TO SUPPLY NEEDS

Jack Wilson, a buyer at a major aerospace company, is not happy. During a break at a training session, he left the room to make several phone calls. After a few minutes he returned visibly upset. When a colleague asked what was wrong, Jack explained that he just called a supplier to ask for some special consideration in the scheduling of an order. Jack's company was asked to adjust a delivery schedule to accommodate a change at an important customer, prompting the request for a change further upstream from this supplier. His contact at the supplier told Jack the change was not possible and that Jack's company should not expect to receive any special treatment compared to or at the expense of other customers. In fact, the contact maintained, this supplier proudly treated all its customers equally. Jack's not-so-subtle reminder that his company was one of the supplier's biggest customers did not seem to carry much weight. While Jack knew that patience was a virtue, he also knew it was a virtue he was about to lose. He told his colleague that he finally lost his temper. "We did not award a single-source contract featuring very attractive volumes to your company to be treated equally," Jack told the supplier in no uncertain terms. "We gave you that contract so we would be treated *unequally*!"

Without question strategy development is fundamental to strategic supply management. It is hard to imagine a company that has gained a competitive advantage from supply management without putting in place formal and rigorous supply strategies. As the opening example illustrates, communicating those strategies to others across the supply chain may be as important as the strategy itself. One reason, but certainly not the only reason, for developing supply strategies is to gain preferential treatment that is not available from traditional purchasing approaches. Often we develop supply strategies with the objective of receiving "unequal" treatment from suppliers—treatment that may not be available to a supplier's other customers.

This chapter explores the topic of supply strategies. A primer to position our thinking about what strategy as a concept means is presented first. The chapter next summarizes the strategy development process at a company that is recognized for its worldwide supply strategies. The chapter concludes with a discussion of the portfolio matrix and relationship continuum—two strategy tools that should be in the tool kit of every supply manager.

A PRIMER ON STRATEGY

Even though strategies are an integral part of strategic supply management, we should not assume that everyone understands this topic, although we have all heard the term. Experts on strategy development may find the following to be somewhat basic. Others may find it helps them better understand what they need to know about developing supply strategies. This primer defines the concept of strategy, discusses the internal and external constraints that supply managers often face when developing strategies, and explains the differences between goals and objectives.

Defining Strategy

The concept of a strategy or strategy development is not at all unique to supply management. In fact, supply management has often lagged in this area compared with groups such as finance and marketing. At many companies, purchasing has simply reacted or responded to requests from internal customers. Historically the idea that purchasing could proactively develop well-thought-out strategies was a bit too much for some people to grasp. Today, a clear indication that a supply management group is pushing itself in the right direction is the presence of strategies that are formalized through supply contracts.

When supply managers are asked to define the term *strategy*, they usually reply it is a longer-term plan. While a plan is an important part of a strategy, it fails to define the concept fully. Richard Vancil of Harvard University provides perhaps one of the better and timeless definitions of strategy.[1] He says the strategy of an organization, or of a subunit of a larger organization, is a conceptualization, expressed or implied by the organization's leaders, of (1) the long-term *objectives* or *purposes* of the organization, (2) the broad *constraints* and *policies* that currently restrict the scope of the organization's activities, and (3) the current set of *plans* and near-term *goals* that have been adopted in the expectation of contributing to the achievement of the organization's objectives.

This definition is easy to summarize: An effective strategy basically consists of objectives, constraints, plans, and goals. The plans that are part of an organization's strategies are also called tactics, which are essential for carrying out any strategy. It is not enough to have a vision about the objectives or purposes of a supply organization. We must understand how to achieve that vision through action. Supply managers must create clearly articulate their objectives, goals, and plans through their written supply management strategies.

Strategy development occurs at different levels. These levels, similar to a continuum, include corporate, business unit, functional, and departmental strategies. Corporate strategies define the businesses in which the corporation expects to participate and the allocation of resources to those business units. Business unit strategies are concerned with the scope of each business and its linkage with the corporate strategy. These strategies are also concerned with how the business unit achieves and maintains a competitive advantage. Increasingly, supply management strategies are part of business unit strategies. The third level, functional strategies, defines how functional strategies will support the desired business level strategy as well as the strategies of other functional groups. The lowest strategy level consists of departmental strategies.

Internal and External Constraints

Every strategy development initiative requires a realistic assessment of the internal and external constraints that create boundaries around what we can do. Constraints should really have a neutral connotation associated with them, although admittedly something that constrains us is usually not viewed positively. There are numerous examples of constraints that place boundaries around our actions. A company may want to outsource the production of an item only to find that its union contract has strict language affecting that decision. Another company may want to develop longer-term contracts with suppliers but lacks any experience in crafting and managing these agreements. A third company may want to expand its sales to Asia but lacks the logistical support required for expansion. All constraints can be classified into one of two categories: internal or external.

A variety of internal constraints can affect the development of supply strategies. These include the following:

- *Corporate policies and objectives.* An effective supply strategy is one that supports the higher-level objectives of the organization. Supply managers must be aware of corporate objectives and policies, partly so they do not violate them. An emphasis on doing business with suppliers that have worldwide capabilities, for example, may conflict with a corporate policy that supports doing business with small and disadvantaged suppliers.

- *Strategy development within other functional groups.* Many supply strategies are developed to support the strategies that are developed by other functional groups. Purchasing is considered a support activity with an extensive array of internal customers that cannot be ignored. For example, a great deal of supply activity may surround the development of new products.

- *Financial resources.* Many strategies require financial resources, particularly for travel and living. A commodity management team that performs site visits to suppliers, for example, will require budget support. Opening and then operating an international purchasing office (IPO) will not be inexpensive. Supply managers must compete against other groups and opportunities for limited financial resources.

- *Human resource capabilities.* A shortage of qualified participants continues to be one of the most serious internal constraints facing many supply organizations.

- *Labor contracts.* Labor contracts may be an issue when supply managers are involved with the development of outsourcing strategies. These contracts often prohibit the outsourcing of work unless certain conditions are met. These contracts may also prohibit suppliers from working on-site.

- *Internal customer demands.* A support function such as purchasing must always be ready to satisfy the demands of its internal customers. Satisfying these demands, many of which are not known until they are made, naturally reduces the flexibility and resources that are available.

Supply strategists must also consider factors that are external to the supply organization:

- *Competitor actions.* At times supply strategies are developed as a response to actions by competitors. We often see this when one company announces a merger with another company. These announcements tend to set off an outbreak of merger activity.

- *Economic conditions.* Economics affect supply strategies because of the increasingly global nature of supply activities as well as the effect these conditions have on supply markets. Currency changes, interest rates, supply and demand, and worldwide growth all influence supply strategies.

- *Laws and regulations.* Domestic and foreign laws and regulations can affect the strategy development of any organizational unit. For example, Chapter 14 will address worldwide sourcing. Strategy development involving international procurement will require an evaluation of which country's laws to apply to an agreement.
- *Customer demands.* Many suppliers have grown because of the demands placed on them by their industrial customers. A customer that expands its operations to Europe will influence how its suppliers form their growth strategies. The objective of many supply alliances is to influence the technologies and strategies that suppliers will develop in the future. Customer demands at all levels of the value chain influence supply strategies. Your customers influence your strategies, and your strategies influence your suppliers' strategies, and so on down the line.

Differences between Objectives and Goals

Effective strategies include objectives and goals, making an understanding of the differences between these terms important. While they are often interchanged, even in the dictionary, fundamental differences exist between objectives and goals. Broadly speaking, it might be best to think of an objective as an aspiration to be worked toward in the future. The major feature of objectives is they provide broad direction. A goal, on the other hand, is an achievement or accomplishment to be realized by some future date. Ideally, goals align with the objectives of the organization as articulated by its leaders. Goals make objectives actionable.

Objectives and goals can differ across one or more of four dimensions: time frame, specificity, focus, and measurement.[2] Within the time frame dimension, objectives are timeless or open-ended, while goals are time-phased and intended to be superseded by subsequent goals. Improving supplier quality, a timeless aspiration, is an objective, while lowering the average supplier's defect level from 5,000 parts per million (ppm) to 2,500 ppm within a two-year period is a goal. The expectation is that a new goal will be put in place once the current goal is achieved.

For specificity, objectives are stated in broad, general terms, while goals are much more specific, stated in terms of a particular result that will be accomplished by a certain date. A desire to reduce purchase costs is an example of a broad objective. Reducing the purchase price of DRAM semiconductors by an average of 15 percent within six months is a specific goal that relates to this objective.

For focus, objectives are often stated in some relevant environment external to the organization, while goals are internally focused and imply how resources shall be used in the future. An organization may have an objective of being regarded (externally) as an environmentally friendly company. A corresponding goal may be to commit 2 percent of pretax profits (internally focused) to waste reduction and recycling efforts.

Finally, for measurement, quantified objectives are stated in relative terms, while a quantified goal is stated in absolute terms. An objective may be to be in the top three in terms of industry market share. The relative aspect of the objective is the comparison of market share to others within an industry. A stated goal in absolute terms is to reduce the procurement overhead budget by $100,000 annually. Effective supply strategies consider both objectives and goals during their development. One needs the other.

THE SUPPLY STRATEGY DEVELOPMENT PROCESS

If strategies are an integral part of strategic supply management, then it makes sense that a process for developing strategies should be in place. Recall from Chapter 1 that a process consists of a set of interrelated tasks or activities designed to achieve a specific objective. In this case, the objective is to develop a set of world-class supply strategies that lead to competitive advantage. While there is no agreed-upon or standardized strategy development process or template to follow, it is important to give thought to a process that enables a supply manager or team to methodically analyze and develop supply strategies.

Not all strategy efforts involve the development of supply contracts, although strategy development and contract development are often part of the same process. A firm could develop strategies, for example, for increasing supplier involvement in product design. And strategy development plays a large part in the supplier evaluation and selection process, a topic that is covered in Chapter 10. Much of the strategy attention in supply management pertains to developing commodity or category strategies, almost all of which are eventually formalized through written contracts.

Table 7.1 summarizes a strategy development process used at a chemical company when developing its strategies and worldwide contracts. Firms that routinely develop formal supply strategies usually have some sort of process that is presented as a sequence of steps. These processes may include as few as five steps or phases or as many as 16. (The company whose strategy development process has 16 steps could perhaps compress its process.)

The process presented in Table 7.1 contains some best practices that are not immediately obvious in the exhibit. An executive steering committee oversees this process and takes an active role in sponsoring strategy initiatives. Executive managers also make budget available to support travel and living expenses incurred

Table 7.1 Sample Strategy Development Process

Step 1: Identify Sourcing and Supply Opportunities

An executive steering committee, working with functional managers, identifies supply strategy development opportunities offering the best return.

Step 2: Establish Strategy Development Teams

The executive steering committee charters cross-functional teams with members from world-wide locations participating. The committee provides resources as required.

Step 3: Evaluate Sourcing Opportunities and Propose Strategies

Teams validate the assumptions underlying the project, verify current volumes and expected savings, determine if qualified suppliers exist, evaluate the current set of specifications between design centers, and propose preliminary supply strategies. The executive committee reviews the recommendations developed by the strategy development teams.

Step 4: Identify Requirements for Supplier Proposals

Strategy development teams, working with other internal participants, prequalify suppliers and develop the request for proposal that suppliers receive.

Step 5: Forward Proposals to Prequalified Suppliers

On average, teams forward proposal requests to six suppliers, with responses expected within six weeks.

Step 6: Evaluate the Technical and Commercial Viability of Proposals

The team performs a commercial and technical evaluation of supplier proposals and conducts supplier site visits as required.

Step 7: Negotiate with the Most Qualified Suppliers

A smaller team negotiates with suppliers at the buying company's U.S. headquarters. Negotiations, which last up to three days, lengthen if the buying company does not achieve its previously established improvement goals.

Step 8: Award Final Contract(s) to Winning Supplier(s)

Information concerning the awarded contract is communicated throughout the company. The steering committee reports expected savings to executive management and finance.

Step 9: Manage Transition to New Contracts and/or New Suppliers

Agreements are loaded into the appropriate corporate and contract management systems. The strategy development team manages the transition if the supplier and/or part numbers change from previous agreements or designs.

Step 10: Monitor Supplier Performance and Review Expiring Contracts

Performance measurement systems assess supplier performance and validate savings. The contract repository system notifies supply managers of expiring agreements six months prior to expiration.

Table 7.2 Questions to Consider when Developing a Supply Strategy

What are the broad objectives of the strategy?

What other functional groups should we involve in strategy development?

What internal customer requirements are we trying to exceed through this strategy?

What are the current expenditures by commodity and supplier?

What are the future volumes for this commodity?

What is the performance of the current supplier(s)?

What other suppliers are in the marketplace, and what are their capabilities?

Do we want a domestic, regional, or worldwide contract?

Should we use a single supplier or multiple suppliers?

If we use multiple suppliers, how will we divide the total spend?

Should we develop a short-term or longer-tem contract?

What are our pricing targets?

What other issues besides price do we need to consider?

What services, such as inventory management or design support,
do we want the supplier to provide?

Who has the power in the market?

What other buyers are competing for supply?

What is our negotiating strategy?

How will we measure supplier performance?

How will this strategy promote continuous improvement?

What are the contract performance risks and how can we manage them?

What type of supplier relationship should we pursue?

Who will be assigned to manage the supplier relationship?

What specific clauses should the contract include?

when developing supply strategies. These managers also require strategy development teams to meet specific milestones before they can proceed to the next step. Teams have to present their progress to the steering committee on a regular basis, with their progress posted on the company's intranet. This company also conducts lessons learned sessions after the completion of every strategy development project to identify what went right and what went wrong.

Most supply strategy development processes, particularly those that result in formally negotiated supply agreements, require the participants to address some important questions. Table 7.2 presents some of the more relevant topics to consider when creating a formal supply strategy.

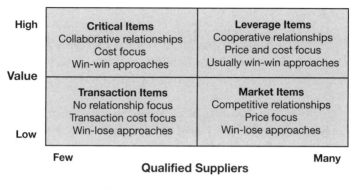

Figure 7.1 Segmenting supply requirements.

THE PORTFOLIO MATRIX—A TOOL FOR DEVELOPING SUPPLY STRATEGIES

Strategy development is not an easy process. If it were easy, then everyone would have a set of fully developed supply strategies in place. What if a strategy development tool was available that provided valuable guidance when crafting supply strategies? Fortunately, such a tool exists and can be used by any organization. The next few pages may be the most important in this book.

Figure 7.1 presents the portfolio matrix, a tool every supply manager should have in his or her tool kit. Presented in the timeless and classic 2 × 2 format, the matrix recognizes that an effective supply organization must apply a variety, or portfolio, of strategies and approaches given different supply requirements. The 2 × 2 matrix has been around for quite a while. This concept, although not this specific tool, was first articulated by Kraljic in his 1983 *Harvard Business Review* article titled "Purchasing Must Become Supply Management."[3]

The use of this tool forces supply organizations to segment their supply approaches and to recognize that one strategy approach does not fit all requirements. This matrix is referenced throughout this book, and later chapters provide company examples that further highlight the use of this approach.

Users of this matrix segment their purchase requirements across two dimensions: the number of active suppliers in the marketplace and the value of the good or service to the buying organization. Both of these dimensions are intentionally vague. For some requirements an active supply market might consist of three or four suppliers. For other items there may be dozens of qualified suppliers. The concept of value also does not have a specific definition. Value can be a function of total dollars spent on an item, or it could be a relatively inexpensive item that has a disproportionate effect on product or service performance.

Perhaps the most important reason for using a tool such as the portfolio matrix is its prescriptive nature. Once a supply manager or team quantifies the total spend for each commodity or category, the good or service can be positioned within the most appropriate quadrant. This will help identify (1) the type of supplier relationship to pursue, (2) whether to engage in a win-lose or win-win negotiation and relationship approach, (3) whether to take a price or cost analytic approach, (4) the types of supply strategies and approaches that should work best given the placement of an item, and (5) how best to create value across different purchase requirements.

Price versus Cost Analysis

A major advantage of using the portfolio matrix is it helps identify when to apply a price versus a cost analytic approach. Fundamental differences exist between price and cost analysis. *Price analysis* refers to the process of comparing a price against another price or against other available information without in-depth knowledge about underlying costs. *Cost analysis*, on the other hand, focuses on the costs that are added together to create a purchase price. By better managing and reducing the elements of cost, a buyer should see the result of these efforts in a lower purchase price compared with prices where cost management did not occur. Chapter 12 addresses price and cost management in detail.

Items that reside in the lower half of the matrix will benefit most from price analytic techniques. At times an item may have such a low value or be part of such a highly competitive market that any analysis beyond competitive price comparisons is not worth the effort. At other times supply managers must apply innovative cost management techniques to manage costs and cost drivers for items that are more important or higher in value. It would be a waste of time to take a cost perspective when a situation requires a price perspective. Conversely, taking a price analytic approach when a situation would benefit from cost analysis can leave some value unrealized.

Types of Supplier Relationships

The portfolio matrix also helps an organization understand what type of relationship to pursue with suppliers. A central theme throughout this book is that a strong understanding of supply relationships is essential for effective supply management. This does not mean that all relationships are equally important. Knowing when, where, and how to apply an appropriate relationship is an area

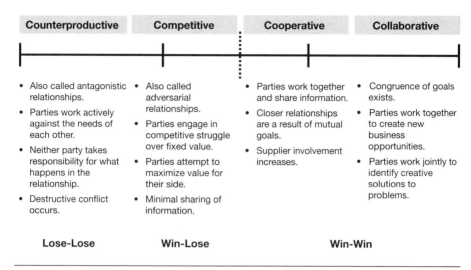

Figure 7.2 The four Cs of supply relationships.

where supply professionals bring value to their organization. Chapter 11 addresses supplier relationship management in detail.

Various models have been developed that provide some order or logic to industrial relationships.[4] Figure 7.2 presents an approach that characterizes relationships based on behavior rather than legal structures. This figure presents relationships along four behavioral dimensions and recognizes that different approaches to supplier management apply to different settings. With buyer-supplier relationships, there is no "one size fits all."

Counterproductive Relationships. Counterproductive relationships, also called antagonistic or lose-lose relationships, feature the parties in a relationship working actively against each other's interests. In addition, neither party feels a need to assume responsibility for what transpires. This scenario not only fails to create new value, it is detrimental to short and longer-term success.

While this type of relationship is never recommended, they do occur. Some buyers have taken legal action against their suppliers recently to prevent material price increases that the buyer contends violate contractual agreements. Suing your supplier is a subtle clue that a relationship is moving toward being counterproductive.

Competitive Relationships. Competitive relationships, also referred to as distributive, win-lose, or adversarial relationships, feature supply chain members acting primarily in their own self-interests. The parties compete over a fixed amount of value (win-lose) rather than pursuing activities that create new value or opportunities for both parties (win-win), such as innovations that lead to increased market share. While it seems wrong to say, many relationships should be competitive. Beyond the transaction or arm's-length activities taking place, few benefits result from a closer relationship. The reality is that a majority of a buying firm's relationships should be competitive. The total value of the goods and services provided by these suppliers usually does not make up a majority of total expenditures.

Cooperative Relationships. Cooperative relationships, also referred to as integrative relationships, recognize the value of closer interaction and open sharing of information. These relationships are most often associated with suppliers who are expected to be longer-term members of a reduced supply base. Relationships with these suppliers are often formalized through longer-term contracts that lead to discussions about how to improve cost, quality, delivery, packaging, inventory management, product innovation, and service—all factors that can affect performance. Cooperative relationships often feature early supplier involvement during product development.

Collaborative Relationships. Collaborative relationships, sometimes called creative relationships, involve a very limited number of suppliers that provide items or services that are essential or unique to a firm's success. A willingness to work jointly to identify better ways to operate or to compete in the marketplace is characteristic of a collaborative relationship. These relationships, which should be relatively few across the supply base, represent the most intensive relationship possible between a buyer and seller. They feature executive-to-executive interaction, joint strategy development sessions, and a sharing of resources. Supply chain alliances and partnerships, for example, are collaborative by design. The parties ideally share a co-destiny and recognize that the value they receive would be far less than if the collaborative relationship did not exist. Chapter 15 addresses supplier alliances, which are a special form of collaborative relationships. Cooperative and collaborative relationships should, by definition, be win-win.

Understanding the Four Quadrants

The portfolio matrix contains four quadrants where we position or place goods and services. Part of the value that supply managers bring is an understanding of their organization's purchase requirements and then knowing how to pursue an appropriate supply strategy. There is also value in understanding how to shift items across quadrants to realize even greater value. Table 7.3 summarizes the characteristics of each quadrant.

Transaction Quadrant. The goods and services in the transaction quadrant have a lower total value with a limited supply market. Reducing the transactions

Table 7.3 Portfolio Matrix Characteristics

Critical	Leverage
• Fewer capable suppliers providing unique or custom-designed items • Collaborative or interdependent relationships • Unable to move easily between suppliers • Joint cost analysis yields benefits • Unproven, undeveloped, or evolving technology • Focus on win-win opportunities and projects • High supplier switching costs	• Active supply market • Medium to high annual dollars combined into commodity families • Cooperative relationships featuring win-win approaches • Extensive use of longer-term agreements • Developed quality and technology of items • Less able to switch between suppliers • Focus on cost and price analysis
Supply Management's Value Contribution: Identifying and forming alliance-type relationships that should lead to competitive advantage	*Supply Management's Value Contribution:* Selectively developing longer-term supply agreements that provide unique value to the buyer
Transaction	**Market**
• Fewer capable suppliers within a region (the cost of a search outweighs the value of the search) • Low-priority items with fewer total dollars spent • May consume a disproportionate amount of time and resources to acquire • Developed quality and technology of items • Able to move easily between suppliers	• Greater number of suppliers in the marketplace • Relationships are largely competitive • Low to medium annual dollars • Able to move easily between suppliers • Developed quality and technology of items • Focus primarily on price analysis
Supply Management's Value Contribution: Developing low-dollar purchase systems that remove transactions costs and allow internal users to obtain items as required	*Supply Management's Value Contribution:* The use of buying approaches, such as competitive bidding, that rely on market forces to identify the most efficient producer

cost of the purchase is the primary way for supply professionals to create value here, usually through electronic systems or procurement cards. Even when an item has many potential suppliers, the cost of comparing sources outweighs the value resulting from the search. Any price analysis that occurs is cursory because of the low value of the good or service. In reality, relationships are not even a concern in this quadrant, which is why transactional relationships are not part of Figure 7.1. Negotiation rarely occurs for these items, since supply managers should not involve themselves in their direct acquisition. Supply managers may be involved, however, in negotiating with the vendors that supply low-dollar purchase systems, such as a procurement card provider.

The actual number of suppliers that reside in this quadrant should not be a major concern to supply managers. It is simply not worth the effort to get bogged down with transaction items and suppliers. Too many firms commit a disproportionate amount of time managing these relatively unimportant items. This takes away from managing the items that are important. Miscellaneous office supplies, one-time purchases, magazine subscriptions to trade journals, and emergency tools needed at remote locations usually qualify as transaction items. Reducing the transactions cost of a purchase is the primary way to create value in this quadrant.

Market Quadrant. The market quadrant includes standard items or services that have an active supply market, lower to medium total value, many suppliers that can provide substitutable products and services, well-defined specifications, and low supplier switching costs. Commodity chemicals, fasteners, corrugated packaging, and other basic raw materials that do not have an unusually high dollar value are logically part of this quadrant. Any negotiation that occurs in this quadrant is lower level and focuses on price and delivery.

Price rather than cost analytic techniques usually work best when obtaining these items. Competitive bid or price comparisons, spot buys, shorter-term contracting, reverse Internet auctions, and blanket purchase orders are often-used techniques when obtaining market items. Relationships with the providers of market items are typically competitive (i.e., win-lose) and price focused. The buyer should use the power of the marketplace to have suppliers actively compete for business in this quadrant. A buyer at a Midwest company, for example, began to market-test selected items on an annual basis. The threat of switching suppliers because of the market test prompted a current supplier to reduce its price by 20 percent to retain its business.

Some of the buying approaches employed in this quadrant may actually increase the number of suppliers that a buying firm does business, something that seems to counter a broader objective that most firms have of reducing their overall supply base. Chapter 12 will highlight some price analytic approaches that may actually result in using a greater number of suppliers. Like the transaction quadrant, it might be counterproductive to get too caught up with supplier numbers here. The big dollars and returns lie in the upper half of the portfolio matrix, not the lower half.

Leverage Quadrant. The upper right quadrant, or the leverage quadrant, includes those items where consolidating purchase volumes and reducing the size of the supply base should lead to a range of benefits. This quadrant features the extensive use of longer-term contracts, a subject that is covered in Chapter 8.

Examples of leverage items include any grouping or family of items whose volumes can be combined for economic advantage, such as plastic injected molded parts, transportation services, electric wiring harnesses, and facility maintenance services. Market quadrant items that are grouped into commodity families can be treated as leverage quadrant items.

Since leverage items are often candidates for longer-term agreements, supply managers should engage in intense negotiations with suppliers over issues beyond price. The development of longer-term contracts should lead to discussions about cost, quality, delivery, packaging, logistics, inventory management, and service—all factors that can affect supply chain performance. Supply chain managers leverage their requirements not only to obtain favorable pricing but also to gain advantages in other non-price areas. Depending on the leveraged item, a cost rather than a price focus should begin to emerge in this quadrant.

The management of leverage items, particularly due to the longer-term nature of the contract, will benefit from relationships that are cooperative. This includes an extensive sharing of information between parties being the norm rather than the exception. While this quadrant will not have the most suppliers in terms of numbers, the dollar value of the leverage items should be quite high. It is not unusual today for fewer than 100 suppliers to receive 80 percent or more of total purchase dollars.

Critical Quadrant. The critical quadrant includes goods and services that consume a large portion of total purchase dollars, are essential to a service or product's function, or offer differentiation to the end customer that he or she values. This quadrant also features fewer suppliers that can satisfy a purchaser's requirements, which often involves customization rather than standardization. At times a supplier is critical simply because it has a patent right to a good or service that the buying company must have.

Although critical items usually represent a small portion of total transactions and part numbers, they often have a disproportionate effect on product cost or performance. Relationships with suppliers that provide critical items should be, by design, collaborative. In fact, this is the quadrant where we see true supply alliances, a topic that Chapter 15 covers. The following example illustrates how a buying company has approached an item that truly is critical.

In 2000, Boeing's board of directors approved the development of two longer-range versions of the popular 777. These planes are capable of flying over 10,000 miles without refueling. No one would argue against the notion that the engines that Boeing and Airbus use are extremely valuable and are available from a limited supply base—Pratt & Whitney, General Electric, Rolls-Royce, and a joint venture between GE and Snecma. What makes this new plane unique is that Boeing only equips the longer-range 777s (as well as a new version of its popular 737) with engines made by General Electric. The development of the new 777s featured a very different approach to sourcing that highlights the special nature of the Boeing–GE relationship. GE shared in the plane's development costs and is sharing revenue with Boeing from each plane sold. This is not a standard long-term agreement.

Shifting between Quadrants

At times the marketplace determines the position of an item within the portfolio matrix, which may limit a company's flexibility to reposition an item to its advantage. At other times a buying company, through its strategy development process, consciously positions an item in a desired quadrant. While a good or service may be treated historically as belonging within a certain quadrant, this does not mean it must always remain a permanent resident of that quadrant. Let's look at some examples that show how supply managers can modify their strategies in their quest for greater value.

Shifting between the Transaction and Market Quadrants. Almost every buying organization has an established procurement card program. At one private university the academic departments rely on procurement cards to obtain a wide range of items and services that do not justify the use of a purchase contract. Departments require miscellaneous supplies and services that may or may not be similar to other departments across the university. As Chapter 5 noted, procurement cards help drive out transactions costs through their ease of use and provide simplified data reporting and billing. Procurement cards have become a popular approach for obtaining transaction items.

A major assumption here is that the card is used for items that truly belong in the transaction quadrant. An analysis of the spending patterns at this university revealed some interesting findings. While no single department required an unusual amount of goods or services obtained with procurement cards, there was enough overlap *between* departments to justify a different buying approach. The procurement manager blocked some items from the procurement card that had commonality between departments and instead created new blanket purchase orders to obtain those items. The manager made a conscious decision to shift some items from the transaction quadrant to the market quadrant. Competitive bidding and blanket purchase orders now became appropriate approaches for managing these newly shifted items. The result for the university was better pricing and payment terms compared to when the items were obtained with procurement cards.

The university's analysis revealed another interesting finding. About half of the university's 350 blanket purchase orders showed no activity during the previous year. The procurement manager, who has a small support staff, found he was committing far too much time reestablishing unnecessary contracts on an annual basis. This prohibited him from focusing on areas that would provide greater return. The decision was made to cancel over half of the university's blanket purchase orders and to use procurement cards in the event these items were required. Again, the procurement manager made a conscious decision to shift items between quadrants. In this case the shift occurred from the market quadrant to the transaction quadrant.

Shifting between the Market and Leverage Quadrants. This next example relates to the aftermarket packaging facility of a major manufacturing company. This facility uses corrugated boxes to package parts for aftermarket sale through the company's dealer network. At first glance corrugated boxes are a classic market item—no individual box is high in value, switching costs are relatively low, the technology to make a box is well established, and many producers are available within a geographic region. A logical supply approach, particularly if all that is needed is a box, is to rely on competitive bidding to identify the most efficient producers. And for many years this is exactly how this company managed corrugated boxes.

In one part of its packaging facility, this company relied on six suppliers to provide 50 box sizes. Unfortunately, spreading volumes across this many suppliers and sizes meant that the company did not have any clout or leverage. A decision was made to purchase high-speed packaging equipment and to shift thousands of part numbers from a manual pack area to the new equipment. Because the new equipment had a significant setup charge each time a carton change took place, the number of box sizes for the new equipment was reduced from 50 to 12. A decision was also made to rely on a longer-term contract with a single supplier for all 12 box sizes. The company decided to leverage its purchase volumes.

What exactly did shifting this item from the market quadrant to the leverage quadrant get this company? Almost overnight the buying company went from having minimal influence with any one supplier to being the selected supplier's most important customer. Besides the double-digit price reductions that resulted from larger volumes, the buying company became the welcome recipient of many non-price benefits.

Consider the benefits the corrugated supplier now bestowed upon the buying company. The supplier agreed to deliver twice a week instead of the more traditional weekly deliveries. More frequent deliveries allowed the buying company to reduce its average inventory levels. Next, order lead times were reduced. This allowed the buying company to shorten its ordering cycle time, which helped reduce forecast uncertainty through better planning. The buyer also received preferential scheduling in the supplier's production queue. The supplier also provided design support for new corrugated applications, helping to compensate for a lack of design resources at the buying company. The supplier also began to send higher-level managers and technical people to meet with the buying company to help identify new corrugated applications. No longer were meetings about "selling" with salespeople. And finally, the supplier became more active in helping manage the buyer's corrugated inventory.

This example highlights the benefits of shifting from a market approach to a leverage approach. It also highlights the value of "thinking outside the box." A review of the benefits reveals that most have nothing to do with the physical product. Combining similar market items into larger-volume contracts is probably the most prominent shift that occurs within the portfolio matrix.

The logic of shifting from quadrant to quadrant to gain additional value does not hold up as well when the shift occurs between the leverage and critical quadrants. A buying company does not want to see too many items in the critical quadrant unless it is fully prepared to actively manage these relationships. Critical items feature intensive supplier relationship activities and a power relationship that often favors the supplier. Chapter 15 on supplier alliances provides a realistic assessment about what it takes to manage these relationships.

CONCLUDING THOUGHTS

While supply strategies are a major element of strategic supply management, forming strategies is no guarantee these strategies will deliver the desired results. Effective supply strategies share some important characteristics. They result from an iterative process involving different groups and personnel, they provide a proper match between opportunities and resources, and they support and align with original corporate objectives. They are also drafted (at least partially) by those who are responsible for their attainment, they provide operational guidance to supply managers across an organization, and they are dynamic and subject to review and/or change as conditions warrant. But perhaps most importantly, well-executed strategies result in a wide range of performance outcomes that allow companies to place strategic and supply management in the same phrase.

SUMMARY OF KEY CHAPTER POINTS

- Developing supply strategies is an essential part of strategic supply management.

- The concept of a strategy or strategy development is not unique to supply management. Supply management has often lagged in strategy development compared with other functional groups.
- An effective supply strategy consists of a number of parts—objectives, constraints, plans, and goals.
- Every strategy development initiative requires a realistic assessment of the internal and external constraints that create boundaries around what a buying company can do.
- A well-thought-out process for developing supply strategies is an important part of strategic supply management. While similarities often exist, no agreed-upon or standardized strategy development process or template for supply managers to follow is available.
- The portfolio matrix recognizes that an effective supply organization applies a variety, or portfolio, of strategies, approaches, and relationships to different supply requirements.
- An understanding of supply relationships is essential for effective supply management. Knowing when, where, and how to apply an appropriate relationship is an area where supply professionals bring value to their organization.
- While a good or service may be treated historically as residing within a certain quadrant, supply managers can shift items between quadrants during strategy development in an attempt to create new value.
- The logic of shifting items from quadrant to quadrant to gain additional value does not hold up as well when the shift occurs between the leverage and the critical quadrant. This is due to the intensive requirements for managing critical items.

ENDNOTES

1. The discussion in this section on strategy draws from R. F. Vancil, "Strategy Formulation in Complex Organizations," *Sloan Management Review* 17, no. 2 (Winter 1976): 1–18.
2. Vancil, 1–18.
3. Peter Kraljic, "Purchasing Must Become Supply Management," *Harvard Business Review* (September 1, 1983).

4. For example, see L. M. Rinehart, M. B. Myers, and J. A. Eckert, "Supplier Relationships: The Impact on Security," *Supply Chain Management Review* 8, no. 6 (September 2004): 52.

8

CONTRACTING FOR THE LONGER TERM

Several years ago a logistics company entered into a five-year agreement that called for a supplier to place people and equipment at each of the buyer's many sites to perform fleet maintenance. In the second year of the agreement, it became painfully obvious that the supplier was unprepared to ramp up and support a contract of this magnitude. The buyer had to quickly qualify a second service provider, a process that required time and money. While the buyer's attorney had insisted the agreement contain a termination clause with 30 days' notice, this did little to help the situation once the supplier was physically located at several dozen sites. Contract switching costs had become very high and disruptive. What started as a way to create new value and reduce risk did not achieve the desired outcome. As a result, this company rarely considers the use of five-year agreements. And capacity issues now receive a bit more attention during supplier selection.

This chapter could easily have started with an example of how a longer-term contract wildly exceeded the expectations of those who crafted the agreement, and these agreements certainly do exist. But that is not how life always works. While most supply managers believe that longer-term supply agreements are a good thing, they can also lock in mistakes for many years. The crafting of longer-term contracts is another endeavor where activity and accomplishment may not always be related.

Well-crafted longer-term agreements with selected suppliers are an essential part of strategic supply management. These agreements provide a foundation that supports the development of more advanced supply approaches. This chapter approaches longer-term contracting by defining the concept, identifying the reasons for using longer-term agreements, and presenting the potential risks from their use. The role that negotiation plays in the contracting process and a set of good contracting practices are presented next. The chapter concludes with a case that shows how longer-term supply contracts helped a business unit exceed a corporate financial mandate.

UNDERSTANDING LONGER-TERM CONTRACTING

A longer-term agreement is a legal contract between two or more parties that is expected to be in effect for a time period greater than a year and that usually addresses a greater range of price and non-price issues than shorter-term or standard "boilerplate" agreements. Longer-term agreements formalize the supply strategies developed in Chapter 7.

The 1990s witnessed a major growth in the use of longer-term contracts. From 1990 to the latter 1990s, the dollar value of purchases represented by longer-term contracts increased from 34 percent to 50 percent of total purchase dollars.[1] The percent of total spend under contract is a common metric used when evaluating a supply management organization. This growth has continued through the 2000s.

Notice that the term *longer-term* rather than *long-term* is used here. This is done purposely to reflect agreements that are longer than a year but are not defined by any standard length. No established duration formally defines a longer-term contract. However, experience with many companies indicates that longer-term agreements are often three years in length. Two years is usually not long enough given the time and resources required to craft and roll out these agreements, particularly worldwide contracts. Agreements that are four or more years begin to expose the buying company to a higher level of uncertainty and risk.

Longer-term contracting is an area where supply managers can exercise a tremendous amount of creativity. U.S. commercial law is quite generous regarding what two or more parties may agree to in a contract. Virtually anything is negotiable as long as a contract satisfies four basic conditions:

- *Offer and acceptance.* An offer is a proposal to do something and acceptance is agreeing to the offer.
- *Consideration.* Each party must agree to give up something of value during the performance of the contract.
- *Legality of subject matter.* Contracts can only cover topics that are legal.
- *Legal capacity.* Only those individuals who are legally or mentally qualified to enter into a contract may do so. In purchasing this deals with legal agency.

Ten years ago the use of longer-term supply contracts was considered an innovative supply practice. Today their use hardly elicits a yawn. This does not mean we should discount their importance. In fact, the opposite is true. Besides creating new opportunities for the parties, longer-term agreements form the foundation that allows a company to pursue supply activities that are exciting and innovative. Many of the approaches presented in later chapters simply are not possible without a longer-term contract underlying the buyer-seller relationship.

Supply managers should enter into longer-term contracts only after asking a simple question: What value do these contracts provide that traditional or short-term contracts do not provide? Forming longer-term contracts simply because there is a belief they are inherently good or everyone else seems to be doing it are not good reasons. As with many of the topics presented throughout this book, care has to be taken not to mix up activity (forming longer-term agreements) with accomplishment (what the agreement brings in terms of new value).

Why Use Longer-Term Agreements?

Why are supply managers increasingly using longer-term contracts with suppliers? During the 1990s buying companies began to appreciate the economic value of combining volumes across their buying units. The companies that began to aggregate their requirements also understood the need to address many issues with suppliers besides price. The shift toward relying on fewer suppliers with a higher amount of value-add received from key suppliers was well underway.

Chapter 7 argued that longer-term agreements are logical as firms leverage their purchase volumes. At some point most buying companies have come to realize that frequent supplier switching and adversarial supplier relationships do not provide the highest return from their supply management investment. It is difficult to develop solid relationships with suppliers when the supply base is constantly being churned. A longer-term contract is a visible means of showing commitment to a longer-term relationship.

Longer-term agreements address many issues or topics that are not present in traditional purchases or shorter-term contracts. These include, but are certainly not limited to, the following:

- Quality, delivery, and cycle time expectations
- Technical support
- Joint improvement activities
- Extended warranties
- Additional services provided by the supplier
- Problem resolution mechanisms
- Supplier-provided investment and resources

- Volume commitments
- Guarantees of supply when demand changes
- Nonperformance penalties and continuous improvement incentives
- Agreement on allowable costs
- Risk and reward sharing
- Agreement exit clauses
- Protection of intellectual property

The use of longer-term agreements is also a tangible way that supply managers support the principles of total quality management (TQM). In particular, longer-term agreements are ideal for conveying the requirements of the buying (i.e., the customer) company. Contract compliance can also be measured, which relates to the principle of relying on objective rather than subjective assessment. Effective longer-term agreements and the contract management process are also ideal ways for striving for continuous improvement within the buyer-seller relationship.

Longer-term agreements also benefit suppliers. Smaller and medium-size suppliers can present these contracts to financial institutions to obtain loans to finance their working capital requirements. These agreements should also help a supplier to better plan capacity, demand, and investment requirements. And if the supplier is contracting on a longer-term basis with world-class buying companies, the supplier should strive to leverage the advantages of that relationship. These include marketing advantages (it looks great to have great customers), continuous improvement (demanding buyers will push their suppliers to higher levels of performance), and growth (grow along with your key customers). All of this assumes that suppliers have not been pressured into accepting a contract that is not in their best interests. Suppliers, as well as buyers, can enter into poor agreements.

Table 8.1 presents the advantages and disadvantages of longer-term contracting. Given that longer-term contracting as a practice is not going away anytime soon, it becomes imperative for supply managers to recognize the benefits as well as the risks of this important part of strategic supply management.

Longer-Term Contracting Risks

With the opportunity for reward comes the possibility of risk. Perhaps the biggest impediment to longer-term contracting is an inability for most firms to predict what will happen in the future. What will prices be in three years? Which suppliers will be the technology leaders? Will another company, perhaps even a competitor, buy the supplier? Will we lock ourselves into a bad situation? As a classic bumper sticker says, and slightly reworded here, "Stuff Happens." And the longer a company looks into the future, the probability increases that "stuff" will happen. Supply managers must work to prevent any unintended consequences

Table 8.1 Potential Advantages and Disadvantages of Longer-Term Contracting

Potential Advantages	Potential Disadvantages
Assurance of supply.	Requires greater relationship management resources.
Access to supplier cost information, technology, and capacity.	Could commit to a poorly negotiated agreement.
Focus on many non-price issues.	
Supplier may be willing to make relationship specific investments.	Harder to switch suppliers if the wrong supplier is selected.
Better able to focus on developing longer-term relationships.	Markets or technologies may change and the supplier does not stay current.
Likelihood of joint improvement efforts increases.	Other suppliers may not bring new ideas because the longer-term supplier "owns" the business.
Pursuit of win-win business opportunities.	Buying organization is not familiar with the nuances of developing or managing longer-term contracts.
Less supply base churning or switching.	
Should enhance the probability of becoming a preferred customer.	Buyer and seller become complacent over time.
	Inability to predict the future makes longer-term planning difficult.

from their longer-term agreements. Two potential unintended consequences are complacency and shutting out new ideas from the supply market. Complacency is a risk when the parties to an agreement believe that good things will happen because of the agreement. As a result, the parties may not be as diligent as they should be in monitoring performance outcomes or the external marketplace. The contracting best practices in the latter part of this chapter provide ways to protect against complacency.

Longer-term agreements usually cover the more important supply items in terms of dollar value and importance. Buying companies may rely on only a few suppliers or even a single supplier to support 100 percent of their requirements for an item. But what happens when a nonincumbent supplier has a new innovation or idea? Does the longer-term agreement shut out that supplier from approaching a buying company? Do other suppliers believe the current supplier has the business locked up? Unfortunately the answer can be yes, and the risk is that innovative ideas will work their way to a competitor. Shutting out new ides from suppliers becomes an even greater concern when alliances are formed with a select group of suppliers.

How do we capture the benefits of longer-term contracting while preventing any unintended consequences? Supply managers can prevent the shutting out of new ideas by relying on more than one supplier for items that have a rapid rate of change. This helps maintain a level of competition between suppliers. Supply managers can also open up new business opportunities to nonincumbent suppliers. In other words, the supplier with a longer-term agreement must earn the new business. Incumbent suppliers, while clearly having their "foot in the door," are not guaranteed new business opportunities.

Another way to prevent the shutting out of new ideas, and a technique that is often used by high-technology companies, is to hold technology demonstration days. A company that produces personal computers identifies a technology requirement each quarter and then invites suppliers to present their ideas. The message to suppliers is clear: Future business is possible if you have an idea or application that will benefit us.

Entering into a longer-term contract with suppliers, while an essential part of the strategic supply management process, does not guarantee better outcomes. Consider the following examples of companies that entered into longer-term agreements and relationships with the best of intentions that somehow went astray.

General Motors and Bethlehem Steel. In 1999 General Motors entered into a longer-term supply agreement with Bethlehem Steel.[2] The two companies agreed on a four-year contract with a 3 percent to 5 percent price decrease with fixed pricing covering 18 million metric tons of cold-rolled steel annually. Historically, steel contracts covering one year in duration were the accepted industry practice. GM's contract was part of the company's overall strategy for managing *$12 billion* of annual steel purchases.

GM correctly viewed steel as a leverage item during strategy development. The company consumes massive amounts of steel, making it a high-value item. The steel market also features many worldwide producers. In fact, GM does business with dozens of steel producers on a worldwide basis. Steel is also not a rapidly changing item from a technological or growth perspective. Unlike aluminum, automakers are searching for ways to *remove* steel from their vehicles to reduce weight.

GM's steel contract with Bethlehem Steel is a textbook example of using a longer-term agreement for a leverage item. The agreement also changed the way the supply market typically operates by shifting from one-year agreements, which more closely resemble how companies manage market items, to multiyear agreements, which are characteristic of leverage items.

At this point astute readers should proclaim loudly that Bethlehem Steel is no longer in business! What good is a contract with a company that no longer operates? This brings us to the second part of the story. GM entered into a longer-term agreement with a *financially distressed* company. During the GM contract, Bethlehem Steel entered into bankruptcy and its assets were purchased by Integrated Steel Group (ISG). ISG was then purchased by a foreign firm (Mittal) that now controls a disproportionate share of the worldwide steel market.

What is the lesson learned here? A detailed assessment of Bethlehem Steel's financial health would have indicated the company was in distress. (Chapter 10 will present a tool for predicting a supplier's financial condition two years out.) Buying companies should evaluate longer-term suppliers as if they were buying the supplier, not just buying the supplier's output. In other words, progressive supply managers should perform something that approaches *due diligence* when selecting their longer-term suppliers. While GM continued to receive steel shipments, how many companies want to do business with suppliers that are in bankruptcy?

Ford Motor Company. One of the more public supply contracting missteps occurred at Ford Motor Company.[3] Just how big was this misstep? In the end Ford had to write off $1 billion worth of precious metal inventory and was sued by shareholders who alleged the company misled them about the risks from Ford's handling of precious metals. This story was so important it was featured on the front page of the *Wall Street Journal*. Fortunately for Ford, only several million people a day read that paper.

Let's step back and talk about a relatively unknown element called palladium. For years auto companies used platinum in catalytic converters for emission control. However, in anticipation of tougher emission rules by the U.S. government, auto companies began to design palladium into their pollution control equipment, suddenly making up over half the world's palladium demand. Besides being more effective at cleaning vehicle exhaust, it was also less expensive (at the time) than platinum.[4] The end of the Cold War left a large stockpile of inexpensive palladium, particularly in Russia.

As engineers created designs that replaced platinum with palladium, the worldwide price of palladium became very volatile. As demand skyrocketed, palladium peaked at almost $1,000 an ounce, with each vehicle requiring almost 1 ounce of palladium. At this point macro economics should kick in, as high-commodity prices encourage suppliers to provide more output, helping to bring supply and demand closer to equilibrium. Unfortunately, several factors helped ensure a move toward equilibrium would not be smooth. First, the two primary supply sources of palladium are Russia and Africa, two areas not known for their supply stability. In Russia, the size of the palladium stockpile is a state secret. The Russian government also showed a willingness to "delay" releases from its stockpile, thereby creating major supply and price disruptions. Second, palladium occurs in nature with other elements. It is mined with platinum in Russia and with nickel in Africa, and the amount of palladium present is less proportionally than platinum or nickel. A producer would have to increase the production of platinum and nickel to increase the output of palladium. That would drive down the price of nickel and platinum as new supply flooded the market with no change in demand.

Now, let's get back to Ford. Assurance of supply and a fixed price were clearly the procurement group's primary objectives as it developed its precious metals strategy. Ford entered into a longer-term palladium contract with a high fixed price at near record levels. As Ford's buyers stocked up on expensive precious metals, Ford's engineers, as well as engineers at other companies, figured out how to reduce by half the amount of palladium required in each vehicle. The net effect of these engineering changes was to dramatically lower total palladium demand, and lower demand resulted in a lower per-ounce cost. The value of the inventory that Ford locked into and stockpiled was now worth much less. The eventual $1 billion write-off for precious metals clearly upset some shareholders.

Palladium's high total value and limited supply base clearly places this item in the critical quadrant of the portfolio matrix presented in Chapter 7. So, what was Ford's mistake? The company's *procurement managers treated palladium as a leverage item, similar to steel and copper, rather than the critical item that it truly resembled.* Treating palladium as a critical item would likely have resulted in some strategy changes. Procurement did not consider the input of finance (who probably would *not* have recommended a high fixed-price contract) or engineering (who might have casually mentioned something about the ongoing effort to reduce the amount of palladium required in each vehicle). Ford's CFO later said the purchasing staff did not take the sort of precautions sophisticated buyers routinely take to hedge risk in volatile markets.[5]

Remember a critical point here: Procurement is a functional activity, while strategic supply management is organizational. There are good reasons why important supply initiatives, including longer-term contracting, involve groups besides procurement. In this example procurement lacked the expertise to source this volatile element on its own. While it is easy to look afterward at what went wrong, there are still valuable lessons to take forward.

NEGOTIATING LONGER-TERM AGREEMENTS

It would be incomplete to ignore the role of negotiation when crafting longer-term agreements. Almost all longer-term agreements, at least initially, are negotiated, making this a relevant subject for supply managers. Negotiation as a general process is so important that dozens of books have been written on the subject. Its treatment here is cursory at best.

The difference between a good and poor longer-term agreement may very well center on the effectiveness of the negotiator. Negotiating longer-term agreements is such an important part of the contracting process that some firms use trained negotiators or teams that are separate from the strategy development team. These individuals do not become involved with strategy development until it is time to plan for the negotiation.

Theoretically, negotiation as a process is designed to explore options and to create new value from a relationship. The heavy-handed way that some supply managers approach negotiation can actually work against their longer-term interests. A survey of European automotive suppliers revealed the desire of some to shift business away from customers that have costly and time-consuming negotiating processes.[6]

Effective negotiators know they must plan diligently for a negotiation, understand thoroughly their needs as well as those of their counterpart, and know when and how to use negotiating tactics and concessions. At some point the parties within a relationship may become so comfortable with the sharing of information, for example, that price negotiation takes a back seat and is replaced by a cooperative effort to achieve a preestablished target price.

CONTRACT MANAGEMENT GOOD PRACTICES

Supply managers sometimes have the mistaken notion that negotiating a formal supply agreement is the end of the process. The agreement sits in a desk or file cabinet, and as long as nothing bad happens, there really is no reason to open the agreement. In reality, contract management is an active process designed to ensure the reality of an agreement matches or exceeds the expectations of the agreement. Signing an agreement is a commencement activity.

Contract management is the process of ensuring that the parties to a legally agreed-to contract fulfill the requirements, expectations, and terms and conditions of the agreement. There are two primary dimensions at work here. The first involves the development of contracts, while the second involves managing and monitoring these agreements. Any company that realizes competitive advantages from supply management understands the importance of active contract management. The following presents a set of good contracting management practices.

Good Practice 1. Involve Internal Customers during Contract Development. This practice supports the total quality management principle of understanding customers and their requirements. In this case the customers are internal and can be located at individual company sites or be from functional groups that the supply manager is assigned to support.

This practice should not be that difficult. The company featured at the end of this chapter uses electronic communications to involve internal customers when developing company-wide agreements. The supply manager in charge of contract development electronically informs personnel at all sites about a pending supplier negotiation. Internal sites or customers identify "must have," would like to have," or "do not need" contract items. The supply manager then considers these specific needs when negotiating a supply agreement.

Good Practice 2. Enter into Agreements with World-Class Suppliers. This practice seems obvious—who wants to do business with poor suppliers? This practice also addresses the topic of trust. One of the results of doing business when trust and performance are concerns is lengthier contracts. Performance and trust shortfalls require the buying company to more aggressively protect its interests during the contracting process. This practice recognizes the importance of supplier selection as a core business competency. It makes sense to rigorously select qualified suppliers to *prevent* contract compliance problems later.

Good Practice 3. Develop Complete Contracts Whenever Possible. Developing complete contracts does not mean negotiating the dreaded 60-page agreement with a team of 15 lawyers reviewing the agreement over a six-month period. Contract completeness simply refers to how well the obligations of the parties to a contract are specified. Research evidence suggests that when contracts describe what actions a supplier should take and what outcomes should be achieved, the risk of contract failure and the costs of monitoring the contract relationship are lower. With incomplete contracts, the parties face potential opportunistic behavior that may entail very high monitoring costs or costly bargaining later.

Good Practice 4. Obtain Contract Performance Feedback from Internal Customers. Oftentimes the best perspective about a supplier's performance comes from internal customers, who should have a wealth of day-to-day experience with suppliers. There are others who likely have a better idea about a supplier's performance, including adherence to a contract, than the supply manager.

If internal customers should play a role during the assessment of a supplier's contract performance, then the question becomes how best to formalize that role. Some firms use an intranet that allows internal customers to post comments directly about a supplier's performance, either for contract review meetings or during the development of supplier scorecards. Supply managers can also go out and meet face-to-face with their internal customers. The bottom line is that internal customers should be regularly surveyed about their satisfaction with suppliers, including in areas directly related to a contract.

Good Practice 5. Assign a Relationship Manager to Each Contract with Performance Accountability. Recall from Chapter 3 the most widely used organizational design feature involved the assignment of specific individuals to manage supplier relationships. Two key points are important here. As mentioned elsewhere in this book, the level of the individual assigned to manage the relationship changes with the importance of the relationship. Buyers might manage market items on a short-term or traditional contract, a supply manager or cross-functional commodity team might manage leverage items on a longer-term agreement, and an executive might be assigned to manage a relationship with an alliance supplier. Next, accountability is critical. Some companies evaluate the performance of relationship managers based on the performance of the suppliers and contracts they manage. This is a sure way to convey the importance of this role.

Good Practice 6. Measure and Report Internal Customer and Site Compliance with Company-Wide Agreements. An issue that can expose the buying company to liability is the failure to follow through on committed contractual volumes. Suppliers that do not receive their promised volumes will argue, and probably rightfully so, that they quoted a price at volumes that did not materialize. There have been instances where suppliers have sued their customers to make up for profit shortfalls due to lower volumes that affected their cost structure.

Today, most firms that use company-wide, longer-term contracts do not make them voluntary. Unless a business unit or site can make a compelling case why it should be exempt from using a corporate agreement, it is required to follow that agreement. Until the day comes when complying with corporate agreements is a regular practice, buying companies should measure and report internal customer compliance with corporate agreements. Executive leaders should review site and business unit compliance with these contracts.

Good Practice 7. Develop a System That Compares Prices Paid against Contracted Prices. An efficient way to compare prices paid against an established contact or baseline price should be a feature of any contract management system. The finance group should help develop or at least sign off on any methodology used for price comparisons. Contract management becomes more objective when price and savings data are readily available. All transactions and costs over a 12-month period need to be captured, compared against a baseline, aggregated across commodities, and reported to executive management.

Good Practice 8. Measure Real-Time Performance. Most performance measurement systems do a poor job of reporting supplier performance, including performance against specific contract requirements. While the reasons for this shortfall are discussed elsewhere in this book, part of the problem is the lag in these systems between cause and effect. Few systems are capable of capturing and then comparing supplier performance data against an agreed-upon requirement.

Measuring real-time performance requires extensive linkages to other systems and groups across the supply chain. An inbound logistics group must provide real-time supplier receipt data that are compared to a promised delivery date, quality assurance groups must post the results of quality samples and nonconformances that occur further down the supply chain, and accounts payable must provide data to support comparisons of invoices against contracted prices. Real-time data support the objective management of supplier contracts.

Good Practice 9. Conduct Regular Contract Performance Review Meetings. Regular contract review meetings, conducted at least annually, should be the responsibility of relationship managers. During these meetings the relationship manager should compare the supplier's performance relative to other suppliers and against agreed-upon performance targets. External reviews should address not only current contract performance but also ways to improve future performance as well as the buyer-seller relationship. The relationship manager should also conduct regular review sessions with internal customers to gain input and feedback about a contract and its supplier(s).

Good Practice 10. Utilize Contract Management Systems and Systems Technology. In the not too distant past, contract management involved signing an agreement and then placing it in a desk or file cabinet. Unless something really bad happened, the agreement often did not see the light of day. This labor-intensive and hands-off approach to contract management is not an example of a good contract management practice.

Companies need to develop company-wide contract management systems, including systems that act as contract repositories, to better manage their longer-term agreements. A key feature of these systems is a notification sent to the appropriate contract manager about an expiring contract that needs to be reviewed. It is likely that many contracts have been quickly renewed over time simply because of oversights regarding their expiration dates.

Increasingly, third-party software providers are developing contract management software (CMS) applications. Automated contract management systems are networked-based software platforms that provide visibility to contracts. Historically these systems have been used more on the selling side than the buying side of the business.

Good Practice 11. Benchmark Contract Management Practices against Other Leading Companies. Supply managers face similar issues as they attempt to manage their contracts. Good contracting practices are certainly not limited to any one industry. Supplier managers should routinely benchmark their contract management practices against leading firms or with their industry contacts.

Good Practice 12. Double-Translate Contracts Involving Foreign Suppliers. As the growth in international purchasing continues, the chance that contract misunderstandings due to language differences becomes very real. Some firms manage this risk by double-translating contracts involving foreign suppliers.

Here's how double translation works. Let's assume a U.S. company negotiates a contract in English with a Chinese company. The English contract is given to a *competent* translator (and the competent part here is important) to translate into Chinese. Then the Chinese version is given to another competent translator to translate back into English. Any inconsistencies between the original English contract and the double-translated English contract indicate areas where contract problems may occur. While this practice is burdensome, it may help prevent problems caused by language and interpretation misunderstandings.

CREATING NEW VALUE THROUGH LONGER-TERM CONTRACTING

A number of years ago the executive leadership at a major raw materials company directed its business units to begin concentrating on return on net assets (RONA) as a key performance indicator. All units were directed to achieve a specified RONA rate or risk possible divestiture by the parent company. This example focuses on how the purchasing group that represents the combined interests of five subsidiary railroads relied on longer-term contracting to change the way the railroads managed both repair inventory and contracts. These railroads support the movement of goods into, within, and out of the parent company's vast geographic locations.

The corporate mandate to improve financial returns forced different functional groups at the railroads to work together to improve RONA. Figure 8.1 presents the RONA formula used by this company along with the expected contribution of various groups. The purchasing group focused primarily on the denominator of the equation, although price reductions obtained through leveraged agreements helped improve earnings before interest and taxes. The functional groups met monthly to discuss their initiatives and to chart their progress against their RONA target. The RONA target became a unifying target for the different functional groups, or what some call a superordinate goal.

Procurement's plan for improving RONA relied extensively on the development of longer-term systems contracts that featured consignment inventory. A systems contract covers multiple items on the same agreement. In this case each contract covered about 25 items. Consignment involves deferring ownership and payment for an item until an internal user at a rail yard physically takes possession of an item from storage. Negotiated contracts also required suppliers to replenish rail yards within 24 hours for out-of-stock items and to physically unload and store material in each rail yard. Previously, railroad employees performed this task.

Marketing and Sales: Focus on *increasing revenue* from non-parent company operations.

Operations: Focus on *improved forecasting*, better *management of capital equipment requirements*.

Finance: Track, validate, and *report overall* progress.

Return on Net Assets =
$$\frac{\text{Earnings before Interest and Taxes}}{(\text{Inventory} + \text{Accounts Receivable} + \text{Plant Property and Equipment} + \text{Other Current Assets}) - \text{Accounts Payable}}$$

Procurement: Focus on longer-term systems contracts featuring *lower prices* and *consignment inventory*.

Accounting: Focus on better *management of receivables* and **payables.**

Figure 8.1 Managing return on net assets—a cross-functional approach.

Longer-term systems contracts have changed the way the railroads conduct business with suppliers. Standard operating procedure historically involved each railroad issuing one-year purchase orders to suppliers. At the end of the year the supplier would typically inform the buyer of the next year's price increases. Knowing this practice was not creating the type of value that comes from leveraging a company's volumes, a central purchasing group located at the parent company stepped in to analyze the combined needs of the five railroads. The three-year agreements that resulted featured fixed pricing with price reductions. Before long, the railroads, acting as a single voice to suppliers, had 30 systems contracts in place.

These changes did not come easily. In fact, some suppliers, and even some buyers at the railroads, argued quite vocally against these new agreements. Some suppliers contacted the president of the railroads to voice their displeasure. The idea of the supplier maintaining ownership of the inventory in the rail yards was hard for some to understand. And the railroads, which historically operated in a highly decentralized fashion, perceived centralized purchasing as a challenge to their power and authority. Table 8.2 presents the lessons learned from the shift from short-term contracting to longer-term systems contracting.

How were these challenges overcome? First, the purchasing group briefed the president of the railroads regularly about the new initiatives. He quickly endorsed this new approach when suppliers called to express their discontent. Second, the

Table 8.2 Longer-Term Systems Contracting Lessons Learned

Accurate demand estimates are critical.	Accurate demand was critical, since each railroad agreed to take ownership of any consigned inventory not used at the end of a year. Also, accurate demand estimates were essential when negotiating prices with suppliers.
Communicate continuously with user groups.	Electronic tools were used to efficiently identify internal requirements at each site, receive feedback about supplier performance, and improve relationships with each operating unit through frequent communication.
Negotiate a broad range of issues.	Longer-term contracting is a creative process. The belief is almost anything in longer-term contracts should be open to negotiation.
Determine baseline prices before pursuing longer-term contracts.	To prevent suppliers from raising prices to cover consignment or any other costs, document current prices in detail before beginning any contact with suppliers.
Planning and analysis are critical.	The supply manager relied extensively on spreadsheets to record current prices, analyze supplier proposals, calculate company-wide requirements, identify potential systems contract candidates, determine inventory investment data, and plan negotiation strategy.
Gain executive commitment.	Meet frequently with executive leaders to inform them of the intent and progress of systems contracting.
Recognize the supplier has needs to meet.	Trying to understand the needs of suppliers through a win-win approach to contract negotiation is important for reaching an agreement that all parties can endorse.

suppliers that remained in the supply base soon realized, with reminders from purchasing, that they were receiving volumes that were higher than when they dealt with the individual railroads. These higher volumes created economic advantages that helped offset the price reductions as well as the cost of the consignment inventory. Furthermore, transactions costs, or the cost of doing business with the buyer, also declined due to the longer-term nature of the contracts. Most suppliers soon realized that life could be good under the new system.

Overcoming resistance to change at the railroads meant involving users, usually electronically, during the planning phase of contract development. Care was taken to ensure that the requirements of individual railroads were considered during contract negotiations. When necessary, an addendum was added to the master systems contract to reflect an individual railroad's unique needs. The railroads were also enlightened after seeing the effect that consignment and price reductions had on their operating budgets. The ritual of annual price increases had become a thing of the past. This new approach to contracting has helped the railroads reduce prices, achieve almost a 40 percent reduction in inventory investment, reduce transaction costs through streamlined ordering and payment, improve cash flow, and downsize as suppliers assumed responsibility for delivering and placing physical inventory in storage.

Longer-term contracting is a continuous process. While the early emphasis was on forming and maintaining an initial set of systems contracts, supply managers soon broadened their list of items to include. Also, since a small number of suppliers did not take seriously the goals of this process, purchasing targeted these suppliers for elimination or "reeducation" as these agreements came closer to renewal.

By working together toward a common goal, the different functional groups achieved net asset returns of 50 percent, easily surpassing the RONA target established by the parent company. And how has the parent company performed? It continues to fall well short of its own RONA targets, prompting some at the railroads to joke that perhaps they should divest themselves of the parent company.

CONCLUDING THOUGHTS

Longer-term agreements provide the foundation upon which to build the strategies that truly define strategic supply management. By design, these agreements feature cooperative relationships that focus on win-win opportunities, address topics that traditional purchasing approaches do not address, and create new value for the parties to the agreement. Their use should only continue to grow.

SUMMARY OF KEY CHAPTER POINTS

- A longer-term agreement is a legal contract between two or more parties that is expected to be in effect for a period greater than a year and that usually addresses a greater range of issues compared with shorter-term or standard "boilerplate" agreements.
- Longer-term contracting is an area where supply managers can exercise a tremendous amount of creativity.
- Longer-term agreements provide the foundation upon which to build the relationships and strategies that truly define strategic supply management.
- While no set duration defines a longer-term contract, experience with many companies indicates the typical duration of a longer-term agreement to be three years.

- Longer-term contracting is a tangible way that supply managers support the principles of total quality management.
- Perhaps one of the biggest challenges to longer-term contracting is an inability for most firms to predict what will happen in the future. Other challenges involve preventing unintended consequences from longer-term contracting, including complacency and shutting out new ideas from the supply market.
- Supply managers sometimes have the mistaken notion that crafting a strategy and then negotiating a formal supply agreement is the end of the process. Signing an agreement is the beginning of relationship and contract management.
- Contract management is an active process designed to ensure the reality of an agreement matches or exceeds the expectations of the agreement.

ENDNOTES

1. R. M. Monczka and R. J. Trent, "Purchasing and Supply Management: Key Trends and Changes throughout the 1990s," *International Journal of Purchasing and Materials Management* 34, no. 4 (Fall 1998): 2–11.
2. P. Galuszka, "An Ironclad Deal with GM," *BusinessWeek* 3619 (March 8, 1999): 36.
3. G. L. White, "Precious Commodity: How Ford's Big Batch of Rare Metals Led to a $1 Billion Write-Off," *Wall Street Journal*, February 6, 2002, A1.
4. Ibid., "Unruly Element: Russian Maneuvers Are Making Palladium More Precious Than Ever," *Wall Street Journal*, March 6, 2000, A1.
5. Ibid., "Precious Commodity: How Ford's Big Batch of Rare Metals Led to a $1 Billion Write-Off," A1.
6. J. Snyder, "European Suppliers Play Favorites," *Automotive News*, May 16, 2005, www.autonews.com.

9

OUTSOURCING FOR COMPETITIVE ADVANTAGE

To hear the "experts" explain it, a firm that does not outsource just about everything where it does not add unique value is destined to fail. Furthermore, companies should outsource way more than they currently outsource. If there ever was a topic where we should step back, take a deep breath, and approach it methodically, outsourcing may be that topic. While many companies have used outsourcing to gain competitive advantage, the process is not without serious risks. Consider the following, which is one manager's account of how a poorly executed outsourcing decision caused his company's demise:[1]

> *Our parent company, with the help of a consultant, determined that weldments were not critical to our primary business of designing industrial vacuuming systems. When we eliminated welding operations, I had to find suppliers to handle our welding requirements. The good news was that we were able to purchase complete welded assemblies from suppliers for 25 to 40 percent less than our in-house costs. I was responsible for two business units that benefited from outsourcing. Since welding was a large part of the cost structure in my area, we were able to become more competitive. My staff and I even received bonuses for record bookings, sales, and profits. Unfortunately, things weren't going as well for the rest of the company.*
>
> *A major problem had to do with how we allocated overhead. Our accounting system was designed to liquidate overhead against direct labor.*

By eliminating the welding shop, we assumed that overhead would decrease in proportion to the decrease in direct labor hours. The reality was quite the opposite. We eventually realized that the weld shop required very little support and its elimination had almost no effect on total overhead. Almost all of our overhead, such as our engineering center, remained, but we now had less direct labor. As a result, overhead rates increased from $62 per hour to $110 per hour in three years. This made our factory incapable of competing in any category, including products made on our CNC equipment. We outsourced welding so we could become more competitive, not less competitive!

Before a company can make a decision to outsource, it must make sure the accounting system properly reflects the true cost associated with making a part. Our company would have been better served by an activity-based accounting system that charged all services to the work center that consumed them so we would have a more accurate cost picture. This would have provided a better estimate of where our true costs were and how outsourcing would have impacted those costs.

There were other problems. We were a union shop, and when the weld shop was eliminated morale plummeted, productivity and quality were affected, and there was vandalism. One of the employees threw a rock at my head in the parking lot. Fortunately, his aim was off.

Eventually our company was sold and our plant was closed. The large CNC equipment was moved to the Czech Republic, where the hourly labor rate was much lower. The large capital equipment product lines were eliminated, and the only remaining labor was an assembly group at a smaller U.S. facility, which represented just 15 percent of the original workforce. The company recently announced that facility will also close. In four years sales dropped almost 70 percent and 250 people lost their jobs. I hear the company is now thinking about producing in China.

Outsourcing is something that if performed well offers tremendous opportunities for realizing some serious performance gains. Conversely, it is also a topic that if not performed well, as the above scenario illustrates, can have serious consequences.

This chapter addresses the interesting world of outsourcing. First, a variety of topics are presented to aid in understanding this phenomenon. Next, a set of macro trends and changes that are affecting outsourcing are presented, followed by a structured approach for conducting outsourcing analyses. The chapter would be incomplete without a discussion of core competencies and their relationship to outsourcing. The chapter concludes with a set of lessons learned from a company that saw its core competency, and eventually its business, disappear.

THE OUTSOURCING PHENOMENON

In *Strategic Outsourcing: A Structured Approach to Outsourcing Decisions and Initiatives,* Maurice Greaver II writes that "outsourcing can be a slapdash affair that stirs up trouble among employees and fails to deliver bottom-line results. Or, it can be a potent business tool for creating a focused, robust organization."[2] Greaver defines outsourcing as "the act of transferring some of an organization's recurring internal activities and decisions rights to outsiders, as set forth in a contract."[3]

A firm should concentrate internally on those components, assemblies, systems, or services that are critical to its end products and where it possesses a distinctive or unique advantage. Conversely, an organization should consider outsourcing when suppliers offer a unique advantage. Supplier advantages may result from economies of scale, process specific investment, higher quality, innovative technology, or lower costs.

Once something is outsourced, a company usually loses the ability to bring it back without making a major investment. And outsourcing does not necessarily mean offshoring, although we often think of it that way as we watch the stampede of U.S. firms shifting their requirements to China and India. The supplier that ends up providing an outsourced good or service can be located just about anywhere.

Some items and services have and will always be outsourced. Who wants to make their own office supplies or build their own power-generating equipment? The difference today is we are witnessing outsourcing in areas that not too long ago were safely performed in-house, including services. As an example of how far outsourcing decisions have evolved, Boeing sold its facilities that make aircraft fuselages to a Canadian company. In the past, selling this facility might have resulted in a strike against the company. Agere Systems (now part of LSI Logic) designs and sells semiconductor chips yet does not own a single production facility. Many computer companies never touch the PCs they sell.

Years ago outsourcing decisions were part of a tactical decision-making process called "make or buy." What's different today is the scope of the decisions that are being made. Debating whether to keep or outsource a component now seems almost trivial. The discussion today is about shifting responsibility for designing and making entire products or for managing entire parts of the value chain. Outsourcing decisions have assumed their place as a key part of the *strategic* planning process.

The move toward outsourcing is also affecting services. Dozens of major companies have turned over the management of their global logistics network, for example, to third-party suppliers. *BusinessWeek* reported that DuPont now uses legal services provided by a Philippine provider called OfficeTiger.[4] DuPont expects to save 40 percent to 60 percent on the review and classification of documents related to a $100 million lawsuit against insurers. Examples of services that

Table 9.1 Level of Outsourcing by Activity Area

Value-Chain Area	Outsource Area
Supply-side activities	• Distribution/fulfillment—32%* • Manufacturing/operations—24% • Procurement/supply management—15%
Corporate support activities	• Information technology—36% • Legal/regulatory—30% • Human resources—16% • Finance and accounting—9%
Research and technology activities	• Engineering/detailed design—22% • Research—14% • Product and service development—12%
Demand-side activities	• Customer call center—22% • Marketing—17% • Field service—16% • Sales—7%

*Interpret this figure as 32 percent of firms have outsourced at least a quarter of their distribution/fulfillment requirements. Interpret all other percentages accordingly.

Source: Adapted from Robert M. Monczka, William J. Markham, Joseph R. Carter, John D. Blascovich, and Thomas H. Slaight, *Outsourcing Strategically for Sustainable Competitive Advantage*, Tempe, AZ: CAPS Research, 2005, p. 20.

are increasingly being outsourced include customer support and service, legal services, payroll, security services, management of temporary labor, travel services, administration of medical plans, IT management, warehouse management, transportation, human resource outplacement, food services, janitorial services, grounds maintenance, risk management and insurance, printing, operational procurement, physical plant maintenance, and sometimes even procurement.

We often take it as a given that an outsource provider can perform a service better than these services can be performed internally. While a specialist should perform better than a nonspecialist, outsourcing, like most other supply management activities, comes with no guarantee of better performance. Outsourcing contracts require extreme care when crafted and then continuous monitoring over the life of the agreement. Outsourcing agreements, which can be quite complex, also require a set of metrics that tell the buyer how the provider is performing. Consumers have become increasingly vocal, for example, about the lack of service received from call centers staffed in foreign locations. While call center costs may decrease, the number of frustrated customers increases. How does this frustration affect a company's brand?

Table 9.1 reports the magnitude of outsourcing across 14 areas. The data are part of a broader study on outsourcing conducted by CAPS Research. This table

Table 9.2 Achieving Outsourcing Goals

Goal Area	Falling Short	Meeting	Exceeding
Reduce capital investment.	9%	61%	30%
Obtain competitive intelligence.	10%	61%	29%
Meet downsizing requirements.	12%	62%	26%
Reduce development costs.	13%	62%	25%
Turn fixed costs into variable costs.	14%	62%	24%
Grow revenue.	20%	58%	22%
Increase speed to market.	21%	60%	19%
Improve customer response cycle time.	22%	55%	23%
Increase flexibility and responsiveness.	29%	49%	22%
Improve quality.	30%	55%	15%
Gain access to markets.	31%	54%	15%

Source: Adapted from Robert M. Monczka, William J. Markham, Joseph R. Carter, John D. Blascovich, and Thomas H. Slaight, *Outsourcing Strategically for Sustainable Competitive Advantage*, CAPS Research, Tempe, AZ, 2005, p. 24.

identifies the percent of companies that currently outsource at least 25 percent of their requirements for each area listed. For example, 36 percent of respondents have outsourced at least a quarter of their IT requirements to external third parties.[5]

Why Do Companies Outsource? One expert argues that the reasons to outsource fall primarily into six categories:

- *Organizationally driven reasons.* To enhance overall effectiveness by allowing an organization to focus on what it does best
- *Improvement-driven reasons.* To improve operating performance and gain access to expertise, skills, and technologies that would otherwise not be available
- *Financially driven reasons.* To reduce the investment in assets and free up resources for other uses
- *Revenue-driven reasons.* To accelerate expansion by tapping into a supplier's capacity, processes, and systems
- *Cost-driven reasons.* To turn fixed costs into variable costs
- *Employee-driven reasons.* To increase commitment and energy in core business areas

While cost improvement is and will always be a major benefit sought from outsourcing, it is certainly not the only possible benefit. Table 9.2 summarizes the percent of firms exceeding, meeting, and falling short of their outsourcing goals. While the news overall is favorable, some outcomes are not as well realized as others.

Table 9.3 Factors Supporting Insourcing

Favorable costs to produce internally.

Desire to absorb fixed overhead costs through higher capacity utilization.

Desire to maintain design secrecy or protect intellectual property.

Desire to maintain control over production and quality.

Lack of reliable suppliers.

Item or service is core to the business.

Union or other restrictions limit outsourcing options.

Desire to maintain workforce stability.

Outsourcing may encourage new competitors.

When Do Outsourcing Decisions Arise? Outsourcing decisions arise at many different times. Outsourcing considerations are increasingly part of the corporate strategic planning process. Decisions at this level address what businesses to be in, what product lines to introduce, and in what geographic regions to operate. Outsourcing decisions also arise during the new product development process.

Outsourcing discussions may also occur due to poor internal performance (just as insourcing decisions may occur because of poor supplier performance). Changing technology may also encourage an outsourcing discussion. During the 1990s, printing technology changed to the point that Federal Express decided not to make an investment in its internal printing capabilities, motivating FedEx to outsource its printing operation. Geographic expansion, product line expansion, and changing product demand patterns may also encourage outsourcing discussions.

Factors Affecting the Outsourcing Decision. While many, if not most, outsourcing decisions are based on cost savings, there are many factors affecting whether to insource or outsource. These decisions are becoming so important that anything less than a thorough analysis before reaching a final decision could have longer-term consequences. Tables 9.3 and 9.4 identify some of the more important factors affecting whether something stays or goes. The CAPS Research outsourcing study revealed that loss of control, activities are core to the business, and the protection of intellectual property are the three most cited reasons for not outsourcing an activity.[7]

Outsourcing Risks. Outsourcing decisions, like the other topics presented in this book, can be carried out poorly. This process carries a number of risks that we need to understand. Perhaps one of the most cited risks involves the potential for creating new competitors. Airbus recently announced it intended to build an assembly plant in China, even though the Chinese government has openly stated its desire to become a major player in the global aerospace industry.

Table 9.4 Factors Supporting Outsourcing

Desire not to add new employees.

Desire to reduce capital assets or avoid taking on new assets.

Specialized supplier capabilities provide advantages.

Item is routine and widely available.

Item or service is not core to the business.

Product life cycle is mature or declining.

Lower volume requirements.

Capacity constraints at the buyer.

Shorter product life cycles discourage investment.

Unfamiliar with producing an item or service.

Forecasting and volume uncertainty.

Decades ago U.S. television manufacturers decided to abandon the production of black-and-white televisions to the Japanese so they could focus on the more profitable and growing color television segment. Apparently the Japanese were not content with taking over a declining market. The rest, as they say, is history. While the United States is competitive across many industries, consumer electronics is not one of them. The potential for creating new competitors is a risk that must always be considered during outsourcing. For most firms, the allure of quick cost savings from outsourcing often overshadows any concerns about longer-term consequences.

The decision to outsource often seems quite clear. The execution of the decision is sometimes not quite so clear, making poor execution a risk. What seems logical on paper may not seem logical to a workforce that resists change or to a management team that has never managed the transition from insourcing to outsourcing. Many companies simply do not have experience operating a business model that features higher-level or system outsourcing.

Another risk involves incorrectly allocating overhead costs during the outsourcing analysis. In fact, the inability to accurately allocate overhead charges was one of the driving forces behind the development of activity-based costing systems. What costs will stay and which will really be eliminated if we outsource? How valid are the numbers? Will the remaining fixed costs be allocated over fewer total units, leading to decreased competitiveness within other product lines? As the opening to this chapter illustrated, incorrect cost allocation is not an insignificant issue.

Perhaps one of the most significant risks surrounding higher-level outsourcing is that it is part of a new business model that is largely untested. Never in history have so many companies outsourced so many parts of their value chain.

Component Outsourcing ➡	**Strategic Outsourcing**
Characteristics:	**Characteristics:**
❏ Manage thousands of component part numbers and suppliers.	❏ Manage 100 or fewer key suppliers.
	❏ Manage collaborative relationships.
❏ Manage hundreds of standard contracts.	❏ Develop alliances with select suppliers.
❏ Manage transactions.	❏ Pursue cross-organizational integration opportunities.
❏ Employ many buyers.	
❏ Practice traditional supplier relationships.	❏ Practice value-creating supply activities.
❏ Participate in make-or-buy analyses.	❏ Rely on systems suppliers to manage component suppliers.

Figure 9.1 Supply management's changing role.

Outsourcing does not mean something is not important. It simply means the company has decided not to provide a good or service internally. If something were unimportant, a company would likely find a way to eliminate its need for it.

Supply Management's Role. It would be reasonable to ask why a chapter on outsourcing appears in this book. What does outsourcing have to do with supply management? The answer is, more than you think. The world of supply management changes radically under today's model of outsourcing. Figure 9.1 compares an environment featuring component buying to one featuring systems or higher-level outsourcing. The two environments are vastly different.

An important question is whether an organization has the capabilities to operate on the right side of this figure. Managing a smaller number of strategic supply relationships is certainly different than managing thousands of component suppliers. Relationship management takes on an entirely different level of importance when a company is pursuing a systems outsourcing strategy. Most of this book relates to the right side of Figure 9.1.

Outsourcing entire system or service areas, such as logistics management, means that supply managers need to be involved early during the strategic planning process. This process demands the expertise of supply managers when making supplier selection decisions that have high switching costs and risks associated with them. Outsourcing also demands that supply managers become early participants in the product development process. Who, after all, is supposed to go out and find these outsource suppliers?

MACRO CHANGES AND TRENDS PROMOTING OUTSOURCING

Some well-defined changes and trends are promoting ever-higher levels of outsourcing. Understanding these will help us better understand the outsourcing phenomenon.

The Pressure to Reduce Costs Is Severe and Will Continue to Increase. Cost reduction pressures are forcing companies to use their resources more effectively. Studies show that most executives perceive the need to reduce costs to be constant and growing. As a result, executive managers will increasingly look to outsourcing as a way to lower costs.

Firms Are Becoming More Highly Specialized in Product and Process Technology. Increased specialization leads to focused investment in a process, technology, or capability, which should lead to greater cost differentials between firms. Consider the case of engine manufacturer Cummins. This company historically produced most of its pistons internally. In fact, piston production was part of its industrial heritage. However, an analysis identified several companies that specialized in piston production and who were investing three or four times the amount that Cummins invested in piston technology. Are pistons a critical engine component? Absolutely! Is the production of pistons the best use of Cummins' valuable investment resources? Probably not.

Firms Will Increasingly Focus on What They Excel at while Outsourcing Noncore Areas. More and more companies are formally defining their core competencies to help guide their outsourcing decisions (a later section formally defines the concept of a core competency). A focus on core competencies and cost reduction pressures may be the strongest drivers behind the current outsourcing movement. Several years ago, for example, Procter & Gamble made the decision to sell the plants that made the liners for disposal diapers, even though these plants were profitable. P&G decided this was not where they wanted to invest over the long term. Making diaper liners, even though liners are critical to the end product, is not part of P&G's core business.

The Need for Speed and Responsiveness in the Marketplace Is Promoting Outsourcing. The way that companies win in the marketplace is increasingly through speed and responsiveness. Shorter cycle times encourage greater outsourcing with less vertical integration. The time to develop a capability or capacity internally may exceed the window of opportunity available to exploit an opportunity. In a recent cover story, *BusinessWeek* maintained that speed to market is now the ultimate competitive weapon.[8] Performed properly, outsourcing can help a company be fast, flexible, and responsive to market opportunities.

Wall Street Recognizes and Rewards Firms with Higher Return on Assets. Since internal control usually requires an assumption of fixed assets and increased human capital, pressures from financial analysts are causing managers to look to outsourcing as a means to avoid assets and human resources. Improving ROA is motivating many companies to rely on a supplier's assets through outsourcing.

THE OUTSOURCING PROCESS

The probability of making effective outsourcing decisions will increase if companies take a structured approach to the analysis. Greaver proposes a seven-step planning and implementation methodology to support effective outsourcing:[9]

1. *Planning initiative.* Form a cross-functional team to study and implement the outsourcing option; be open internally with intentions each step of the way.
2. *Exploring strategic implications.* Determine how outsourcing fits with your company's strategies and how it works with other transformational approaches.
3. *Analyzing costs and performance.* Measure the existing costs of activities against the costs of outsourcing, including future costs; analyze current and future performance.
4. *Selecting suppliers.* Identify qualified suppliers; prepare detailed RFPs; evaluate proposals and select a prime provider candidate.
5. *Negotiating terms.* Reach agreement on specific terms, including scope of services, performance standards, pricing, and contract management; draft a binding agreement.
6. *Transitioning resources.* Address the human resource issues; transfer factors of production to the outside provider or dispose of as required.
7. *Managing relationships.* Monitor performance, evaluate results, and resolve problems; build a strong, committed relationship with the supplier.

Part of approaching outsourcing methodically is having a structured approach so that outsourcing results in a focused, robust organization.

THE (MISUNDERSTOOD) CONCEPT OF CORE COMPETENCIES

Probably one of the most misunderstood concepts among managers today is the notion of core competencies. A core competency is another one of those buzzwords that we all wish we had a dollar every time the term was tossed about. When asked to define what a core competency is, most respondents will reply that it is something that a firm does well. This, unfortunately, is incorrect.

C. K. Prahalad and Gary Hamel originally put forth the idea of core competencies in their *Harvard Business Review* article titled "The Core Competence of the Corporation."[10] They defined a core competency as the collective learning in an organization, especially how to coordinate diverse skills and integrate multiple streams of technologies. They further refined this concept by saying that in the long run, competitiveness derives from an ability to build, at lower cost and faster than competitors, the core competencies that spawn unanticipated products and services. Conceiving of the corporation in terms of core competencies widens the domain of innovation. A company that organizes around competencies does not envision itself as a group of unrelated businesses.

Prahalad and Hamel offered three basic yet powerful tests for determining if a collective learning should be considered a core competency. First, the core competency must provide access to a wide variety of markets. Second, the competency should make a significant contribution to the perceived customer benefit of end products or services. Finally, a core competency should be difficult to imitate.

Here are some examples to illustrate this concept. Many at FedEx will argue the company's ability to deliver packages overnight is a core competency. However, if we apply Prahald and Hamel's three tests, we will see that overnight package delivery no longer qualifies as a core competency. While FedEx's ability to deliver packages overnight is valued by customers and provides access to a wide variety of markets, it is no longer hard to duplicate. A host of other companies, including the U.S Postal Service, offer overnight package delivery service. Overnight delivery, while important to FedEx's business model, has shifted from being a core competency to a core capability. With so many companies offering this service, overnight package delivery has become a commodity.

Let's now consider a company that has a true core competency. Casio makes hundred of products, including calculators, watches, and musical instruments. While its product line appears diverse, each shares a core competency, or collective learning, that is difficult to imitate, is valued by customers, and provides access to a wide variety of markets. That competency is the *ability to miniaturize* electronic components. Casio does this as well as anyone in the world.

What do core competencies have to do with outsourcing? During the strategic planning process, core capabilities and competencies are something to be protected and nurtured. Areas that are not core to the business rapidly become candidates for outsourcing. Much of what executive leaders focus on today relates to decisions about what to keep and what not to keep. At the highest planning levels the concepts of core competencies and capabilities are influencing the development of supply strategies and relationships. We have moved away from a make or buy model that focused on basic components to an outsourcing model that requires supply managers to operate at an entirely different level.

CORE COMPETENCIES AND OUTSOURCING AT POLAROID

Imagine it is the mid-1990s and you are a supply manager working for the once-proud company called Polaroid.[11] While the rest of U.S. industry is enjoying steady growth, your company has been struggling. The 1990s, which featured the longest period of industrial expansion in U.S. history, were not rewarding for Polaroid. The company experienced eroding profit margins due to intense global competition, mature product lines, and several costly product launch failures. With some difficulty, the company was forced to change its culture to respond to the demands of a new marketplace, forcing a transformation from a "technology push" to a "marketing pull" company.

Polaroid's traditional business model, which featured the development of a limited number of breakthrough products requiring four to five years to develop, succeeded for many years. Unfortunately, the company's measurement and reward system, which was a reflection of the company's culture, rewarded basic rather than applied research. Polaroid's founder is one of the most prolific inventors of the twentieth century. The emphasis on basic rather than applied research resulted in many patents "sitting on the shelf" without ever being commercialized. While having strong research capabilities, Polaroid often lacked a customer and marketing focus.

After Polaroid's CEO retired, a new management team arrived to reenergize the company. This led to the development of several new philosophies. The first was the need to introduce and market quickly a greater numbers of new products. The second was to streamline the organizational structure so it could support faster product development. A third philosophy was the need to nurture and innovate within the company's primary core competency and capability areas while outsourcing those items where the company did not add significant value. These emerging beliefs caused Polaroid to outsource products and services that it historically produced internally.

Something that Polaroid did have going for it was a true core competency that was shared with only one other company in the world (Fuji). This competency involved the ability to acquire images instantly. The collective knowledge about instant image acquisition was designed into all of the company's products, was valued by customers, and was difficult to imitate. Instant image acquisition with film qualified as a true core competency.

Procurement responded to the operating philosophies introduced by the new CEO by introducing a host of changes. Polaroid organized its supply efforts around three primary groups: indirect purchasing, raw materials purchasing (any materials that are required directly for production), and contract or finished goods purchasing. This case addresses the outsourcing efforts of the contract purchasing (i.e., finished goods) group, although the other two groups also actively pursued their version of strategic supply management.

Finished Goods Outsourcing

Virtually all of Polaroid's products used complex components referred to as *media*, which is central to the company's core competency. The decision was made to control the design and production of media while outsourcing the assembly and casings for finished products (think of the plastic housing for a camera), which design engineers referred to as *hardware*, to trusted third-parties. Most of the innovation valued by customers occurred within media rather than hardware, making media a primary area to focus research and development efforts. Furthermore, the margins for media products were higher than the margins for hardware products. From an investment and financial perspective, limited corporate resources were best allocated to media rather than hardware.

Asian suppliers eventually provided all outsourced hardware requirements using media components and systems designed and produced by Polaroid. Outsourcing to Asian suppliers offered two major benefits: access to technology and lower cost.

The Genesis of the Outsourcing Group. Starting in the late 1990s, Polaroid began to search for outsourcing partners for hardware requirements. Unfortunately, there was no organization in place to formally support that effort. While a small OEM group worked to locate contract manufacturers from the 1970s to late 1990s, there was no formal endorsement or focus on outsourcing as a corporate strategy. As a result, creating an outsourcing organization was not a high priority.

A procurement director approached several key executives to discuss the need for greater contract manufacturing. He argued for the creation of a group that would be responsible for managing worldwide hardware outsourcing. As a result of these discussions, the company created a finished goods outsourcing group. This group had responsibility for identifying and qualifying outsource partners, managing product quality, and working with contract manufacturers during new product development.

The finished goods outsourcing director was primarily responsible for managing strategic relationships with contract manufacturers and pursuing early-involvement opportunities with these suppliers. He reported to the vice president of new product delivery while maintaining a dotted-line reporting relationship to the vice president of purchasing.

The outsourcing director also had responsibility for two Asian international purchasing offices (IPOs). The primary mission of these offices was to identify and work with potential and existing partners. The Asian IPOs reported to the outsourcing director in the United States as well as to a regional manager. These offices helped identify potential contract manufacturing suppliers or identified available suppliers during the sourcing of indirect requirements and raw materials.

Linking Finished Product Outsourcing with Marketing and Technical Groups. Coordinating the activities of the outsourcing group with marketing and technical groups was also critical. The corporate marketing group was divided by market application—a consumer youth segment, a business segment, a professional/technical segment, and the traditional consumer market. Consistent with this company's shift from technology push to marketing pull, increasing numbers of new product ideas were originating from marketing. Marketing had even become responsible for market testing new product ideas generated by R&D, something that was unlikely in the past.

Product ideas that emerged from the marketing groups had to have a defined commercial applicability. Operations and technical representatives, who reported to the vice president of new product delivery, were physically colocated within each marketing group to ensure the operations and technical voices were represented during the generation of new product ideas. The contract purchasing director conversed with the operations and technical people weekly to gain insights into new product ideas that might affect the development of strategic outsourcing plans.

This company also created a futures group. This was an advanced-technology development group that met weekly to address media and hardware requirements. The group, created by the CEO, was given a broad charter of developing medium- to longer-range product strategies. The Futures Media Group, driven by research and development and headed by a vice president, also included marketing, finished products outsourcing, and operations. One indication of this group's importance was that it reported directly to Polaroid's CEO. Being part of a futures group provided the outsourcing director with insight at the concept stage of product and technology development.

The End of an Era. Even though this discussion focused on a single group, there is no question that all three procurement groups played a major role in supporting Polaroid's turnaround. And for a while things were turning around nicely, just like a textbook would suggest. Unfortunately, the reader might notice that this case is written largely in the *past* tense. In 2001 Polaroid entered bankruptcy and subsequently had its assets purchased by an affiliate of One Equity Partners. Many of the Polaroid products we see on television or on the company's Web site are simply finished goods branded with the Polaroid name. The Polaroid we see today is not the Polaroid of yesterday.

Why should we talk about a company whose best days are past? What can we learn from this case? First, supply managers should play an active role during the strategic outsourcing process. Within Polaroid the finished goods procurement group was instrumental in changing the way the company viewed itself and how it conducted its business. And for a while this group helped the company again become profitable. Second, all the good supply management intentions in the world will not be enough to save a company when technology or market conditions change abruptly. The rapid transition from instant image acquisition from film to digital was cruel to Polaroid. While there is still a small market for instant film, the company has nothing distinctive to offer in the digital arena.

We should also realize that core competencies are not necessarily permanent or ensure success. They are subject to the same destructive forces of creativity and competition that affect all parts of a business. The famous Austrian-American economist Joseph Schumpeter once said that capitalism is a process of creative destruction. The change in instant image acquisition from film to digital was simply too much for Polaroid to overcome. The creative destruction was complete.

CONCLUDING THOUGHTS

Outsourcing is not a topic that is exclusive to the domain of supply management. It is a topic, however, that will continue to affect the thinking and activities of supply managers for a long time to come. A focus on outsourcing is not going away anytime soon. Readers who want a more detailed evaluation of strategic outsourcing should obtain a copy of the report "Outsourcing Strategically for Sustainable Competitive Advantage" published through CAPS Research. This study assesses the state of outsourcing as it is practiced today, provides a prescriptive model for strategic outsourcing, takes a closer look at procurement outsourcing, and addresses how to think strategically about this topic.

SUMMARY OF KEY CHAPTER POINTS

- Outsourcing is the act of transferring some of an organization's recurring internal activities and decisions rights to outsiders, as set forth in a contract.
- While some items and services have always been provided externally, the difference today is we are witnessing outsourcing in areas that not too long ago were safely performed in-house.

- A firm should concentrate internally on those components, assemblies, systems, or services where it possesses a distinctive or unique advantage. Once a company outsources something, it usually loses the ability to bring it back in-house without making a major investment.
- Outsourcing is not the same as offshoring, although a great deal of outsourcing is occurring with China.
- Outsourcing considerations are increasingly part of the corporate strategic planning process. Outsourcing decisions also occur during product development, when experiencing poor supplier or internal performance, when technology changes, during geographic and product line expansion, and during changing product demand patterns.
- Outsourcing is not without risk, including the potential for creating new competitors, poor execution of outsourcing decisions, incorrectly allocating overhead costs during the outsourcing analysis, and attempting to manage a new business model that is largely untested at most firms.
- Some well-defined changes and trends are promoting an emphasis on higher-level outsourcing, including pressure to reduce costs, increased specialization, a focus on areas where companies excel, a need for speed and responsiveness, and pressure to generate higher asset returns.
- A seven-step planning and implementation methodology to support effective outsourcing includes planning, exploring strategic implications, analyzing costs and performance, selecting suppliers, negotiating terms, transitioning resources, and managing relationships.
- During strategic planning, core capabilities and competencies are something to be protected and nurtured. Areas that are not core to a business are candidates for outsourcing.

ENDNOTES

1. The author would like to thank Terry Fennell for his contribution to the opening section.
2. M. F. Greaver II, introduction to *Strategic Outsourcing: A Structured Approach to Outsourcing Decisions and Initiatives* (New York: AMACOM, 1999).
3. Greaver, 3.
4. P. Engardio, "Let's Offshore the Lawyers," *BusinessWeek* 4001 (September 18, 2006): 42.

5. R. M. Monczka, W. J. Markham, J. R. Carter, J. D. Blascovich, and T. H. Slaight, "Outsourcing Strategically for Sustainable Competitive Advantage" (Tempe, AZ: CAPS Research, 2005), 20.

6. Greaver, 4–5.

7. Monczka et al., 23.

8. S. Hamm, "Is Your Company Fast Enough?" *BusinessWeek* 3977 (March 27, 2006): 68.

9. Greaver, 24–29.

10. C. K. Prahalad and G. Hamel, "The Core Competence of the Corporation," *Harvard Business Review* 68, no. 3 (May/June 1990): 79–91.

11. The information in this example was obtained from interviews with Polaroid supply managers.

10

BUILDING A WORLD-CLASS SUPPLY BASE

Imagine you work for a firm where organizing around traditional functional groups and activities has been the norm. Imagine further that your CEO has assembled her key managers, of which you are one, to announce a major restructuring—a restructuring that is sure to involve major change. The CEO has asked you to visualize an organizational model that features the widespread sharing of information, a flattened decision-making hierarchy, and, perhaps most importantly, a design that is centered around processes that are your organization's source of value creation.

One outcome from this scenario should be the identification of those processes that will have the greatest impact on performance. A second outcome should be the realization that the changes required by this transformation, which will be dramatic in scope, will allow attention to fewer rather than many processes. As organizations take on a process-centered orientation, and there is evidence that suggests this is happening, identifying those processes that are the most likely sources of value creation becomes critical. As a supply manager, you know quite well that the activities required for building a world-class supply base include some of the most important processes your firm should have in place.

This chapter addresses several topics that are essential for building a world-class supply base. The first part of the chapter covers what may be one of the most important organizational processes in place today—evaluating and selecting suppliers. This includes a seven-step selection process, a set of tools that support supplier selection, and suggestions for taking time out of the process. The second part of the chapter addresses the important role that supply base optimization plays when creating a world-class supply base.

163

EVALUATING AND SELECTING SUPPLIERS

Supplier selection is one of the most important responsibilities of supply managers and commodity teams. This process is too often an afterthought performed by buyers who are measured by their ability to obtain the lowest price rather than the lowest total cost or highest value. With a growing reliance on fewer suppliers to provide greater value-add, and with the use of longer-term contracts continuing to grow, the cost of making an incorrect selection decision can have long-lasting consequences. As external suppliers begin to command 50 percent or more of a firm's total revenue, the logic behind creating a world-class evaluation and selection process becomes even clearer. Besides the obvious impact on cost, suppliers affect a broad range of end-customer requirements.

Too many leaders have viewed suppliers and the process that selects them with relative indifference. Purchasing simply was not part of the executive radar screen. A strategic emphasis on core capabilities and competencies, which often results in the outsourcing of major requirements, now makes supplier evaluation and selection a critical *organizational* process.

Not all selection decisions are created equally or warrant comparable effort. Firms that excel at supply management understand the need to approach the selection decision based on the attributes of their requirements. The way that buying firms subsequently manage their suppliers will also differ from requirement to requirement. Segmenting supply requirements using the portfolio matrix approach presented in Chapter 7 begins to define the intensity of the search, the contracting approaches and performance measures to employ, and the kind of relationships to pursue with selected suppliers.

The primary objective of the selection process should be a reliance on suppliers that become a source of competitive advantage. For the most important goods and services, firms should use cross-functional teams to evaluate first-hand a supplier's financial condition, capacity, global capabilities, logistical networks, cost structure, supply management practices, process capabilities, technology innovation, and design and engineering capabilities.

Firms that practice total quality across their supply chain should see the connection between the selection process and some very important quality management principles. A cross-functional approach for evaluating and selecting suppliers is an ideal way for pursuing quality at the source, emphasizing prevention rather than detection, stressing objective rather than subjective decision making, and making quality everyone's responsibility. Supplier selection is a process we really want to get right.

A Methodical Approach for Selecting Suppliers

The supplier selection process incorporates many of the topics presented in earlier chapters, including strategy segmentation and development, measurement, longer-term contracting, and negotiation. Most observers will agree that each selection decision has some level of uniqueness—there is no one way to evaluate and select suppliers and no two selection decisions are exactly alike. However, all selection decisions should follow a logical flow from recognizing that a selection need exists to reaching agreement with the selected supplier. The following summarizes a seven-step selection process.

Step 1. Recognize a Supplier Selection Need. As an internal service provider, supply managers have an obligation to link with internal customers around the company. Instead of sitting in an office or cubicle waiting to be informed that a selection need exists, supply managers need to become more proactive to selection needs. The following presents some of the ways that supply managers recognize a supplier selection need exists:

- Through participation on new product development teams
- From internal customer requisitions
- During supplier switching, perhaps due to poor performance
- During supply base reduction or optimization
- Due to notices of expiring contracts
- During strategy development, including during the development of global strategies or when supporting the strategy needs of other groups
- During market testing of standard items
- During outsourcing
- From early insights gained through colocation with internal customers
- During geographic or capital expansion

Step 2. Identify Supply Requirements. This step is critical because it begins to define the criteria against which potential suppliers are eventually evaluated. While two selection decisions may be similar, no two are completely alike. The involvement of internal and sometimes even external customers is essential for identifying the correct set of attributes, and eventually their weights, that will be used during a formal assessment. For example, the ability of a supplier to adjust capacity quickly due to changing demand might be a critical requirement for the marketing group. Or a supplier's ability to provide engineering resources might be important to product design engineers. For other items a basic package of cost, quality, and delivery performance attributes is all that is needed.

Step 3. Determine Supply Strategy. Chapter 7 and 8 discussed extensively the idea of developing supply strategies. In this part of the selection process, participants must consider a number of questions as they *formally* articulate a supply strategy within the context of the selection process. Some of the more important questions include the following:

- Should we use a single source or multiple supply sources?
- Should we consider foreign suppliers?
- Should we enter into a shorter-term or longer-term contract?
- What type of relationship best fits this supply requirement?
- Is this an item that will benefit from early supplier involvement during product design?
- What value-added services do we want the supplier to provide?
- How much and what type of information must be shared?
- Do we want regional agreements or a global agreement?
- Are we willing to use a supplier that is also a competitor?
- Are there any corporate policies affecting the selection decision?

Step 4. Identify Potential Suppliers. In years past it was more of a challenge to identify potential suppliers that might be able to support the supply strategy developed in Step 3. Now Web-based search technology and electronic databases may provide us with too much information. In this step we are identifying rather than qualifying potential supply sources. The extent of the search process for potential suppliers is a function of several variables. Is the item new to the buying company? Is the item basic or complex? Do we have a preferred supplier that is already part of the supply base? The existence of a preferred supplier that everyone agrees upon is a strong choice may make the selection decision short and sweet.

The most efficient resource for locating potential suppliers today is the Internet. Online directories contain an abundance of information about potential supply sources. Consider a tiny fraction of the supplier directories that were identified through a Google search:

- *www.thomasnet.com.* This site contains perhaps the most comprehensive directory available for identifying information on North American suppliers.
- *www.indiamart.com.* This site contains an online business directory and yellow pages of several hundred thousand suppliers in India.
- *www.ism.ws/SupplierDirectory.* This resource is maintained by the Institute for Supply Management and helps buyers locate possible supply sources.

- *www.staffingindustry.com.supplier_directory*. This database features information on providers of services such as payroll, Web design, drug and background screening, accounting services, and so on.
- *www.made-in-china.com*. This site provides a directory with leads about Chinese manufacturers and suppliers.

Other possible sources that might be helpful when locating potential suppliers include sales representatives, trade shows, other internal business units, trade journals, foreign consulates, and internal databases.

Step 5. Reduce Suppliers in Selection Pool. This step requires the narrowing of the potential supplier pool to a manageable number, such as three to five suppliers. This step is not as critical if the supply pool is already limited.

One approach for limiting the supplier pool is to evaluate each supplier's financial condition. A supplier financial analysis is performed basically for two reasons: to manage business risk and to eliminate marginal suppliers from the evaluation process. Many firms require suppliers to achieve a certain level of financial stability before they can receive further consideration. Evaluating a supplier's financial health is a risk management technique that all supply managers should practice.

As an aside, financial assessments should also occur for incumbent suppliers, perhaps every six months. Existing suppliers that are under financial duress should be placed on a "watch list." Do we really want to rely on suppliers that will be bankrupt or insolvent in a year or two? Exceptions to this certainly exist. A supplier's financial problems may be temporary, or the supplier is developing a new technology that is vital to the buyer. The supplier may also be the only source available.

A supplier's health is often assessed through the calculation of financial ratios. While dozens of ratios exist, most fall into one of four categories. Figure 10.1 presents these categories along with a sample of ratios within each category. A challenge when analyzing a supplier's financial health is obtaining reliable information, particularly for private companies. A variety of resources provide information about companies, including company-published annual reports, Web sites such as www.finance.yahoo.com, 10-K and 10-Q reports, Dun & Bradstreet reports, TRW credit reports, trade and business journals, and supplier provided data obtained through RFIs.

Some words of caution are in order when calculating ratios. Data access and reliability is often a concern, particularly for private and foreign companies. Furthermore, ratio analysis is simply a tool that should be part of a broader evaluation and selection process. Like measurement, ratio analysis is not a substitute for good management or sound decision making. Care must also be taken when comparing companies from different industries. Finally, financial statements,

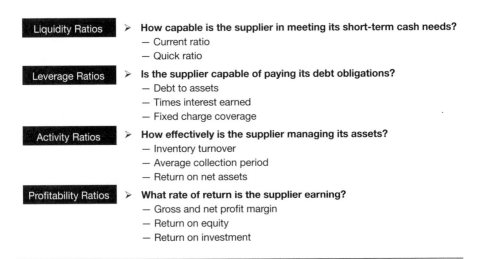

Figure 10.1 Supplier financial ratio analysis.

which provide the basis for most ratios, are only for a point in time (the balance sheet) or a relatively short period of time (the income statement). Multiple time periods should be considered to identify possible trends.

There are other reasons for removing a supplier besides concerns about financial health. These include, but are certainly not limited to, a history of poor performance, lack of available capacity, pending litigation involving the supplier, a supplier is a direct competitor, the supplier has environmental or other workplace infractions, the supplier demonstrates relative indifference about doing business with the buyer, and unfamiliarity with the buyer's industry.

Step 6. Conduct a Formal Evaluation. At this point of the process, a buying firm has identified a set of suppliers that will undergo a more formal assessment. As mentioned in Chapter 4, supplier evaluation is one of the major times when supply measurement occurs. Sometimes the selection decision is based on a relatively easy comparison of competitive bids. At other times the decision is made only after a time-consuming formal supplier assessment involving supplier site visits.

Supplier evaluation and selection decisions are becoming considerably more complex and important today. Given the performance demands placed on suppliers and the extremely high cost of switching suppliers after selection, the use of site visits to evaluate supplier capabilities is an important part of the selection process. These visits, however, require a major commitment of time, cross-functional support, and budget for travel and living. Visits to more than one supplier may also occur, since these visits may determine which suppliers are invited to final negotiations. And, if the company is considering a global supplier, buyers must consider and likely visit multiple sites around the world. While the cost of making worldwide site visits is high, the cost of making a poor selection decision is even higher. A buying firm should perform due diligence by acting as if it were buying the supplier rather than buying the supplier's capabilities.

Step 7. Select Supplier and Reach Agreement. In a perfect world the objective assessment performed in Step 6 will reveal the optimal selection choice. Unfortunately, even with the most rigorous assessment, the decision about selecting a supplier, like hiring personnel, is not always obvious. For critical items this step usually requires a variety of cross-functional perspectives before reaching a final decision.

Part of this step involves deciding how to reach agreement with the targeted supplier(s). When thinking about how to reach agreement, keep in mind that a recent survey of European suppliers revealed their willingness to shift business away from customers that have costly and time-consuming negotiating processes.[1] The negotiating process can become quite adversarial if not managed properly. It would be disappointing to go through the previous steps only to reach a deadlock at this point. At times reaching agreement simply involves an offer by a buyer and an acceptance by a seller that is formalized through a purchase order.

The end of Step 7 is only the beginning of what could be a very long buyer-seller relationship. The focus must shift from evaluating and selecting suppliers to managing and developing suppliers.

Tools That Support the Selection Process

A variety of tools are available to support the selection process. Progressive organizations are constantly searching for best practices they can incorporate into their selection process. The following is a small sample of the kinds of tools that should be made available to support supplier selection.

Company-wide Selection Templates. Many firms have developed Excel-based templates that can be tailored to match the unique requirements of the selection decision. These templates are used for more important selection decisions (i.e., longer-term, critical suppliers, complex items). The advantage of pre-developed supplier selection template is twofold. First, these templates ensure that those responsible for supplier selection are using rigorous tools to support their decisions. Second, preestablished templates help avoid duplication of effort. Most commodity teams will develop some methodology to follow when evaluating potential suppliers. Reinventing a tool to support supplier evaluation is not where value is being created in the selection process.

Supplier selection templates will include different evaluation categories, the ability to weigh each category, and the metrics that define each score within a performance category. No standard assessment applies to all selection decisions. For example, a supplier that will assume some product development responsibilities should have its design and technical capabilities weighted more heavily than a supplier that will produce according to a provided specification. Some less critical selection decisions may be based on standard evaluation categories like cost, quality, and delivery performance.

Z-Score Analysis. Perhaps the best tool for assessing supplier financial health is the Z-Score. Developed by Dr. Edward Altman of New York University, the Z-Score combines a series of weighted ratios for public and private firms to predict financial health. The Z-Score is almost 90 percent accurate in predicting bankruptcy one year in advance and 75 percent accurate in predicting bankruptcy two years in advance.

The Z-Score has two things going for it that make this tool a must for every supply organization. The first is its simplicity. Only four ratios are needed to calculate the Z-Score for private firms and five are needed for public firms. Second, the Z-Score provides a single score that can be used during the preliminary evaluation of potential suppliers. The following are the Z-Score formulas for private and public firms:

Private Company:

$$\text{Z-Score} = 6.56 \times \frac{\text{Working capital}}{\text{Total assets}} + 3.36 \times \frac{\text{Retained earnings}}{\text{Total assets}} + 6.72 \times \frac{\text{EBIT}}{\text{Total assets}} + 1.05 \times \frac{\text{Net worth}}{\text{Total liability}}$$

where:

Z-Score < 1.1   Red zone—Supplier is financially at risk.
Z-Score between 1.1 and 2.6   Yellow zone—Some area of financial concern.
Z-Score > 2.6   Green zone—Supplier is financially sound.

Public Company:

$$\text{Z-Score} = 1.2 \times \frac{\text{Working capital}}{\text{Total assets}} + 1.4 \times \frac{\text{Retained earnings}}{\text{Total assets}} + 3.3 \times \frac{\text{EBIT}}{\text{Total assets}} + 0.6 \times \frac{\text{Net worth}}{\text{Total liability}} + 1.0 \times \frac{\text{Net sales}}{\text{Total assets}}$$

where:

Z-Score < 1.8   Red zone—Supplier is financially at risk.
Z-Score between 1.8 and 3.0   Yellow zone—Some area of financial concern.
Z-Score > 3.0   Green zone—Supplier is financially sound.

Third-Party Data. Dun & Bradstreet (www.dnb.com), an organization that makes its living compiling information on public and private companies, offers various reports that support the supplier selection process, particularly in the evaluation of private or smaller suppliers. Its *Comprehensive Insight Plus Report* offers detailed information on U.S. suppliers across a number of areas, including financial norms, ratios, and benchmarks; forecasts of future credit worthiness; the likelihood of a supplier experiencing financial distress over the next year; financial condition comparisons to similar businesses; and a dashboard view of key risk indicators. Other reports are available that are a subset of D&B's most comprehensive report. These reports are best suited for quickly prequalifying or limiting suppliers in the selection pool. They are not good sources of information about a supplier's cost, quality, or delivery performance.

Decision Support Tools. Various tools are available to support decision making when more than one choice is available. One of the best-known approaches is the Kepner-Tregoe Matrix. This approach supports unbiased decision making by providing a structured methodology for identifying and ranking the factors that are critical to a decision. This tool, developed by Charles Kepner and Benjamin Tregoe and presented originally in their 1965 book *The Rational Manager: A Systematic Approach to Problem Solving and Decision Making*, is used to help make decisions of all sorts, including site selection, supplier selection, and product development decisions. A Kepner-Tregoe analysis comprehensively evaluates alternative courses of action to arrive at a desired state based on explicit objectives. This approach follows a specific sequence of steps:[2]

1. Prepare a decision statement having both an action and a result component.
2. Establish strategic requirements (the musts), operational objectives (the wants), and constraints (the limits).
3. Rank objectives and assign relative weights.
4. Generate alternatives.
5. Assign a relative score for each objective on an objective-by-objective basis.
6. Calculate a weighted score for each alternative and identify the top two or three.
7. List adverse consequences for each top alternative and evaluate their probability (high, medium, low) and severity (high, medium, low). Make a final, single choice between top alternatives.

Tools for Making Group Decisions. Since many supplier selection decisions are made by teams, it is likely these teams will benefit from a variety of techniques that share a common objective: They are designed to help make a decision. Each of the following is far less complex than the Kepner-Tregoe approach but still can be effective during the decision-making process:

- *List reduction.* Subjects a large list of ideas or options to a pre-established set of criteria.
- *Balance sheet.* Requires the identification of the pros and cons of a variety of options.
- *Criteria rating forms.* Uused to evaluate options head-to-head against various criteria.
- *Weighted voting.* Used to quantify the position or preference of group members.
- *Paired comparisons.* Used to select a preference for every combination of possible decisions or choices.

These tools are not only inexpensive, they are easy to use and often quite effective.

Mathematical Models. Operations researchers have developed a host of techniques that employ very complex mathematical models that support the selection decision. Researchers have explored mathematical modeling to aid supplier selection, including mixed-integer nonlinear programming models to solve multiple-sourcing problems, stochastic integer programming approaches for simultaneous selection of suppliers based on loss functions and capability indices, a comparison of suppliers using data envelopment analysis, linear programming that considers tangible and intangible factors in selecting the best suppliers with optimum order quantities identified, and multicriteria supplier selection using fuzzy logic and an analytic hierarchy process. While these approaches are outside the scope of this book, it is still worthwhile to appreciate some of the more complex approaches that exist.

Taking Time out of the Selection Decision

It's surprising how rare cycle times are measured, including the concept-to-customer (C-to-C) cycle time for new product development. The ability to reduce cycle times, especially for the times associated with supplier selection, customer order fulfillment, and new product development, is increasingly defining how companies win in the marketplace today.

While not always the case, many supplier evaluation and selection decisions occur during product development. Given that development times for new products and services are declining rapidly, it seems logical that any supporting cycle times must also decline. Gone are the days when supply managers could spend months to evaluate, select, and negotiate supplier agreements. Major selection decisions often have to occur in weeks, perhaps even days. Supplier selection is a process that must not only be performed well but also performed quickly.

There are many creative ways to shorten supplier selection cycle time without reducing the quality of the process. Figure 10.2 highlights some of these ways. Identifying ways to reduce cycle time should actually improve the effectiveness of

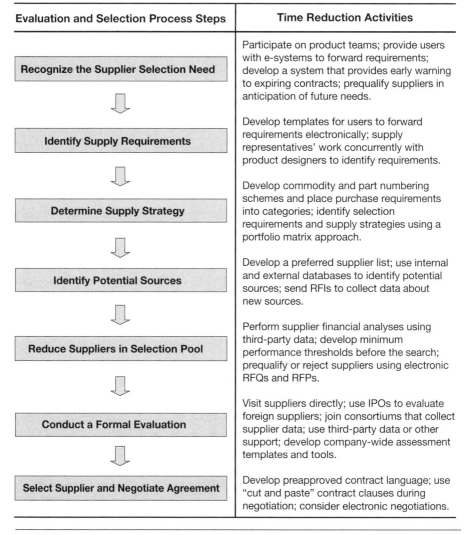

Evaluation and Selection Process Steps	Time Reduction Activities
Recognize the Supplier Selection Need	Participate on product teams; provide users with e-systems to forward requirements; develop a system that provides early warning to expiring contracts; prequalify suppliers in anticipation of future needs.
Identify Supply Requirements	Develop templates for users to forward requirements electronically; supply representatives' work concurrently with product designers to identify requirements.
Determine Supply Strategy	Develop commodity and part numbering schemes and place purchase requirements into categories; identify selection requirements and supply strategies using a portfolio matrix approach.
Identify Potential Sources	Develop a preferred supplier list; use internal and external databases to identify potential sources; send RFIs to collect data about new sources.
Reduce Suppliers in Selection Pool	Perform supplier financial analyses using third-party data; develop minimum performance thresholds before the search; prequalify or reject suppliers using electronic RFQs and RFPs.
Conduct a Formal Evaluation	Visit suppliers directly; use IPOs to evaluate foreign suppliers; join consortiums that collect supplier data; use third-party data or other support; develop company-wide assessment templates and tools.
Select Supplier and Negotiate Agreement	Develop preapproved contract language; use "cut and paste" contract clauses during negotiation; consider electronic negotiations.

Figure 10.2 Reducing supplier evaluation and selection time.

supplier selection decisions. When performed correctly, a faster selection process requires supply managers to redesign the process by reducing time and waste.

Be aware that there can be a dark side of cycle time reduction. Cutting corners to save time is not the same as properly redesigning a process. For example, let's say you have two alternatives for awarding a $100 million contract. These alternatives are cleverly named Supplier A and Supplier B. Quick—make a selection decision! So, you picked Supplier A (or perhaps Supplier B) in a matter of a second or two. While you were fast and efficient (you are a decision-making machine), were you also effective? Was your choice the right one? Do not lose sight of the time-accuracy trade-off.

OPTIMIZING THE SUPPLY BASE

A second part of building a world-class supply base involves determining the right mix and number of suppliers to maintain for each purchase item, category, or commodity. Talking about the right mix and number leads us to supply base optimization, or as it is sometimes called, supply base rationalization. The technical definition of *optimize* is to make something as perfect, effective, or functional as possible. So, supply base optimization is a process that seeks to create a supply base that is as perfect, effective, or functional as possible.

Many supply managers will associate supply base optimization with supply base reduction. This is because most U.S. firms historically have maintained a very large supply base. During the 1990s over three-quarters of firms surveyed decreased the total number of suppliers they maintained, some by up to 90 percent.[3] Another survey reported that over the last several years almost 50 percent of companies have reduced their supply base by 20 percent, another 15 percent reduced their supply base between 20 and 60 percent, and fully three-quarters of buying firms now commit 80 percent or more of their total purchase dollars with fewer than 100 suppliers.[4]

The logic for reducing the size of the supply base from historically high levels is based on two beliefs. The first belief is that the costs associated with maintaining multiple suppliers for each purchased good or service usually outweigh any perceived reduction in supply risk. Firms have historically maintained a larger number of suppliers to reduce risk. We now know that risk has many dimensions and that maintaining too large a supply base in itself can increase rather than decrease supply chain risk and costs. Multiple suppliers for a single item create additional opportunities for variability and higher costs due to reduced leverage.

The second belief is that optimization is a critical prerequisite for the development of the leading-edge activities that can truly lead to a competitive advantage. Supplier involvement in new product development, collaborative longer-term agreements, and joint performance improvement initiatives are difficult with a cumbersome supply base. One hundred key suppliers will be easier to work with than 2,000 suppliers that you hardly know.

Early supplier reduction efforts by U.S. firms were often too cosmetic to offer any real payback. Do you want to know the quickest way to reduce your supply base? Identify those suppliers that have not received an order in the last two years, and remove them from the database. Wham—say goodbye to hundreds of suppliers! Next, identify duplicate supplier records. Zap—there goes a bunch more! During its supplier optimization efforts, one company discovered its number one supplier in terms of purchase dollars was IBM, its number five supplier was I.B.M. (with periods), and its number seven supplier was International Business Machines. While cleansing the database should be a regular occurrence, we know that the corresponding reduction in the number of suppliers is, at best, superficial. This activity is required, however, to arrive at a true picture of the supply base.

Initial reduction efforts by U.S. firms usually resulted in keeping a smaller group of suppliers from the original supply base. This was due partly to the need to reduce the supply base quickly in response to oversees competition. While the use of existing suppliers minimized switching costs, it also precluded the consideration of potentially better suppliers that were not currently part of the base. Since many companies within the same industry went through the optimization process at the same time, any supply base improvements were not necessarily unique to any one participant. What a supply organization does after completing its primary optimization efforts will define the winners and losers.

A misconception surrounding optimization is that reducing the size of the supply base means fewer total supply chain members. At most companies, supplier reduction corresponds only to a reduction in the number of first-tier suppliers. As buyers rely on larger, full-service suppliers to design and build entire systems, the first-tier component suppliers get pushed to the second or third tier of the supply chain. The systems supplier is slotted into the first-tier position. However, the need to source components did not go away. The responsibility for sourcing these components now often resides with the new first-tier "super" supplier. Even though the purchaser maintains fewer first-tier suppliers, an emphasis on strategic supply management demands a keen interest in second- and third-tier suppliers.

Another point is that most firms do not establish strict goals regarding how many total suppliers to maintain. As mentioned in Chapter 1, for some items, it is not worth the time to be concerned with how many suppliers provide relatively insignificant items. If numerical targets are set, they should correspond to the upper half of the portfolio matrix (the leverage and critical items) that was presented in Chapter 7. That is where the action is today.

Supply base optimization is a continuing process. There will always be a need to "tweak" the number of suppliers that a buying organization maintains. At some point firms will want to replace "good" suppliers with even better suppliers, even if this means searching outside the current base. Furthermore, shifting demand patterns, changing supplier ownership, the introduction of new products, global expansion, and mergers and acquisitions all have a continuous impact on the size of the supply base.

Optimization Success Factors

Like any process, supply base optimization requires certain factors to be successful. And, as usual, number one on the chart is having the time to pursue optimization. Supply base optimization usually requires a detailed analysis that is not normally part of the supply management process. The importance of supply base optimization also mandates that managers draw upon a variety of cross-functional skills. Many companies will assign this responsibility to their commodity teams. If a team is considering evaluating suppliers that are not currently part of the supply base, then all the resources that support supplier selection, including site visits and a defined selection process, will also be important here. The optimization process also requires an extensive amount of data to support objective decision making.

Benefits and Risks of an Optimized Supply Base

Perhaps the most significant benefit from an optimized supply base is that it allows supply managers to pursue leading-edge supply management activities. The activities that can create a competitive advantage simply are not feasible with an unruly supply base. Another benefit is the opportunity to develop closer relationships with the remaining suppliers. If performed correctly, supplier reduction efforts should also result in better supply chain performance and reduced risk as survival of the fittest takes over. Who would get rid of their best suppliers? And finally, fewer suppliers per item allow a company to more easily leverage purchase volumes.

Optimization is not without risk. Perhaps the two greatest risks are selecting the wrong supplier to be part of an optimized supply base and, if optimization means supply base reduction, cutting the supply base too deeply or too quickly. Removing too much capacity from the supply base has come back to haunt more than one firm.

Some organizations have strict guidelines regarding single sourcing during the optimization process. These firms are concerned about a supplier becoming too dependent on the buyer's business, a shift of power from the buyer to the seller, a supplier not staying current with technology, or complacency. One advantage of maintaining several suppliers for an item is the sense of competition that should exist between the remaining suppliers. A company that builds heavy-duty

Competency Staircase Approach	Improve or Else Approach
• Suppliers must pass a series of performance hurdles similar to climbing a staircase. • Hurdles can include performance requirements in quality, technical capability, cost, responsiveness, etc. • Purchaser defines the hurdles and their required performance levels.	• All suppliers have a chance to remain in the supply base. • Suppliers have a specified period to meet stringent performance requirements. • Suppliers that fall short may soon become ex-suppliers.
Triage Approach	**20/80 Approach**
• Place suppliers into one of three categories. • Category One includes suppliers incapable of meeting performance requirements. • Category Two includes suppliers that would benefit from supplier development support. • Category Three includes near-perfect suppliers.	• Requires an analysis to identify the 20 percent of suppliers receiving the majority of purchase dollars, or the minority of suppliers causing the majority of problems. • The large majority of supplies that receive fewer dollars are candidates for elimination. • This approach often assumes the best suppliers receive the majority of purchase dollars, which may not be true.

Figure 10.3 Approaches for optimizing the supply base.

trucks optimized its supply base to a single supplier to provide cab assemblies. Unfortunately, this "partnership" deteriorated to the point where the buyer had to make a costly switch. According to supply managers, the incumbent supplier abused its power position as the single source of a very critical item.

Optimization Approaches

Various approaches support optimization. The most appropriate approach often relates to how quickly or how urgently the buying company needs to optimize its supply base. Keki Bhote, an architect of Motorola's Six Sigma quality process, presents four basic approaches that support supply base optimization, which Figure 10.3 summarizes.[5] While a supply organization can put its own spin on these approaches, the point is that optimization should follow some coordinated logic rather than move along haphazardly.

Figure 10.4 illustrates the approach taken by a leading company to support its optimization efforts. This approach closely resembles the triage approach in Figure 10.3 and effectively combines reduction goals with supplier development goals. This company ranks its suppliers against specific performance criteria. Suppliers

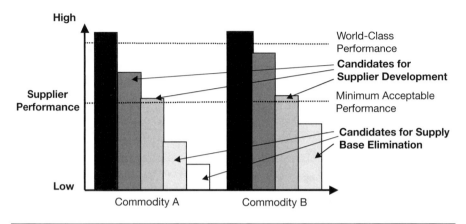

Figure 10.4 Identifying supply base optimization and supplier development candidates.

that are incapable of meeting minimum performance targets are eventually invited to leave the supply base. Remaining suppliers that are not performing at world-class levels are targeted for supplier development support, a topic the next chapter covers. This company then takes great care to nurture its relationships with its highest-performing suppliers. Optimization must be part of a broader, coordinated process.

CONCLUDING THOUGHTS

Few could logically argue that the inputs received from upstream suppliers do not affect the ability to satisfy or even exceed the requirements of downstream customers. We know that producers are afforded minimal forgiveness when they fail to satisfy demanding customer requirements. Building a world-class supply base recognizes that meeting customer needs requires attention to the inputs and relationships that originate far upstream in the supply chain. Leading firms would never ignore the relationship between the effectiveness of their selection decisions and the effectiveness of their value chain.

SUMMARY OF KEY CHAPTER POINTS

- Supplier selection is one of the most important components of building a world-class supply base. Supplier evaluation and selection is too often an afterthought.
- Firms that practice total quality should see the connection between a world-class supplier selection process and TQM.

- Supplier selection can be displayed as a seven-step process that consists of recognizing the need to select a supplier, identifying supply requirements, determining the supply strategy, identifying potential suppliers, reducing suppliers in the selection pool, conducting a formal evaluation, and selecting the supplier and reaching agreement.
- There are many ways to anticipate a supplier selection need, including electronic linkages with internal customers and supply involvement on new product development teams.
- The involvement of internal and sometimes even external customers is essential for identifying the correct set of attributes, and eventually their weights, that will be used during a formal supplier assessment.
- One approach for limiting the number of suppliers under consideration is to evaluate each supplier's financial condition. A financial analysis is performed to manage business risk and to eliminate marginal suppliers from the evaluation process.
- Perhaps one of the best tools for assessing supplier financial health is the Z-Score, which combines a series of weighted ratios for public and private firms to predict financial health.
- Since most cycle times are shortening, it makes sense that supplier evaluation and selection times must also decline. There are many ways to accelerate the evaluation and selection process without sacrificing quality or effectiveness.
- Supply base optimization or rationalization is concerned with the right mix and number of suppliers to maintain. Most supply managers will associate supply base optimization with supply base reduction, since U.S. firms have historically maintained a very large supply base.
- The logic for reducing the size of the supply base is based on two beliefs: The costs associated with maintaining multiple suppliers usually outweighs any perceived reduction in supply risk, and optimization is a critical prerequisite for the development of leading-edge supply activities.

ENDNOTES

1. J. Snyder, "European Suppliers Play Favorites," *Automotive News*, May 16, 2005, www.autonews.com.
2. Adapted from "Kepner-Tregoe Matrix," 12manage Web site, www.12manage.com/methods_kepner-tregoe_matrix.html.

3. R. M. Monczka and R. J. Trent, "Purchasing and Supply Management: Key Trends and Changes throughout the 1990s," *International Journal of Purchasing and Materials Management* 34, no. 4 (Fall 1998): 2–11.

4. A. Reese, "eProcurement Takes on an Untamed Supply Chain," *iSource* (November 2000): 108.

5. K. Bhote, *Strategic Supply Management* (New York: American Management Association, 1989), 75.

11

MANAGING SUPPLIER PERFORMANCE AND RELATIONSHIPS

Imagine enjoying a cup of coffee as you sort through the day's mail. In front of you is a letter from one of your biggest customers, a major tier one supplier to the medical equipment industry. As you read the letter, your mouth drops and your stomach tightens. It becomes obvious that things are about to change for your company.

The purpose of the letter is to request that immediate action be taken to protect the future of your business. The letter explains that improvements from suppliers at all levels have not kept pace with the improvements demanded by the OEMs. The author of the letter explains that while his company has tried to work collaboratively with suppliers, and he proceeds to list a variety of programs with impressive-sounding names, the results have been "disappointing." As a result, your customer has decided to reestablish prices with all suppliers and to conduct market tests for every purchased item. Your customer is demanding *double-digit* price reductions retroactive to the beginning of the year, or a period of about two months. This is not going to be fun.

The letter goes on to say how important suppliers are to this company's success. It is only with the full support and participation of suppliers "as our *partner* will we reach our objectives." The letter concludes by stating that suppliers who contribute significantly to the cost reduction effort will solidify their position in the long-term supply base and share in new business opportunities, which are anticipated to be significant.

The example highlights three important points about managing supplier performance and relationships. First, the activities that supply managers put in place, even if they do have impressive-sounding names, are no guarantee of better outcomes. Second, relationships that can take years to nurture can change almost overnight. Here, relationships with suppliers that this buying company called collaborative quickly turned adversarial. While this buyer will argue that desperate times call for desperate measures, unilateral action taken in the short term often has longer-term consequences. Third, the term *partner* is sometimes tossed around so freely that it is easy to become cynical when someone uses it.

This chapter focuses on ways to manage supplier performance and relationships. We first link a set of quality management principles to specific supplier management activities. The second section presents supplier development as an approach for improving supply chain performance. The important topic of managing supplier relationships is presented next. The chapter concludes with one of the most interesting cases of supplier management in recent history.

APPLYING A TQM APPROACH TO MANAGING SUPPLIER PERFORMANCE

Managing suppliers is one of the most important, and often challenging, responsibilities facing supply managers. The switching or churning of suppliers is simply not as great as it once was, making it important to work with a set of suppliers that will be around for a while. Once a firm brings a supplier on board, the emphasis should shift from supplier evaluation and selection to supplier management and development. Supplier performance management consists of the approaches and activities that supply organizations put forth to ensure a steady stream of conforming, and hopefully improving, products and services from suppliers. As such, there is no one activity or approach that defines supplier performance management or supplier relationship management. Rather, these concepts are composed of many different activities.

Supply managers should never assume that suppliers will always perform as required or that supplier performance is not vital to supply chain performance. Lapses in supplier performance can tarnish even the world's most powerful brands. In a case that gained widespread attention, European soda drinkers became ill after consuming Coca-Cola products, prompting government officials to ban the sale of the company's products for a period of time.[1] Coke's chief scientist said that a major culprit was quality lapses at a Belgian bottling plant that allowed contaminated carbon dioxide to enter into Coke's products. A spokesman for Coke confirmed that the Belgian plant did not test the carbon dioxide provided by its supplier. The supplier that provided the gas said that Coke never asked for a certificate of analysis verifying the quality of the gas. In other examples, defective batteries made by Sony have clearly hurt Dell's image in the marketplace. Tainted lettuce from a key supplier has also caused significant harm to Taco Bell and its customers.

When we think about how to manage supplier performance, it is worthwhile to apply a total quality management perspective. The principles that define TQM are still some of the most powerful ever developed, and these principles should guide managers in their supplier management efforts.[2] Even today we still experience the power of TQM, as these principles form the foundation of Six Sigma quality programs.

While the various experts have put forth dozens of different quality principles, it is possible to streamline these principles into a more manageable set. Table 11.1 presents eight quality principles based on the thinking of W. Edwards Deming, Philip Crosby, and Joseph Juran, three of the most respected leaders in the total quality movement.[3] Along with each principle is a set of activities that will help supply leaders put each principle into practice. The ability to recite these principles from rote memory is far different than systematically applying them. The following elaborates on these eight principles.

Principle 1. Define Quality in Terms of Customers and Their Requirements. One of the primary causes of poor supplier performance involves the inconsistent communication and misunderstanding of specifications, expectations, and requirements between supply chain members. A leading quality expert argues that the incomplete or inaccurate development and communication of specifications has a disproportionate effect on supply chain quality. He argues that at least half or even more of the quality problems between a buyer and a supplier are caused by vague or arbitrary specifications, for which the buying company is largely responsible. The first cure for poor supplier quality is to "eliminate the tyranny of capricious specifications."[4]

A clear understanding of requirements has two dimensions. The first is the ability of the buyer to specify his company's requirements. One reason that supply managers, as well as suppliers, should be part of product development teams is to obtain first-hand knowledge about internal customer requirements. The same is true for colocating supply personnel with internal customer groups. The second dimension is the buyer's ability to effectively communicate these requirements to the supplier.

Principle 2. Pursue Quality at the Source. Quality at the source occurs whenever value is added to a product or service as it moves through the supply chain. The value-add points or activities represent "sources" that require careful management. In particular, value creation within the supply chain occurs during

Table 11.1 TQM Principles and Supply Management Activities

Total Quality Principle	Examples of Supply Management Activities
Define Quality in Terms of Customers and Their Requirements	• Identify internal customers and establish communication linkages. • Communicate requirements to suppliers through RFPs. • Conduct face-to-face supplier performance review meetings. • Create measures that relate to key expectations and requirements. • Use formal contracting to define requirements.
Pursue Quality at the Source	• Perform supplier selection site visits. • Develop a consistent selection process and methodology used across all buying centers. • Involve suppliers early in product and process design. • Develop supplier performance capabilities.
Stress Objective Rather than Subjective Measurement and Analysis	• Develop fact-based supplier performance measurement systems. • Develop total cost of ownership measurement systems.
Emphasize Prevention Rather than Detection of Defects	• Perform rigorous preselection supplier site visits. • Use supplier corrective action requests to prevent future problems. • Certify supplier quality capabilities and processes. • Require ISO 9000 certification. • Require supplier-provided testing and verification of shipments.
Focus on Process Rather than Output	• Perform rigorous preselection supplier site visits. • Demand evidence of supplier process. capability. • Develop a consistent source selection process.
Strive for Zero Defects	• Perform rigorous preselection supplier site visits. • Develop fact-based supplier scorecards. • Rationalize the supply base.
Establish Continuous Improvement as a Way of Life	• Upwardly migrate supplier scorecard targets. • Develop supplier performance capabilities. • Use longer-term contracts selectively. • Offer performance improvement incentives. • Conduct value analysis projects with suppliers.
Make Quality Everyone's Responsibility	• Establish supplier residency and colocation programs. • Involve suppliers early in product development. • Conduct joint strategy development sessions. • Create an executive supply council with supplier involvement.

Source: Adapted from Robert J. Trent, "Linking TQM to SCM," *Supply Chain Management Review*, May–June 2001, p. 72.

product and process design and at various points as material and information progresses through the chain. Perhaps more than any other group, supply managers have the ability to affect quality at the source because of their ability to determine the source for most supply chain inputs. A supply management group that practices quality at the source will have processes in place to perform site-based supplier evaluation visits and to integrate key suppliers into new product and process development, two major supply chain source points.

Principle 3. Stress Objective Rather Than Subjective Measurement and Analysis. An executive responsible for coordinating Xerox's successful drive for the Malcolm Baldrige National Quality Award stated that one of the keys to achieving total quality is recognizing that facts rather than subjective judgment must predominate.[5] Hence, if facts predominate, the need for objective measurement becomes evident.

Why is objective data so important to supplier quality? Performance data allow supply managers to develop a preferred supplier list for awarding future business, identify continuous performance improvement opportunities, provide feedback that supports corrective action or future development, identify which suppliers to include or eliminate from the supply base, and track the results from improvement initiatives. Performance measurement systems are also an ideal way to communicate performance expectations. Organizations are increasingly referring to their supplier performance reports as *supplier scorecards*, which Chapter 4 discussed.

Principle 4. Emphasize Prevention Rather Than Detection of Defects. Prevention is the avoidance of nonconformance in products and services by not allowing (i.e., preventing) errors or defects to occur. While preventive activities take many forms, each stresses the need for consistency and reduced variation. An emphasis on prevention makes reliance on appraisal, inspection, and detection less likely. A rigorous approach to supplier evaluation and selection is an ideal way to ensure that selected suppliers have the systems, processes, and methods in place to prevent defects.

Supplier quality certification, another way to pursue defect prevention, is the formal process of verifying, usually through an intensive site audit, that a supplier's processes and methods produce consistent and conforming quality. While certification should contribute to a better understanding of supplier performance, the resources required to develop and execute a certification program can be extensive. Furthermore, some firms have become complacent once they grant certification to a supplier. In one instance, a major automotive company had to discontinue business with 40 certified suppliers due to poor performance. This is not only embarrassing, it also reveals some serious flaws in that company's certification process. A positive feature of ISO 9000, which has become a standard quality certification across many industries, is the requirement for recertification at regular intervals.

Principle 5. Focus on Process Rather Than Output. Perhaps the most radical difference between traditional and total quality thinking surrounds a shift from a product to a process orientation. TQM demands that our focus be on the processes that create output rather than the output itself. Since processes create output, shouldn't we logically focus on the process of creation rather than the result? An emphasis on process rather than product demands that suppliers provide evidence of process capability on a regular basis.

Let's assume that an organization evaluates and awards business based primarily on competitive bids and supplier samples. Relying on output (i.e., the sample) rather than the process raises a number of questions. What supplier would knowingly submit a poor sample? How many pieces did the supplier produce to get a good sample? Did the supplier use the same process, methods, and materials that would be used during normal production? Did the supplier actually produce the sample, or was it subcontracted? Do samples tell the buyer anything about the supplier's capacity, process capability, financial condition, labor relations, supply management capabilities, and so on? Focusing on the process means minimizing a reliance on samples unless a timely and comprehensive method exists to validate sample conformance.

Principle 6. Strive for Zero Defects. Philip Crosby argued that the performance standard that defines total quality is zero defects, which he defined as *conformance* to requirements. Genichi Takuchi further argued that any deviation from a target value carries with it some level of opportunity loss due to scrap, rework, and dissatisfied customers. While the pursuit of zero defects can be frustrating, supply chain performance should be better off because of the pursuit.

Striving for zero defects, however defined, can be operationalized in several important ways. A well-designed and rigorous supplier evaluation and selection process is one way to identify and do business only with suppliers that strive for zero defects. Measurement systems also help identify improvement opportunities and progress. Another major approach, and also one of the fastest ways to achieve higher supply chain quality, is through supply base rationalization. Maintaining a large supply base creates variability across lead times, material consistency, interpretation of specifications and requirements, transportation and delivery, and the quality of relationships. Fewer suppliers should naturally result in less overall variability and move an organization closer to zero defects.

Principle 7. Establish Continuous Improvement as a Way of Life. While the pressure to improve is severe and relentless, there are many ways to make continuous supplier improvement a way of life. One approach involves the aggressive migration of supplier performance targets. Some supply managers believe that achieving incremental goals, however worthy, invites suppliers to perform the same processes incrementally better. Another way is to help develop supplier performance capabilities. If a firm has reduced its supply base to a manageable level, then continuous improvement will occur primarily by developing the capabilities of current suppliers rather than supplier switching. Many companies rely on longer-term agreements with remaining suppliers to support continuous supplier performance improvement. These agreements enhance the likelihood that suppliers will get the financing they require to improve operations. Effective longer-term agreements should also strengthen supply chain performance by stipulating annual improvement requirements.

A producer can also offer rewards to encourage continuous improvement. Offering performance-related rewards recognizes that a direct link exists between the reward and improvement. Traditionally, purchasers demanded supplier improvement but were reluctant to share the resulting benefit, which encouraged suppliers to look out only for their self-interests. Table 11.2 provides examples of various rewards that should encourage continuous supplier improvement. Supply managers should be creative in how they promote continuous improvement.

Principle 8. Make Quality Everyone's Responsibility. This principle requires that internal and external supply chain members assume ownership for quality across the total chain. Some ways to ensure that suppliers assume ownership for supply chain quality include establishing supplier on-site residency and colocation programs, involving suppliers early in product development, conducting joint strategy development sessions, and creating an executive supply council with supplier involvement.

While other competitive factors, such as mass customization and flexibility, are increasingly becoming today's order winners, the ability to design, produce, and sell high-quality products and services will always remain important. Poor quality that starts with upstream suppliers and works its way through the supply chain is perhaps the quickest way to tarnish a company's brand image. With so many choices available, industrial customers and consumers are not that forgiving of poor quality.

DEVELOPING SUPPLIER PERFORMANCE CAPABILITIES

One activity that most U.S. firms have not pursued rigorously is the active development and improvement of supplier performance capabilities. Supplier development is a broad concept that *represents any activity or effort on the part of the buying company to improve the performance of suppliers.* Development efforts primarily fall into three categories: working with suppliers to resolve a

Table 11.2 Continuous Supplier Improvement Incentives and Rewards

Incentive and Reward Examples
Award longer-term purchase contracts.
Offer a greater share of total purchase volume to superior performers.
Publicly recognize superior suppliers, including "supplier of the year" awards across different categories.
Share the cost-savings resulting from supplier-initiated improvements or suggestions.
Provide suppliers with access to new technology.
Provide early insight into new business opportunities and product development plans.
Invite suppliers to participate early in new product development projects.
Allow suppliers to purchase off the buyer's supply agreements to obtain favorable pricing.
Invite suppliers to participate in executive-level buyer-supplier councils.
Create a preferred list of suppliers that receive the first opportunity for new business.

Source: Adapted from Robert J. Trent, "Linking TQM to SCM," *Supply Chain Management* Review, May–June 2001, p. 73.

problem (reactive), working with suppliers to continuously improve a performance capability (proactive), and working with suppliers to create a performance capability where none previously existed (proactive). Regarding the third point, a number of years ago an automotive OEM helped a supplier develop the capability to make exterior mirrors. This supplier previously produced only interior mirrors. Now one trusted supplier performs the work of two suppliers.

Part of the reason for not pursuing supplier development activities relates to the confrontational nature that has characterized too many buyer-seller relationships. The need to focus on supplier development is clear if we can agree about several assumptions. First, most firms have reduced the size of their supply base to a more manageable level and are actively (or should be) pursuing more cooperative relationships with the remaining suppliers. Second, the amount of supplier switching that occurs should lessen as a buying firm converges on a set of suppliers it views as critical to longer-term success. Third, the need for continuous supply chain improvement is never ending. With fewer remaining suppliers, improvement will occur primarily through the improvement of existing supplier capabilities rather than from large-scale supplier switching.

A strong argument can be made that the majority of supplier development initiatives to date, particularly for U.S. firms, have been reactions to performance problems. A supply organization that puts in place a world-class supplier evaluation and selection process will likely prevent future problems that force reactive supplier development activities. When this occurs, supply managers can focus on opportunities that stress continuous improvement and the development of new capabilities.

Like most major topics presented throughout this book, supplier development also benefits from taking a systematic process view. And like all processes supplier development can be displayed as a series of steps:

Step 1. Identify improvement opportunities.

Step 2. Target specific suppliers that should benefit from development activities.

Step 3. Meet with the supplier's executive leadership to obtain buy-in, agree on the development opportunity, and develop project plans and clear measures of success.

Step 4. Identify the type of supplier development support to provide.

Step 5. Make development resources available.

Step 6. Perform the development project.

Step 7. Measure and report the ROI from supplier development.

There are many examples of supplier development activities, including allowing suppliers to attend a buyer's education and training programs, placing support personnel at suppliers, and providing equipment and technology. Conducting kaizen (i.e., continuous improvement) workshops to improve supplier operations, conducting Six Sigma quality improvement projects, and providing capital support, particularly to smaller suppliers, also qualify as legitimate development approaches.

Interestingly, research from the late 1990s revealed that the most common types of supplier development support as articulated by U.S. supply managers included enhancing working relationships with suppliers, requiring supplier capability improvements, and increasing supplier performance goals.[6] These can hardly be classified as hands-on or direct types of supplier development.

Companies that pursue development activities should be aware of three best practices associated with supplier development. The first is that a central system should be established for controlling and monitoring the development efforts. This is done to ensure that development efforts are not diffused, uncoordinated, or underreported. Second, development efforts should be set up as projects with widespread visibility across an organization. This allows the use of project management tools. Finally, supply managers should calculate the ROI from their development efforts. This last point demands the involvement of finance.

It is important for supply leaders to convey the notion that supplier development represents an investment rather than expense. Executive leaders who view development activities as an expense are often quick to cut these initiatives when business declines. Most supply organizations budget limited resources to their development efforts, so it becomes critical to manage these resources carefully and to demonstrate a strong return from the effort.

Some suppliers are world-class and will not benefit greatly from development efforts. Conversely, no amount of supplier development efforts will transform some suppliers into star performers. It is important to carefully segment the supply base in terms of development initiatives. And some suppliers may not want any development support. Forcing your vision of supplier development may only harm a relationship. It is important to target carefully those suppliers and performance areas that will provide the greatest ROI.

Supplier development must become a more routine part of strategic supply management. Not only must executive management be convinced that committing company resources toward development activities is a worthwhile risk, but suppliers must also be convinced that is in their best interest to accept direction and assistance. This assumes, of course, that a buying company has the expertise to provide direction and assistance!

MANAGING SUPPLIER RELATIONSHIPS

A major part of strategic supply management involves managing supplier relationships. We have to be careful here—talking about relationships makes it sound like buyers and sellers should stand in a circle, join hands, and gently sway while singing "Kum Ba Yah." And if a relationship experiences some problems, a trip to Dr. Phil should work wonders. Like transaction costs, supplier switching costs, and the accounting concept called goodwill, relationships are not always tangible. They are, however, very real.

Even with the seemingly intangible nature of industrial relationships, most firms would benefit from a more enlightened approach to managing their supplier relationships. One could easily argue, and a diverse set of research supports this view, that supplier relationships can be so important they become a source of competitive advantage.[7] As a result, many firms are focusing on SRM, which is a broad-based management methodology and set of practices describing how a firm manages its supply base. It is also a philosophy promoted by supply leaders across a company that recognizes the importance of relationships.

Several years ago suppliers complained that the cost-cutting pressures placed on them by DaimlerChrysler were hurting the cooperative relationships the company had so meticulously developed. A strong argument can be made that Chrysler's relationships with its suppliers during the 1990s provided the company with differential advantages compared with Ford and GM. But the times appeared to be changing as we entered the new millennium. An executive at one supplier noted that the give-and-take that had previously characterized the meetings between suppliers and Chrysler had been replaced with one-sided demands by Chrysler, and flexible goals had given way to inflexible goals. *BusinessWeek* noted that Chrysler may be "blowing years of painfully built goodwill for short-term cost savings."[8]

Why Relationships Matter

Identifying the reasons why relationships will become more important is not that hard. Relationships matter because almost every industry is facing changes and trends that make external suppliers a critical part of a firm's value chain. There are at least eight reasons why supplier relationships matter today.

Relentless Pressure to Improve. It is difficult to identify an industry that has not experienced an increase in global competition over the last 15 years, leading to ever-increasing pressure to improve. Even if the number of major competitors in an industry has become smaller, such as in the aerospace industry, sophisticated customers still present their own set of demands. Pressure to improve is relentless and severe, and combined with other changes and trends, it is not hard to envision the role that suppliers will play in the improvement process. Suppliers that have a positive working relationship with their customers should be willing to participate in a buyer's improvement projects, engage in joint problem solving, participate early during product design, and support other activities that lead to better supply chain performance. Suppliers that do not have a positive relationship with a buyer will presumably be less willing to support meaningful changes. These suppliers may even act in a manner that is counterproductive to the buyer's long-term interests.

Reliance on Fewer Suppliers. An unintended effect of relying on a drastically reduced supply base, and one that makes supplier relationships with remaining suppliers important, is an increase in supplier switching costs. As we reduce our supply base for critical requirements to a selected one or two suppliers, place the remaining suppliers on longer-term agreements, and even begin to use global suppliers to satisfy worldwide operating needs, how much supplier switching flexibility does a buying company really have? Supply base reduction, whether buyers recognize it or not, often makes supplier switching more costly. A longer-term reliance on a drastically reduced supply base demands close attention to relationships.

Importance of Early Involvement. For most firms the development of new products and services makes up a major part of their competitive business model. And it's difficult to dispute that an increasing amount of differentiating features and technology in final products and services is originating with suppliers. Consider, for example, the OnStar system in General Motors vehicles, FedEx's tracking technology, and efficient engines and composite materials for Boeing's 787 Dreamliner. These innovations have come largely from suppliers that do much more than design a component according to buyer-provided specifications. Capturing the benefits from early involvement requires a set of suppliers willing to share their expertise and resources as well as buyers who understand how to manage the relationships with these very special suppliers.

Higher-Level Outsourcing. As Chapter 9 noted, the last 10 years witnessed a growing emphasis on core competencies and core capabilities. While outsourced activities or requirements are presumably not part of our internal core capabilities or competencies, they are still essential to success. Can anyone argue that the Asian supplier that produces the iPod does not affect Apple's reputation for quality? Is the logistics provider that helps manage GM's worldwide supply chain not central to GM's success? As third parties assume responsibility for entire "chunks" of the value chain, anything less than a total commitment to strong relationships with outsource suppliers will likely suboptimize performance.

Pressure to Become a Full Product-Service Provider. Industrial customers are showing a desire to work with companies that provide a full range of products and services. The problem for many firms is they lack the capabilities, including geographic capabilities, to market themselves as a full-service supplier. Becoming a full product-service provider rather than a niche player (or a full service-product provider if the primary business is a service) forces firms to consider a number of options. They can develop the required capabilities internally, acquire the capabilities through merger or acquisition, or rely on third-party suppliers to fill in the missing pieces.

Increasingly, we should expect the use of third-party suppliers to be an attractive option. The time and cost required for formal acquisitions or the internal development of a full range of capabilities is often too great, at least in the short term. Furthermore, a reluctance to assume ownership of additional assets from a financial perspective also favors using third-party suppliers. Can a firm that relies on its suppliers to help it compete as a full product-service provider afford not to view relationships as core to its success?

Constrained Supply Markets. Consider some headlines from a report on world supply markets: prices for molybdenum are at historic highs; spot gold predicted to double in coming months; tight cement supply boosts concrete prices; zircon rises as demand exceeds supply; copper leaps to record high; and titanium dioxide is about to rise.[10] While the reasons for the imbalance between global supply and demand are beyond our scope, those who understand supply markets know that when demand exceeds supply, the results are often higher prices, allocation of supply, and a shifting of power from buyers to sellers.

A tightening of supply markets, and the potentially negative effect this tightening can have on an industrial customer's supply chain, should cause a rethinking of traditional supply practices. As market changes shift the balance between supply and demand, do suppliers really have to work with customers that treat them poorly? And if these suppliers continue to work with customers who pursue adversarial relationships, should these customers realistically expect preferential treatment?

Competing Supply Chains. If we believe that competition is increasingly between supply chains, then it makes sense to conclude that effective supply chains feature effective relationships. Descriptors such as aligned, coordinated, and synchronized are all used to describe efficient and effective supply chains. These terms also require a supportive supply base to become a reality. If supply chain management as a philosophy increases in importance, we can conclude that the relationships between supply chain members will also increase in importance.

Fear of a Competitive Disadvantage. Even if the previous reasons do not convince us that supplier-buyer relationships will increase in importance, it is still possible to awaken one day and face competitors that truly understand how to leverage their relationships. Nowhere are supplier relationships receiving more (and sometimes unwanted) attention than in the automotive industry. A recent study concluded that European automotive suppliers are shifting their business to customers they like while making customers they dislike pay more for parts. A second study reported that relationships between automotive suppliers and U.S. OEMs continue to fall far short of Japanese OEMs operating in the United States. The author of the study concludes that Japanese OEMs are applying continuous improvement practices to their supplier relationships just as they have done to their manufacturing processes, and as a result, they continue to win the cost-quality-technology race.[11] While it is easy to discount the importance of supplier relationships, it will not be as easy to discount the advantages gained by competitors who truly understand how to turn their relationships into tangible benefits.

Table 11.3 What Suppliers Want

• A longer-term business arrangement	• Opportunity to become a preferred supplier
• Fair financial return	• Correct material specifications
• Adequate time for planning	• Parts designed to match the supplier's process
• Accurate forecasts	• Smoothly timed order releases
• Sharing of cost-savings ideas	• Sharing of information, including technology roadmaps and business plans
• Minimum number of changes	
• Ethical treatment	• Objective performance feedback
• Early involvement opportunities	• Protection of intellectual property
• Payment in a reasonable time	• Efficient negotiating processes

Source: Adapted from Robert J. Trent, "Why Relationships Matter," *Supply Chain Management Review*, November 2005, p. 58.

What Suppliers Want

If relationships with a company's most critical suppliers increase in importance, and the argument here is that on balance this will happen, then supply managers must understand how to pursue stronger relationships. Table 11.3 presents a set of expectations that begins to define what suppliers want from their business-to-business relationships.

A longer-term business arrangement, the first item in the table, means that suppliers do not want to see their volumes regularly rebid or "shopped around" to other suppliers. While standard items with low switching costs should be market-tested or rebid on a regular basis, buyers might want to consider a more cooperative approach for managing critical or unique items. Using reverse auctions to drive prices lower, for example, quickly sends a message to suppliers about the win-lose nature of a short-term relationship.

Protecting intellectual property is another important expectation. Several years ago an OEM invited suppliers to submit design ideas during the development of a new product. Not only did the OEM fail to compensate suppliers for their efforts (providing design support is part of the cost of doing business with this firm), the winning design was then sent for bid to suppliers, including suppliers in China that did not even participate in the design phase.

A supplier's willingness to do business with a customer correlates closely with satisfying a supplier's expectations in four areas: the supplier's ROI, the customer's support of the supplier, the customer's willingness to reward cost-saving ideas, and the customer's ability to protect proprietary technology.[12]

The likelihood of satisfying each expectation presented here is low. However, supply managers should be aware of these items whenever possible for the sake of longer-term relationships and a smoothly operating supply chain. Satisfying a supplier's expectations should strengthen relationships and trust between suppliers and buyers. The increasing power of suppliers and their willingness to shift business away from less-favorable customers should not be taken lightly.

What Supply Managers Should Do

Although buying firms are the customer in a buyer-seller relationship, and customers are usually the one pursued rather than the pursuer, buyers should be proactive in their relationship management efforts. Table 11.4 presents some ways that supply managers can focus on stronger relationships.

A tangible way to focus on relationships is through an organization's design features. Chapter 3 noted the importance of assigning individuals to manage specific supplier relationships. Furthermore, the organizational level of the individuals who are assigned to manage these relationships should change as the importance of the relationship changes. Progressive firms also establish buyer-supplier councils to share information at the highest organizational levels and include suppliers as part of their product design teams.

Table 11.4 Supplier Relationship Management—What Buyers Should Do

Assign individuals to manage relationships, including executives to manage the most critical relationships.

Provide timely and complete supplier performance feedback in person and through scorecards.

Formally assess the supplier's perception of the buyer as a customer.

Develop longer-term contract agreements that create mutual value.

Invite suppliers to be part of an executive buyer-supplier council.

Emphasize trust-building activities and actions.

Practice cooperative cost management approaches.

Solicit supplier improvement suggestions with joint sharing of savings.

Involve suppliers early during product planning and development.

Implement supplier relationship management (SRM) information systems.

Provide resources to develop supplier performance capabilities.

Meet with suppliers regularly to understand supplier relationship expectations.

Invite suppliers to participate in joint improvement and value analysis workshops.

Share longer-term business plans.

Source: Adapted from Robert J. Trent, "Why Relationships Matter," *Supply Chain Management Review*, November 2005, p. 59.

One outcome from a buyer's relationship management efforts should be the pursuit of activities that promote trust. Perhaps the most critical predictor of successful relationships, *trust* refers to the belief in the character, ability, strength, or truth of a party. Buyers demonstrate their trustworthiness through their actions, including open and frequent communication, following through on promises and commitments, and acting legally and ethically in all dealings. Trust-based relationships also feature acting on behalf of the relationship rather than self-interests, publicizing success stories and personal narratives, especially those that enhance the standing of the other party, and treating information and data confidentially. Enhancing trust across the supply chain is an important objective.

As Chapter 4 noted, an action that few buying firms undertake is a formal assessment of their behavior as a customer. While suppliers are accustomed to receiving regular reports about their performance, it is much rarer for buyers to receive reports about their performance as a customer. These reverse surveys should address how well a buying firm satisfies supplier expectations. The fact that so few buying firms take the time to ask their suppliers why they prefer to do business (or not do business) with them is a good reason to emphasize this activity.

Industrial buyers who pursue adversarial relationships with their most important suppliers will find today's competitive environment different than the 1990s. Those supply managers who fail to develop positive relationships may find their suppliers increasing prices, allocating limited capacity to other firms, or sharing their most innovative ideas with other customers, some of whom may be the buyers' direct competitors.

THE LOPEZ APPROACH TO MANAGING SUPPLIER RELATIONSHIPS

In the early 1990s General Motors was under such financial stress that there were concerns the company might seek bankruptcy protection. In 1992 GM's board of directors removed Robert Stempel as president and quickly replaced him with Jack Smith, the executive who was instrumental in transforming GM's ailing European unit from a divided and expensive operation to one that featured well-managed marketing, distribution, and cost control.[13]

Jack Smith brought with him from Europe his openly emotional and charismatic CPO, Dr. Jose Ignacio Lopez. Given his success at improving purchasing in Europe, some looked at Dr. Lopez almost as a cultlike figure. Viewed as a brilliant cost cutter, Lopez had worked closely with Jack Smith during GM's European turnaround.

Lopez exhibited some interesting practices that further enhanced his mystique within the company. In a dramatic gesture at a dinner party at Jack Smith's house (and in front of other GM executives), he changed his watch to his other arm to signify that times are changing. He announced he would keep it there until GM made record profits from its North American operations. Others quickly switched their watches. Lopez called his top managers "Warriors" and created a diet for them called "Feeding the Warrior." The practice of awarding purchase contracts at GM also changed. *Fortune* magazine wrote that during strategy presentations, "whenever a bid met their pricing target, the Warriors, like Visigoths hearing of a fresh kill, would lustily pound their fists on the table. For many, their loyalty was not so much to GM as to Lopez himself."[14]

While many at GM saw Lopez as their savior, suppliers were seeing things a bit differently. Early after his arrival in the United States, Lopez hosted a meeting at GM's Technical Center in Warren, Michigan. Most suppliers thought the meeting was going to be, in the words of one, a "meet and greet with the new guy." It was not long after the meeting started that those in attendance realized that Dr. Lopez planned to put existing contracts up for bid and expected suppliers to provide double-digit price reductions and major productivity improvements if they expected to keep GM's business. Lopez commented that it was not right for suppliers to be making money while GM was losing money.

At the meeting Lopez also scolded U.S. and European managers for becoming lazy, and he said that Western managers should spend more time trying to figure out how to beat the Japanese and less time out on the golf course. The donuts that only a few minutes earlier were so appetizing were suddenly not so appealing. This meeting was destined to become a defining moment in the history of GM's supplier relationships.

Over the next few months suppliers soon realized that Lopez cared very little for long-standing relationships, including relationships with GM's wholly owned parts subsidiaries. GM was in trouble, and reducing purchase prices was the fastest way to improve cash flow. When suppliers pointed out that tearing up existing agreements and then demanding double-digit price reductions was perhaps a breach of contract, Lopez told them to sue GM. Reportedly, he would remind suppliers about the size of the GM account and that they would long be bankrupt by the time the suppliers' grievances made their way to court. Dr. Lopez also took supplier-provided designs and put them out to bid to other suppliers. GM even stopped sharing savings with suppliers when its engineering teams found improvements at a supplier's facility.

These actions began to take their toll on supplier relationships. A supplier survey that rated automotive OEMs on a scale that ranged from dictatorship to partnership found GM to be the lowest-rated company. Even GM's long-term suppliers were becoming reluctant to share new ideas with the company. Some openly claimed they would offer their best ideas to competitors. And still others said they were looking to drop the company as a customer. Supplier complaints that GM focused only on price also became commonplace. Even though supplier relationships were deteriorating, GM estimated that Lopez's actions saved the company $4 billion. At least in the short term, Lopez was the man.

The Lopez saga quickly deteriorated into a very public, second-rate soap opera. In 1993 he suddenly left GM under almost comical circumstances for Volkswagen, a company he felt was more receptive to his ideas. German police eventually discovered boxes of confidential GM documents in the possession of several of his warriors who had also left the company for Volkswagen. He was eventually indicted by German authorities on industrial espionage charges, and Volkswagen was forced to pay GM some hefty penalties. Rumor has it that Dr. Lopez subsequently went to work as a consultant. Reports that he also teaches a college ethics course are apparently unfounded.

The debate about whether Lopez's approach to supplier performance and relationship management helped or hurt GM will go on for quite a while. In reality, GM's relationships with suppliers have not improved much since Lopez's departure. A survey of U.S. suppliers by Planning Perspectives Inc. rates automotive OEMs on 17 criteria. From 2002 to 2004, GM's Supplier Working Relationship Index score dropped almost 11 percent, while Toyota's improved over 27 percent, making the gap between the best and the worst even wider. Toyota, the highest-rated automotive company by U.S. suppliers, had a score of 399, while GM had the lowest rating at 144.[15] While GM's supply leaders are working hard to correct this situation, the company has a way to go before fully regaining the trust of its suppliers. So, you decide. Did the approach taken by Dr. Lopez help or hurt General Motors? And if it hurt, how could GM have handled suppliers and its financial problems differently?

CONCLUDING THOUGHTS

A recent interview with an executive supply leader revealed an interesting, if not troubling, perspective about what he saw as his central staff's value-added contribution. He said his primary supply responsibility was "to do the deal" and that others throughout the company were responsible for supplier performance and relationship management. In other words, his responsibility involved strategy development but not supplier management.

Supply leadership is about assuming ownership of the entire supply management process. Evaluating and selecting suppliers is only part of the story. Active supplier management, the second part of the story, involves working to ensure suppliers perform and improve as required. Unless there are some great coordination mechanisms in place, foregoing responsibility at a centrally led level for managing key suppliers and their relationships runs the risk that no one will pay attention to this important part of strategic supply management.

SUMMARY OF KEY CHAPTER POINTS

- Lapses in managing supplier performance can tarnish even the world's most powerful brands.
- The principles that compose TQM are some of the most powerful ever developed, and these principles should guide supply managers as they manage supplier performance.
- It is possible to streamline the many quality management principles that exist into a more manageable set that includes defining quality in terms of customers and their requirements, pursuing quality at the source, stressing objective rather than subjective measurement and analysis, emphasizing prevention rather than detection of defects, focusing on process rather than output, striving for zero defects, establishing continuous improvement as a way of life, and making quality everyone's responsibility.
- Supply managers must pursue a set of supplier performance management activities that will put each quality principle into practice. The ability to recite these principles is far different than systematically applying them.
- One activity that most U.S. firms have not pursued rigorously is the active development and improvement of supplier performance capabilities. Part of the reason for not pursuing supplier development activities relates to the confrontational nature that has characterized too many buyer-seller relationships.
- Supply base improvement will occur primarily through the improvement of existing supplier capabilities rather than from large-scale supplier switching.
- A major part of strategic supply management involves managing supplier relationships. A diverse set of research supports the view that supplier relationships can be a source of competitive advantage.
- Supplier relationships matter because almost every industry is facing changes and trends that make external suppliers an important part of a firm's value chain.
- Although buying firms are the customer in a buyer-seller relationship, buyers should be proactive in their relationship management efforts.

- Unless there are some great coordination mechanisms in place, foregoing responsibility at a centrally led level for managing key suppliers and their relationships runs the risk that no one will pay attention to these important obligations.

ENDNOTES

1. N. Deogun, J. Hagerty, S. Stecklow, and L. Johannes, "Anatomy of a Recall: How Coke's Controls Fizzled Out in Europe," *Wall Street Journal*, June 29, 1999, A1.
2. The ideas presented in this section are adapted from Robert J. Trent, "Applying TQM to SCM," *Supply Chain Management Review* 5, no. 3 (May–June 2001): 70.
3. For a complete discussion of Deming, Crosby, and Juran, see M. Walton, *Deming Management at Work* (New York: G. P. Putnam, 1990); P. B. Crosby, *Quality Is Still Free: Making Quality Certain in Uncertain Times* (New York: McGraw-Hill, 1996); and J. M. Juran, *Juran on Quality by Design: The New Steps for Planning Quality into Goods and Services* (New York: Free Press, 1992).
4. K. Bhote, *Supply Management: How to Make U.S. Suppliers Competitive* (New York: American Management Association, 1987), 87.
5. From a presentation made by Jim Sierk at the Michigan State University Purchasing and Supply Chain Management Executive Seminar during the mid-1990s.
6. R. M. Monczka and R. J. Trent, "Purchasing and Supply Management: Key Trends and Changes throughout the 1990s," *International Journal of Purchasing and Materials Management* 34, no. 4 (Fall 1998): 2–11.
7. For two diverse analyses on the importance of supplier relationships, see M. Porter, *The Competitive Advantage of Nations* (New York: Free Press, 1990), and A. S. Carr and J. N. Pearson, "Strategically Managed Buyer-Supplier Relationships and Performance Outcomes," *Journal of Operations Management* 17, no. 5 (August 1999): 497–519.
8. J. Green, "The Tight Squeeze at Chrysler," *BusinessWeek* 3702 (October 9, 2000): 54.
9. The ideas presented in this section are adapted from R. J. Trent, "Why Relationships Matter," *Supply Chain Management Review* 9, no. 8 (November 2005): 53–59.
10. Purchasing magazine's *Price Alert* electronic newsletter, June 27, 2005.

11. M. Verespej, "Detroit Needs a Different Driver," *Purchasing Online* Web site, April 7, 2005.

12. J. Snyder, "European Suppliers Play Favorites," *Automotive News*, May 16, 2005, www.autonews.com.

13. This discussion draws partly on information presented by M. H. Moffett, and W. E. Youngdahl, "Case Study: Jose Ignacio Lopez de Arriortua," *Thunderbird International Business Review* 41, no. 2 (March/April 1999): 179-194, and from the author of this book's attendance at Dr. Lopez's supplier meeting at GM's Technical Center in Warren, Michigan, 1992.

14. From "Bloodfeud," Fortune (April 14, 1997): 92; also appears in Moffett and Youngdahl, 180.

15. Verespej, "Detroit Needs a Different Driver."

12

MANAGING COSTS STRATEGICALLY

Talk about good fortune walking through the door! A young buyer responsible for obtaining materials to package automotive parts sat wondering what he could do to better manage corrugated costs. As he contemplated this very deep subject, a salesperson who had been trying to expand his business with this account entered the buyer's office. Instead of his usual speech about why the buyer should purchase more from him, the salesperson took a different approach. He offered to work with the buyer to help control packaging costs. The buyer, obviously intrigued but somewhat skeptical, asked how that could be done.

The salesman asked about the packaging of camshafts, a major engine component. The buyer responded that camshafts were currently packaged at the rate of about 20,000 a month on a three-person manual line. The camshafts are placed in a corrugated box that costs about $0.55 each. Each box also requires a printed label that is manually attached. The salesman grinned when he heard this information.

It wasn't long before the buyer and the salesperson were on a road trip to Toledo. The salesperson introduced the buyer to an engineer who was developing a machine that packaged items ideally suited for the weight and shape of camshafts. Instead of three operators working on a manual pack line, this machine required only a single employee. And instead of a corrugated box, this machine used a softer corrugated wrap that formed around the camshaft to form a tight package. This new package cost about a third of what the box cost. Besides extensive labor and material savings, more camshafts could be placed in a master shipping container, resulting in fewer loads shipped through the distribution channel. The new machine also printed label information directly on the package, eliminating the need for manually affixing labels.

When the savings and costs were analyzed, this new equipment had one of the fastest paybacks that anyone could remember. Our young buyer was able to report cost savings that made him look like a star. And the salesperson thoroughly enjoyed seeing his corrugated wrap replace someone else's corrugated boxes. Isn't it nice to have a salesperson that looks out for the customer?

The need for supply managers to be effective cost managers is not even in question today. In fact, we could easily replace the words *strategic supply management* with *strategic cost management*. The overlap between the two would be quite significant. Managing costs is such an important topic it could justify its own book. Taking a scaled-down view of the subject, this chapter explores the differences between price and cost management and identifies a set of progressive price and cost management approaches.

DIFFERENCES BETWEEN PRICE AND COST ANALYSIS

A major responsibility of supply managers is ensuring that what they pay for goods and services is fair and reasonable. Many times the need to control costs requires a focus on the cost elements associated with producing an item or service versus simply analyzing price. Examples of cost elements include direct materials and labor, overhead allocations, and supplier profit margins. In other cases, such as the one illustrated in the opening example, it is not necessary to commit much effort or time to understanding costs. Comparing whether a price is fair given competitive market conditions or investigating if better options are available may lead to major savings.

Fundamental differences exist between price and cost analysis, and knowing when and where to apply each type of analysis is an important part of strategic supply management. As touched upon in Chapter 7, price analysis refers to the process of comparing a price against another price, against external price benchmarks, or against other available information without in-depth knowledge about underlying costs. Examples of price analytic techniques include competitive bid comparisons, comparisons against published catalog prices, price behavior relative to external benchmarks, comparisons of historical price behavior, and quantity discount analysis.

Cost analytic techniques focus primarily on the costs that are aggregated to create a price. A cost is a resource sacrificed or forgone to achieve a specific objective. A price is technically a cost, but it is a macro cost composed of the elements that are summed to reach a price. By better managing and reducing the cost elements that make up a price, a buyer should see lower purchase prices compared with prices where cost management did not occur.

Cost analytic approaches require the management of both cost elements and cost drivers. *Cost elements* include the traditional categories of cost such as direct materials, direct labor, overhead, and selling, general, and administrative costs. *Cost drivers* are anything that change cost levels. A change in a cost driver will cause a change in the total cost and often the price of a related product or service. For example, a mandated test by the buyer to certify the purity of a raw material is an example of a cost driver.

A primary difference between price and cost analysis is that cost analysis requires a more technical and detailed understanding of costs. Cost analysis also requires greater cooperation with a seller to quantify costs, identify cost drivers, and develop strategies to improve cost performance. Increasingly, supply chain managers must become skilled at managing costs rather than simply price.

The question of when to apply cost versus price analytic techniques is an important one. The portfolio matrix presented in Chapter 7 helps answer this question. The items residing in the lower half of the matrix, particularly the market items, are those that will benefit most from the application of price analytic techniques. The items in the upper half of the matrix, which includes the leverage and critical items, should benefit from an analysis of cost elements and drivers. It would be unproductive to apply cost analytic techniques when a situation only calls for basic price analysis. Conversely, applying price analytic techniques to situations that would benefit from cost analysis could leave a degree of value or improvement opportunity unrealized.

PRICE ANALYTIC TECHNIQUES

All price analytic techniques share one basic feature: They look at the end price of something as a means of comparison rather than trying to understand what makes up or causes a specific price. These techniques are almost always relative comparisons to something—a comparison of a supplier's price to its previous price, a price change compared against an external index, or a comparison against other suppliers.

One approach to price analysis is simply to demand that a supplier lower its price each year or risk losing its business. While this might be effective in the short term given the right power relationship, we are going to take the view that effective price analysis is more involved than simply demanding price reductions. This section discusses three price analytic techniques: configured supply networks, market testing with competitive bids, and comparisons against external indices. A fourth technique that qualifies as a major price analytic approach is reverse Internet auctions, which Chapter 5 covered.

Configured Supply Networks

A *configured supply network* is not likely a term the reader has heard of, since it was created for this book based on its use at actual companies. At times a buyer will develop systems contracts that cover dozens or even hundreds of items. When configuring a supply network, we analyze price quotations from multiple suppliers and configure the network based on the best quotes from each supplier. While the buyer may have to take on more suppliers than planned, the trade-off of developing a supply network that results in the lowest total price will likely outweigh the costs of maintaining additional suppliers.

Table 12.1 illustrates the concept of a simple configured supply network. In this example, a buyer has requested quotes for five items from four suppliers. For simplicity, let's assume these quotes include transportation costs. By analyzing the quotations, the buyer can identify the best configuration regarding how to source these items at the lowest total price.

This analysis can also be extended to include annual volumes, which the second part of the table illustrates. The best overall total cost based on quoted prices is Supplier A at $193,812. Dividing the five items among the three suppliers yields an expected configured supply network cost of $180,467, which is an 8 percent improvement over Supplier A's quotation. The question now becomes whether it is worth the 8 percent difference to use three suppliers instead of one.

A major assumption when using this approach is that the prices each supplier quotes are independent of each other. This independence is what allows a buyer to "cherry-pick." While this example is for a single buying location, the concept can be extended to identify which suppliers should supply different receiving locations. In reality, a buyer may be dealing with hundreds of standard items from multiple distributors being shipped to numerous locations. The use of spreadsheets will be valuable when crafting a configured supply network. The benefits from this approach are usually worth the effort.

Market Testing with Competitive Bidding

Market testing involves going to the marketplace, perhaps every year or every other year, to request bids from suppliers. It is an important way to ensure you are receiving the best prices available in the marketplace. It is also a great way to introduce competition to existing suppliers, which helps avoid complacency. Like reverse auctions, this approach applies best to standard items where supplier switching costs are low.

Suppliers often complain when they find out they are being forced to rebid business they thought they "owned." What about our relationship? What about all the good times we had together? Didn't we sing "Moon River" together at the annual customer party? Remember: The relationship that covers market-tested

Table 12.1 Creating a Configured Supply Network

Per-Unit Costs

Item/Part Number	Supplier A	Supplier B	Supplier C	Supplier D
442311 Gloves	$1.26	$1.65	$1.45	$1.29
338922 Wax	$7.45	$7.61	$6.15	$6.90
9963782 Glasses	$2.10	$2.54	$2.43	$2.91
746322 "D" Batteries	$.40	$.30	$.36	$.35
854471 Soap	$4.45	$4.01	$4.55	$4.50

Note: Shaded areas represent the lowest price for each item across each row.

Total Dollars Based on Volume

Annual Volume	Supplier A	Supplier B	Supplier C	Supplier D
Gloves—80,000	$100,800	$132,000	$116,000	$103,200
Wax—5,250	$39,112	$39,952	$32,287	$36,225
Glasses—3,000	$6,300	$7,620	$7,290	$8,730
Batteries—30,000	$12,000	$9,000	$10,800	$10,500
Soap—8,000	$35,600	$32,080	$36,400	$36,000
Total	**$193,812**	**$220,652**	**$202,777**	**$194,655**

Note: Each cell = (Price x Volume)

The sum of the shaded areas represents the configured supply network total cost, or $180,467.

items is typically win-lose, which means each party is committed to looking out for its own interests. Deep down the suppliers of these items understand they have to constantly earn a buyer's business. What upsets them is the fact that the buyer has also figured this out.

Comparisons against External Indexes

This approach features the use of objective, third-party information to verify that prices paid are reasonable and are behaving as expected across a marketplace. One Web site that supply managers should become familiar with is www.bls.gov. This site, compiled by the U.S. Bureau of Labor Statistics, contains a wealth of free data and information. For those who venture to this site, the first thing they might

Table 12.2 Producer Price Index Motor Vehicle Parts

Year	Jan	Feb	Mar	Apr	May	Jun	Jul	Aug	Sep	Oct	Nov	Dec
2005	112.8	112.9	112.8	112.7	112.9	112.8	113.2	113.2	113.3	113.4	113.7	113.9
2006	114.2	114.6	115.1	116.2	116.5	116.7	117.7	117.3	117.7(P)	117(P)	117.2(P)	117.3(P)

Source: www.bls.gov

notice is it is perhaps the busiest Web page not only on earth but perhaps in the entire universe. Still, like the universe, it is worth exploring.

For our purposes we are primarily interested in data at the producer level as reflected in the producer price index (PPI) tables. The *producer price index* is a family of indexes that measures the average change over time in selling prices received by domestic producers of goods and services. It contains over 600 industry price indexes in combination with over 5,000 specific product line and product category subindexes. It also contains over 2,000 commodity price indexes organized by type of product and end use.[1]

To use this tool, simply select Producer Price Indexes from the left side of the Web site's main page, then select the third option down the main list on the PPI page (titled Get Detailed PPI Statistics). The supply manager now has pricing index data for thousands of commodities and items. Besides containing a wealth of price index data, this Web site includes general information for using that data. Many supply managers will appreciate the discussion about how to use the indexes as a benchmark in contract escalation clauses. This Web site is well worth the time to explore.

How else might we use this data in supply management? Let's assume you are a buyer of automotive parts to support your company's fleet operations. One of your primary parts suppliers has informed you that prices will likely go up next year by 6 percent, reflecting increases in labor and material costs. Without even looking at the supplier's labor and material cost elements (the Web site will also have information on these items), the PPI might provide some insight whether this increase is realistic. Consider Table 12.2, which is a snapshot of actual PPI changes for motor vehicle parts. The actual tables often provide over 10 years' worth of pricing index data. The "P" in the table means the data are still subject to possible revision.

The numbers in this table are not prices. They are index numbers for motor vehicle parts compared to a base year where the index was established at 100. From January 2005 to December 2005, prices at the producer level for motor parts increased less than 1 percent: (113.9 − 112.8)/112.8! From January 2006 to December 2006, prices increased less than 3 percent: (117.3 − 114.2)/114.2. Compared to some commodities, this is considered stable pricing. The supplier in this case may not be managing costs well or is possibly trying to slip in a price increase. The point here is the supply manager now has objective data to have a heart-to-heart "talk" with the supplier.

COST ANALYTIC TECHNIQUES

In the world of strategic supply management, cost analysis is essential. The common feature of all cost analytic approaches is their emphasis on the elements or drivers that lead to price. While price analysis does not evaluate underlying costs, by definition, cost analytic techniques address cost elements and cost drivers.

Most cost management techniques are best applied when suppliers are willing to share information. At times a cost analysis must be conducted without the support, for whatever reason, of suppliers. These approaches are called *noncooperative* cost analytic techniques. The same cost management technique can be cooperative or noncooperative given the willingness of a supplier to share information. An issue becomes the validity of the data when suppliers are not cooperative.

Like price analysis, the domain of cost analytic techniques is wide. This section presents but a handful of cost analytic approaches, including learning curve analysis, value analysis, target pricing, theoretical best pricing, total cost of ownership models, supplier suggestion programs, and drop shipping.

Learning Curve Analysis

Learning curve analysis is based on the principle that as individuals become more familiar with a task or process, the average amount of direct labor to perform that task or process declines a predictable rate. A supplier that is experiencing learning during its production process should provide a continuous stream of price reductions.

Learning rates represent the predictable reduction in *direct* labor requirements as production doubles from a previous level. For example, a 90 percent learning curve means that the average direct labor required to produce an item decreases by 10 percent as volume doubles from one level to another. An 80 percent learning curve, which is quite steep, means the average direct labor to produce an item decreases by 20 percent as production doubles from a previous level. At most firms, learning curve analysis is applied internally. Applying the concept to a supplier's price, particularly during negotiations, is not practiced as often.

Several words of caution are in order. Learning curves apply only to the direct labor aspects of production, even though the term is often used more broadly. Learning curves also do not apply to simple items or items where the supplier has extensive experience. Even if an item is new to the buyer, it may not be new to the supplier. The analysis works best when a supplier is producing a technically complex item for the first time. Also, the identification of an incorrect learning rate will skew the estimated improvements as a supplier moves along the learning curve. And finally, do not expect to go back to a supplier after a year and expect to see productivity at the same level. There is something called the "forgetting factor" that must be considered.

Perhaps the best way to illustrate this concept is through an example. Table 12.3 presents one way to estimate a pricing change due to learning curves. While material changes may result due to higher volumes, the learning curve analysis only concerns itself with changes due to average direct labor improvements. In this example the buyer calculates an expected price reduction from $112 to $82 per unit. Whether the supplier agrees to this price or methodology is a topic for discussion. In this analysis, learning improvement affected not only the direct labor amount but also the overhead and per-unit profit amount, since they were both presented as a percent of direct labor. This new figure provides a target to work toward with the supplier. Potential improvements in material costs could further reduce this price.

If learning occurs and the buyer does not capture the cost benefits from learning, then it is safe to conclude that the supplier will reap the benefits. A buyer must determine if an item will benefit from learning and then factor that learning into the supplier's pricing.

Value Analysis

Value analysis (VA) is a low-cost technique that evaluates the functionality of a product or service against its cost. In equation form, Value = Function/Cost. The objective of VA is to increase value by affecting the numerator and/or denominator of the value equation. VA is a continuous-improvement approach that is usually applied to existing products and services. Value engineering is the counterpart to value analysis that is applied during new product and service development. Like learning curve analysis, VA has been around for quite a while. This does not mean it is not an effective approach for managing costs.

VA benefits most from a cross-functional team approach that may involve suppliers, customers, packaging, logistics, supply management, design and process engineers, marketing, accounting, and manufacturing. VA teams ask a series of questions to determine if the value that a customer attaches to a product or service can be improved. The types of questions asked include the following:

- Are lower-cost but equally effective materials available?
- Can the design be simplified?
- Are standard components available to replace custom-designed components?
- Can improvements be made to the production process?

Table 12.3 Learning Curve Illustrated

A company is submitting an order to a supplier for 100 units of an engineered item. The buyer estimates the learning curve for this item to be 85 percent. The supplier provides the following per-unit information:

Materials	$28
Direct labor	$32 (2 hours on average per unit @ $16 per hour)
Overhead	$40 (125% of direct labor)
Total costs	$100
Profit	$12 (12% of total costs)
Per-unit price	**$112**

Several weeks later the buyer submits an order for 300 more units (making the total order 400 units). What should the buyer expect to pay per unit for the next order?

Analysis:

If the 100-unit order required an average of 2 hours of direct labor to produce a unit, then a doubling of production to 200 units should require only 85 percent of 2 hours, or 1.7 average hours per unit.* A further doubling to 400 units should require 1.45 average hours per unit (85 percent x 1.7 average hours).

The total direct labor hours required for 400 units should be 580 total hours (400 x 1.45 average direct labor hours per unit). Since 200 direct labor hours were expended to produce the first 100 unit order (2 hours on average × 100 units), these hours need to be subtracted. The 300-unit order should require 380 additional direct labor hours (580 total hours – 200 hours consumed during the first order).

Next, 380 hours × $16 per hour direct labor costs means the next order will consume $6,080 in total direct labor costs. This is equal to $20.27 in labor costs per unit ($6,080/300 units). The new target price with learning factored in becomes:

For the next 300 units:	
Materials	$28
Direct labor	$20.27 ($6,080 direct labor costs/300 units)
Overhead	$25.34 (125% of direct labor)
Total costs	$73.61
Profit	$8.83 (12% of total costs)
New per-unit price	**$82.44**

*Recall that the learning curve principle states that average direct labor hours decline by a predictable rate (called the learning curve or rate) as volumes double from one level to another.

- Can features be added to enhance functionality more than the associated cost increase?
- Are lower-cost suppliers available?
- Is there any functionality currently included that the customer does not want?
- Can packaging or logistics costs be reduced?

VA efforts should follow a process with five distinct phases: information gathering, speculating, analyzing, recommending and executing, and follow-up. Results should be tracked closely, with improvements widely reported across the company. In fact, progressive companies establish annual improvement targets to be achieved through their VA process. When performed correctly, VA becomes a systematic approach for improving value, functionality, and costs.

Target Pricing

A traditional approach to pricing generally assumes that the starting point in arriving at a price is the costs associated with producing an item. Traditional pricing approaches sum the costs associated with producing an item, add on a desired level of profit, and arrive at a selling price. This selling price may not be what the market was expecting. When an automotive company quickly offers rebates and discounts on a newly introduced car, for example, this is a clue that perhaps the selling price missed the intended market segment.

Target pricing (also called target costing) takes a dramatically different approach. Product developers work closely with marketing to identify a selling price that matches the expectations of the target market. Next, a desired profit is subtracted from the selling price to identify the level of allowable costs. The following formulas contrast traditional and target pricing models. Target pricing is used extensively in the auto industry, particularly by Japanese companies.

Traditional Pricing		Target Pricing	
	Costs		Selling price
+	Profit	–	Profit
	Selling price		Allowable costs

What happens next within a target pricing framework? Complex products are broken down into systems, subsystems, and components, each with an assigned cost that rolls up to form the total allowable costs. Eventually, costs are managed at the component and production level. Often buyers and suppliers do not even negotiate prices. The price of a component is assigned as part of the target pricing process. The entire focus in target pricing is on cost management.

It is not unusual during this process to find that current costs are higher than what the model says is allowable. This is where the cooperative part of target pricing really comes into play. The buyer's sub-design teams and suppliers must work together to simplify a product design or production process, search for alternate materials, use standard components instead of custom-designed items, or apply any other approach that addresses underlying cost elements and drivers. It is also possible that savings from one part of a project are used to offset cost deficiencies in another part. Target pricing requires a total systems perspective rather than each part of a development project operating independently.

Theoretical Best Pricing

This approach uses cost data provided by suppliers to identify a theoretical best price. This price represents a composite price after an examination of the best cost elements available across a pool of potential suppliers. Table 12.4 highlights this technique, which can be much more detailed than what is presented here. For example, a buyer may request data about logistics costs, estimated nonconformance costs, production yields, or a breakdown of direct labor charges into rates and hours. Also, what composes the broad category called overhead might also be explored further.

In Table 12.4 the theoretical best price given this set of suppliers is $40.80. No single supplier in this example is lowest in all cost categories. It is possible that a supplier could dominate each category. A supplier may present a quote so low that is not even worth the effort to compare individual cost elements. The theoretical best price should be most effective when evaluating complex purchase requirements where the supplier is providing a significant amount of value.

The use of this technique serves two purposes. The first is to identify a benchmark or target to measure actual prices against. A standardized performance ratio can be created that compares the actual price paid to the theoretical best price. For example, if the price paid for a component is $7.58 and the theoretical best price is $6.32, the ratio is 1.20. This means the buyer is paying 20 percent more than the theoretical best price. The second purpose is to identify specific areas where costs are out of line for each supplier or where possible improvement efforts should be directed. The second part of Table 12.4 presents a standardized ratio of each supplier's cost within each row compared with the best cost for that row. For example, Supplier A's ratio for direct labor is 1.12 ($12.55/$11.22). Calculate all other ratios accordingly by row.

Where do we get data that are reliable enough to identify a theoretical best price? At John Deere, suppliers receive a part quotation form that requires them to break down their costs by category. If a supplier shows a higher-than-expected cost, then Deere may dispatch supplier development engineers to work with that

Table 12.4 Calculating the Theoretical Best Price per Unit

	Supplier A	Supplier B	Supplier C	Supplier D	Best Cost
Direct labor	$12.55	$11.78	$13.10	$11.22	$11.22
Direct materials	$9.78	$9.10	$10.50	$10.75	$9.10
Overhead	$15.06	$11.78	$19.65	$14.25	$11.78
SG&A	$4.90	$5.75	$4.75	$6.04	$4.75
Profit	$4.10	$4.75	$4.50	$3.95	$3.95
Price	$46.39	$43.16	$52.50	$46.21	$40.80

Standardized against the Best Cost

	Supplier A	Supplier B	Supplier C	Supplier D	Best Cost
Direct labor	1.12	1.05	1.17	1.00	1.00
Direct materials	1.07	1.00	1.15	1.18	1.00
Overhead	1.28	1.00	1.67	1.21	1.00
SG&A	1.03	1.21	1.00	1.27	1.00
Profit	1.04	1.20	1.14	1.00	1.00
Price to best price	1.14	1.06	1.29	1.13	1.00

Highlighted areas represent the lowest value in each row.

supplier.[2] Requests for proposal packages should include a supplier cost form. Unfortunately, suppliers sometimes do not know their costs at a detailed enough level to use this approach.

This approach can easily be adapted to arrive at a lowest total cost, especially when estimating the costs of sourcing internationally. In this case the cost elements might include, in addition to unit price, duties, currency management costs, insurance, transportation charges, inventory-carrying costs, ordering and documentation costs, as well as any other cost categories that are part of an international transaction.

Total Cost of Ownership Models

Total cost models are the most sophisticated of all supply measurement approaches. In reality, there is no such thing as a standard total cost system. Three areas where total cost measurement models are often developed include the following:

- *Total landed costs models.* These models include all inbound supply chain costs beyond unit price, including transportation, duties, broker fees, inventory carrying costs, currency costs, and so on.
- *Life cycle cost models.* These models apply primarily to capital equipment purchases. They include estimates of the total cost to operate equipment over an expected life span by considering maintenance requirements, mean time between failure estimates, operating costs, depreciation, and any other relevant cost factors.
- *Total cost performance models.* These models, which are often applied to purchased goods, include unit price plus any nonconformance costs that increase the total cost of a good.

Regardless of where we apply a total cost approach, all systems attempt to capture data beyond unit price. A misconception is that total cost models inherently provide better information than other cost models. Total cost models, like forecast models, almost always have some degree of unreliability. The question becomes how much unreliability is embedded in the model.

The data used in total cost models fall into a hierarchy of categories that conveniently start with the letter "a." The top category, and the most reliable, includes *actual* data. Unit price or tariffs are examples of actual data. Few, if any, total cost models have the luxury of including only actual data. The second category includes *averages* or *approximations*. The costs included here are at least based on data from internal sources. For example, 70 late supplier deliveries last year cost a buying company an estimated $210,000 in total nonconformance costs. The average standard charge for a late delivery in the total cost system therefore becomes $3,000 per occurrence. The usual warnings about using averages apply here. The least reliable total cost data are figures based on *assumptions*. These figures come from external sources that form the basis for applying total costs. For example, let's say a study (not an internal study) concluded that it costs $500 to expedite an order from a supplier. Therefore, each time a buyer must expedite an order, a $500 charge is applied to the total cost model for that item. Be careful not to rely too heavily on total cost models laden with external assumptions.

The remainder of our total cost discussion focuses on a specific model called the *supplier performance index*, or SPI. SPI calculations should become an important part of managing costs.

A virtue of the SPI is the simplicity of the concept. This approach assumes that any quality or performance infraction committed by a supplier increases the total cost of doing business with that supplier. If a supply manager can track these infractions and assign a cost to them, the calculation of a standardized SPI becomes relatively easy. Here's how the SPI is calculated:

SPI = (Cost of material + Nonconformance costs)/(Cost of material)

Assume a supplier ships $10,000 worth of components to a company in the fourth quarter of 2007. The supplier also commits three infractions that quarter: a late delivery, an incorrect invoice, and shipping some defective units. The buying company assigns $750 in total nonconformance charges against the supplier for these infractions. The usual cautions apply regarding whether this $750 is a reliable figure. The supplier's SPI for the fourth quarter of 2007 is 1.075 (($10,000 + $750)/$10,000).

What does an SPI of 1.075 mean? It means the total cost of doing business with this supplier is 7.5 percent higher than the total unit price. If the unit price of a supplier's good is $6.90, then the estimated total cost of that item is $7.42 ($6.90 × 1.075). Because the SPI is a standardized statistic, it allows comparisons between suppliers. A supplier with an SPI of 1.10 has a 2.5 percent higher total cost than the one with an SPI of 1.075. It is important to compare suppliers within the same commodity to ensure "apple to apple" comparisons.

Central to any SPI system is an efficient and accurate way to identify infractions and their appropriate charges. This is harder than it sounds. It can be a major challenge to identify the possible areas where suppliers may commit infractions, capture the infractions on a consistent basis, and assign an accurate charge to those infractions. Since the cost to capture data sometimes outweighs the value of the data, many companies use standard charges. A question will always be present concerning the accuracy of the standard charges that are used.

Accurate SPI calculations are helpful when deciding which suppliers to eliminate from the supply base, tracking supplier improvement over time, and establishing minimum acceptable levels of supplier performance. Unfortunately, the true SPI calculation is not as straightforward as portrayed here. The standard SPI calculation has a built-in bias against suppliers that provide fewer total dollars to a buying company. An example illustrates this bias.

Assume two suppliers commit a single late delivery that resulted in a standard $250 charge within the SPI system. The first supplier provided the buyer with $10,000 worth of goods in a quarter, while the second supplier provided $3,000 worth of goods. The SPI for the first supplier is 1.025 ($10,250/$10,000), while the SPI for the second supplier is 1.083 ($3,250/$3,000). This hardly seems fair—both suppliers committed the same infraction but have different SPI numbers.

The way around this bias is to calculate a "Q" adjustment factor. Essentially, the Q factor allows valid comparisons by removing the inherent small-lot bias within the SPI. It is beyond the scope of this chapter to go into the mechanics of the Q factor calculation.

Supplier Suggestion Programs

Answer this question quickly: How much did your firm save last year from suggestions received through its supplier suggestion program? What? Your company does not have a supplier suggestion program? Or perhaps there is a program but no one knows what it saved? If this is the case, you are certainly not alone. The time has come for most firms to put a supplier suggestion program in place. Thanks to Web-based technology, the challenges surrounding supplier suggestion programs are no longer technical.

Firms that are serious about a supplier suggestion program must be willing to commit resources to evaluate the suggestions they receive. Often this means appointing a program manager or steering committee to oversee the process. It also means making engineers available to evaluate the technical merits of a suggestion. It takes time to evaluate the hundreds, if not thousands, of suggestions that suppliers will hopefully put forth. Suppliers will quickly become disinterested in any program they perceive is a black hole sucking in ideas that are never seen or heard from again. Another challenge is convincing suppliers to participate.

Progressive firms recognize the important linkage between supplier suggestions and rewards. Rewarding supplier participation should lead to greater involvement with the program. Some firms evaluate a supplier's level of participation and include that as part of the supplier's scorecard rating. Other firms share any savings realized from the ideas, either directly as payments to the supplier, as adjustments to the selling price that reflect the supplier's share of the savings, or as credits toward cost reduction commitments. Direct payments require working closely with accounting, since it is often difficult to write a check for a suggestion rather than an invoice.

Best-practice supply organizations track the suggestions they receive from suppliers, respond to suggestions in an agreed-upon time frame, and report to executive managers any savings achieved through the system. The suggestion system should serve as a central repository for all ideas received from suppliers. Developing a supplier suggestion program may be one of the most cost-effective ways to manage costs. It is also an ideal task to assign to a cross-functional team.

Drop Shipping

This technique involves suppliers buying off the contract of larger customers when the larger customer receives a better price. The objective of this approach is to manage costs further upstream from the buying company by forming an informal purchase consortium.

A simple example will illustrate this technique. Let's say your company purchases a plastic injected molded component from a supplier for $1.00. The direct materials required for the part consist exclusively of plastic resin. Your firm happens to be a large buyer of plastic resins for other uses and has negotiated a longer-term contract with favorable prices. Your supplier does not have quite as favorable a contract. In fact, your firm pays 20 percent less for resins than the supplier that provides you with a finished plastic part.

The objective of this technique is to protect but not give the supplier a higher profit. Users of this technique expect a supplier to pass along the savings to the buyer in the form of a lower price that factors in any material savings. Here, a 20 percent reduction from a cost element (direct materials) that composes 30 percent of the final product cost should lead to a savings of 6 percent (20 percent × 30 percent). Savings generated upstream are passed through to the supplier's customer (i.e., the buyer).

The supplier's current and revised cost structure appears as follows:

	Current	Revised
Direct labor	$0.20	$0.20
Direct materials	$0.30	$0.24
Overhead	$0.30	$0.30
Selling, general, and administrative	$0.10	$0.10
Profit	$0.10	$0.10
Selling price	$1.00	$0.94

This approach can be carried out in a number of ways. The larger buying firm can purchase the material from the resin supplier and have it drop-shipped or delivered directly to the component supplier. The buyer will then charge the supplier for the material. It is *not* recommended that the buyer take physical possession from the resin supplier and then forward it to the component supplier. This will create added shipping and handling costs. Another possibility is to have the component supplier purchase resin directly from the resin supplier using the terms of your contract. Since there are accounting, financial, and other legal implications here, it is best to work closely with those groups to determine the best way to handle any transactions.

The resin supplier could object to this idea. It might appear to be too much work from an accounting or logistics perspective. Or the resin supplier might see it as an opportunity for new business, particularly when the buyer gently reminds the supplier how important it is to work together within a relationship. This can become an item for serious discussion and even negotiation among the three parties.

CONCLUDING THOUGHTS

This chapter explored only a few of the many possible approaches for managing price and cost. Examples of other approaches include quantity discount analysis, value stream and process mapping, kaizen workshops, cost reductions from volume leveraging, and approaches for managing the investment in inventory. Supply managers need to appreciate the many ways they can affect prices and costs and then apply the appropriate approaches for ensuring a steady stream of improvements. Price and cost management is one area where supply managers can really show off their creativity. Strategic cost management must become a major part of strategic supply management.

SUMMARY OF KEY CHAPTER POINTS

- The need for supply managers to be effective cost managers is not even in question today.
- Price analytic techniques examine end prices as a means of comparison rather than trying to understand what makes up a specific price. Cost analytic techniques focus primarily on the costs that are aggregated to create a price.
- Understanding when to apply cost versus price analytic approaches is critical. It is unproductive to apply cost analytic techniques when a situation requires price analysis. Conversely, applying price analytic techniques when cost analysis is required could leave some opportunities unrealized.
- A configured supply network involves analyzing price quotations from multiple suppliers to configure a supply network based on the best quotes for individual items from different suppliers.
- Market testing, which involves periodically requesting bids, is a way to ensure your firm is receiving the best prices available for standard items.
- Most cost management techniques work best when suppliers are willing to share information.
- A supplier that experiences direct labor improvements due to learning should provide a continuous stream of price reductions. If learning occurs and the buyer does not work to capture the benefits from learning, then the supplier will likely capture all the benefits.
- Value analysis is a technique that evaluates the relationship between the function of a product or service against its cost.

- Target pricing is a highly collaborative approach for managing costs during product development.
- A theoretical best price can be developed if a supply manager has reliable cost data from suppliers. The theoretical price represents a composite price after examining the best cost elements available across a pool of potential suppliers.
- Other cost management approaches worth considering include supplier suggestion programs, calculating supplier performance indexes, and purchasing off a customer's supply contract when pricing is favorable.

ENDNOTES

1. From descriptions provided on www.bls.gov.
2. D. Smock, "Deere Takes a Giant Leap," *Purchasing* 130, no. 17 (September 6, 2001): 32.

13

INVOLVING
SUPPLIERS EARLY

This is the story of two organizations that took very different paths toward the same goal. The first is a logistics company with employees located around the world. The second is the national postal service of a foreign country. Both organizations have some things in common. Each has thousands of employees who wear uniforms and interact with customers on a daily basis. Each decided it was time to redesign its uniforms. And finally, each operates across a variety of geographic climates with a diverse workforce. A single design would not work from a climate or employee perspective.

At this point, the similarities end. The logistics company, knowing that its expertise did not lie in uniform design, involved its long-time uniform supplier early to lead the design project. The supplier met with employees to understand their uniform requirements (did you know that uniform requirements for Sweden and Arizona are different?), organized fashion shows using the logistics employees to showcase possible designs, created catalogs displaying the new uniforms, placed production plants outside the United States to provide rapid response to regional orders, and developed an online ordering system so local sites could order uniforms quickly and easily. Simplified billing and automatic cross-charging against each location's operating budget also came with the package.

The project resulted in uniforms that employees described as "fashionable," and the entire effort took about half the time as the previous redesign. The experience even strengthened the working relationship between the two companies. Life was good.

The joy was not being felt quite so strongly at the postal service, however. This organization decided it would develop new uniforms without supplier involvement, even though its primary business had nothing to do with designing uniforms. After a lengthy development process featuring limited internal customer or supplier involvement, the new uniforms were received by employees with a less than enthusiastic response. Besides not being too stylish, the company specified fabrics that, when wet, tended to become quite revealing. Unfortunately, and this may come as a shock, mail carriers work in all kinds of weather, including the pouring rain. The postal service was forced to humbly go back to the drawing board with a supplier's help to develop uniforms that were a bit less revealing and a bit more accepting.

While the company that relied on its supplier to lead the development project enjoyed substantial savings, higher internal acceptance, and reduced development times, the one that saw itself as a uniform expert was not quite as fortunate. What is the moral of this story? Tapping into a supplier's expertise early can dramatically alter the outcome of a project. And it's important to know what you don't know.

This chapter explores a critical topic in supply management today—early supplier involvement. It first explores the concept of early involvement and addresses the many issues that surround involvement efforts. A set of practices that separate excellent from average firms when involving suppliers early is also presented. The chapter concludes with a discussion of how one company relies on early involvement when designing and retrofitting its production facilities.

EARLY INVOLVEMENT OF SUPPLIERS

Early involvement is the process of relying on suppliers, either physically or virtually, to provide support early on during strategic planning, demand and supply planning, continuous improvement projects (such as value analysis teams), project planning (such as developing new facilities), and the development of new technologies and products. While early involvement is often associated with new product development, some firms tap into their supplier's expertise when developing technologies that do not yet have a defined commercial application.

The majority of the attention that early supplier involvement has received in research and the popular press centers on new product development. Figure 13.1 presents a generic product development process showing different involvement points. It would be a mistake to ignore the importance of early involvement when developing new products and services. This is especially true since innovation has become one of the hottest topics in business today. Many firms recognize that the source of innovation in their supply chain, particularly for new technology and product features, often comes from suppliers. Failing to tap into sources of innovation early can be a serious mistake—especially if competitors tap into these sources first.

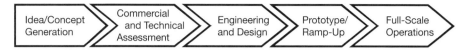

| Idea/Concept Generation | Commercial and Technical Assessment | Engineering and Design | Prototype/ Ramp-Up | Full-Scale Operations |

Early

- Involves complex or critical items or evolving new technologies.
- Suppliers assume responsibility for design leadership.
- Suppliers often provide "black-box designs.
- Involves alliance-type suppliers.
- Suppliers may be formal members of the design team.

Late

- Involves simple items or components.
- Suppliers have minimal opportunity to affect the design process.
- Suppliers works to buyer-provided designs and specifications.
- Relationships are basic.

Figure 13.1 New product development and supplier involvement points. (Source: Adapted from the *Global Procurement and Supply Chain Electronic Benchmarking Network* study of supplier involvement in new product and process development, Michigan State University, 1999.)

As the opening example shows, early supplier involvement can affect the success or failure of important corporate initiatives. While the good news is that various studies have concluded that early involvement can lead to competitive advantage, the bad news is other studies have found that U.S. firms have historically lagged in capturing the benefits of early involvement compared with their foreign counterparts. This is due largely to the many suppliers that U.S. firms maintained (and many still have too many suppliers) combined with an emphasis on adversarial relationships. Early involvement requires trusting working relationships with a smaller set of suppliers.

James Womack, Daniel Jones, and Daniel Roos conducted one of the more thorough studies that highlighted the deficit faced by U.S. firms when involving suppliers during product development. Figures reported in their book, *The Machine That Changed the World*, showed that during the mid-1980s, Japanese producers relied on suppliers for over 50 percent of total engineering during the development of new vehicles, European producers relied on suppliers for 37 percent of total engineering, and U.S. producers relied on suppliers for only 14 percent.[1] Other studies have reported similar kinds of findings.

This historical shortfall does not mean that U.S. managers are unaware of the importance of early involvement. In fact, just the opposite is true. Supply executives indicate their business units plan to increase the use of supplier integration and, as it relates to product design, involve suppliers during earlier stages of the product development process.[2]

Why Involve Suppliers Early?

The logic behind early involvement, like many topics presented throughout this book, is fairly straightforward. At a broad level, the need for continuous improvement demands new ways of doing business. Most firms have yet to tap into the possibilities that early involvement offers. Rest assured your competitors, especially foreign competitors, will not be shy about tapping into their supplier's expertise.

A second reason to consider early involvement is simply because competent suppliers usually have something of value to offer their customers. Suppliers might offer insights about market requirements and changes, improvements in material technology, access to data and information, better ways to manage cost and quality, design capabilities and engineering talent, new product features, or effective problem-solving skills. We should not discount the potential synergies that can result when different companies work together toward a common objective.

Shorter product life cycles, global competition, and demanding customer requirements are all forces behind a dramatic shortening of the time it takes to develop new products and services. The need to develop new products, services, and processes quickly may be the primary driver behind early involvement. Achieving reduced cycle times requires the use of new technology, such as computer-aided design software, as well as new ways of doing business, such as early involvement. A study of America's Best Plants by *IndustryWeek* found that early supplier involvement was one of the most effective ways for achieving concept-to-customer (C-to-C) cycle time reduction.

Consider the pressure that automakers face when they introduce new products. In the late-1980s, U.S. automakers required just over 60 months to design and produce a new vehicle. During the early 1990s, the benchmark for development time became 48 months. By the mid-1990s, world-class producers were aiming for development times of 36 months. By the late 1990s, Japanese companies had reduced development time to 24 months. In 2002 the CEO of Honda was quoted as saying his company needed to reduce development times to 18 months. Over the last 20 years, development cycle times decreased from 60 months to 18 months, or a reduction of over two-thirds. Achieving these targets requires innovative thinking.

Another early-involvement driver is a continuing focus on the outsourcing of noncore capabilities and competencies. A recent study by Mercer Management Consulting, the Fraunhofer Society for Production Technology and Automation, and the Fraunhofer Society for Materials Management and Logistics predicts that by 2015 outsourcing will result in automotive suppliers providing 80 percent of vehicle R&D and production versus 63 percent today. Authors of the study believe that OEMs will focus more on their downstream investment in sales, distribution, and service and be less attracted to capital-intensive investment in technology development and production. The study concludes that development and production will increasingly shift to suppliers.[3] Early involvement will be a necessity when so much of an OEM's content and design originates with external suppliers.

A final driver is a realization that design changes become exponentially more complex and costly as a new product moves through the product development stages. While design costs are a relatively minor part of product development costs, design decisions made early in the process lock in a large proportion of total product costs. Furthermore, as product development progresses, the flexibility to make design changes decreases. Early involvement seeks to bring competent suppliers to the design table early so that better designs will emerge. Projects where key stakeholders agree early on about a design should see fewer design changes later in the process. In the words of the total quality gurus, "do it right the first time." Preventing costly kickbacks of design decisions is a wonderful thing.

For firms that are looking for their next major source of improvement, early involvement is likely a major untapped opportunity area. The Mercer and Fraunhofer study predicts that new forms of collaboration, such as early involvement, will lead to cost savings in the auto industry of between $750 and $1,250 per vehicle. This should result in an increase of 3 percent to earnings before interest and taxes (EBIT) margins. Other industries should assume they also qualify for improvements from early involvement. Financial necessity will be a powerful driver.

Levels of Supplier Design Involvement

Involving suppliers during product design is not a yes-or-no kind of activity—yes we do it or no we don't. Besides the timing of a supplier's involvement, there are varying degrees this involvement can take. A supplier could act in an advisory role, or it could act on behalf of its customer by leading a major portion of a product development effort. Supply managers must understand what supplier best supports a specific need.

Figure 13.2 presents a continuum of supplier design involvement. It would be wrong to assume that moving toward gray- or black-box suppliers is necessarily better. Moving toward black-box designs with *carefully* selected suppliers that excel at design should lead to better outcomes. The challenge is to identify the appropriate design involvement given a particular need and supplier.

Table 13.1 presents findings from a study that focused solely on how firms involve suppliers during product and process development. These findings reveal that earlier levels of supplier involvement do, in fact, translate into better performance results. This study also found that product development projects that rely on suppliers for a greater role, such as that required of black-box design, justify that involvement with even better results.

None	White Box	Gray Box	Black Box
No early supplier design involvement. Supplier produces according to buyer-provided specifications or prints.	Buyer informally consults with supplier about design issues. Supplier is not part of the design team.	Supplier assumes greater design responsibility. Subsystem and system design is a joint effort. Supplier may be part of the design team.	Supplier has responsibility for major portions of product design. Supplier works from buyer requirements, not specifications. Supplier is often a formal design team member.

Increasing Supplier Responsibility and Accountability

Figure 13.2 Continuum of supplier design involvement. (Source: Adapted from the *Global Procurement and Supply Chain Electronic Benchmarking Network* study of supplier involvement in new product and process development, Michigan State University, 1999.)

Suppliers must often be willing to share their black-box designs, including the bill of materials that make up a supplier-designed subsystem or system. It is unreasonable to expect that a customer has to replace an entire system because a single component failed in a black-box design. The supplier should also be willing to identify the component suppliers it relies on during production. Just because an OEM now relies on suppliers to manage component purchases does not make these components any less important. In fact, if not managed carefully, the buyer could subject itself to greater supply chain risk.

Identifying Early-Involvement Candidates

Early involvement should involve a relatively small number of suppliers. Furthermore, the decision about which supplier to involve is a critical one. Selecting the wrong supplier may result in some important indicators, such as product development cycle time, moving in the wrong direction. The issue of early involvement should arise during supplier evaluation for those items that might benefit from early supplier support. Selecting a supplier that will assist or even take the lead during the design phase of a new product or project is quite different than selecting a supplier that will provide an item according to buyer-provided specifications.

It should be obvious now why this topic appears after our discussion on supply base optimization. Imagine trying to identify involvement candidates when 10 or 15 suppliers provide similar materials or services. It is a much different story

Table 13.1 Median Improvements from Supplier Involvement at Different Times*

	Early	Middle	Late
Reduction in material costs	20%	15%	10%
Reduction in development cycle time	20%	20%	10%
Improvement in material quality	20%	15%	15%
Reduction in development costs	20%	10%	10%
Reduction in manufacturing costs	10%	12%	10%
Improvement in product functionality, features, and technology	20%	10%	10%

*Compared to similar projects that did not include supplier involvement

Adapted from R. B. Handfield, G. L. Ragatz, K. J. Petersen, and R. M. Monczka, "Involving Suppliers in New Product Development," *California Management Review* (Fall 1999): 59–82.

when 60 suppliers provide 80 percent of total purchase requirements. The domain to choose from is much smaller. This assumes there are qualified suppliers within the smaller supply base.

A number of questions should be asked during supplier selection when there is a possibility of involving that supplier early, particularly during product design and development:

- What is the supplier's design and engineering capabilities?
- What design software and platform does the supplier use? Is it compatible with our system?
- Is the supplier developing technology that aligns with our future needs?
- How much does the supplier invest in research and development?
- Does the supplier have experience with early involvement and taking on design responsibilities for its customers?
- Is the supplier currently supporting the design efforts of other companies, including our competitors?
- Is the supplier willing to commit resources specific to our development needs?
- Will this supplier safeguard proprietary information?

Table 13.2 identifies four items that will help identify early-involvement candidates within an existing supply base. The first item is somewhat obvious—it does not make sense to involve a supplier early unless a reasonable payback is expected. It also makes sense that adversarial relationships are not conducive to early involvement. These initiatives require trust and open sharing of information.

Table 13.2 Identifying Early Supplier Involvement Candidates

	Limited		Moderate		Extensive
Performance improvement potential due to early involvement	1	2	3	4	5
	Adversarial		**Cordial**		**Cooperative**
Relationship between the buying company and the supplier	1	2	3	4	5
	Not Willing		**Somewhat**		**Very Willing**
Willingness of the supplier to participate in early involvement	1	2	3	4	5
	Not Capable		**Moderately**		**Very Capable**
Capability of the supplier to support early-involvement activities	1	2	3	4	5

The third item in Table 13.2 is not so obvious. Some supply managers over-estimate how much a supplier wants to commit to their early-involvement efforts. Suppliers usually have many customers that differ in relative importance. They also have limited resources to commit to these kinds of initiatives. Perhaps the best way to get a supplier's attention is to be a customer the supplier cannot do without. This does not mean a buying company has to be 30 percent or more of a supplier's business. While definitive numbers are hard to come by, being 2 to 3 percent of a supplier's total business should be more than enough to receive the benefits accorded an "A" account.

The last item relates to the questions raised earlier about a supplier's ability to be an early participant. This should not be an unknown issue if it's evaluated properly during supplier selection.

Early-Involvement Barriers

Early involvement with suppliers is not easy. If it were easy, every firm would routinely be practicing it. Research reveals that the two largest barriers holding U.S. firms back are a fear of exposing proprietary information to outsiders and a lack of understanding regarding how to involve suppliers early.[4] Fortunately, neither of these barriers violates the laws of physics. They can be managed.

Confidentiality is a concern for at least three reasons. Historically the relationship between suppliers and buyers in the United States has been less than ideal. It is hard to talk about early involvement when a lack of trust permeates the supply chain. It is also hard to talk about an intense process like early involvement becoming a reality when a buying company maintains thousands of suppliers. Who do we know well enough to involve early? Who do we trust? Furthermore, a shift toward global sourcing means many internal locations are dealing with new and usually unfamiliar suppliers who may reside outside their home region. Language and cultural issues become a concern, as does the protection of intellectual property. Finally, some industries feature suppliers who are customers who are also competitors. This is common in the global electronics and aerospace industry, for example. Involving these suppliers early can be a challenge.

The confidentiality issue can be managed in a number of ways. The possibility of pursuing early involvement with a supplier should be something that is evaluated during supplier selection. The use of longer-term agreements should also lead to some stability within the supply base to the point that it becomes apparent who are the logical candidates for early involvement. A variety of trust-enhancing activities, which Chapter 11 discussed, can also support early-involvement objectives. Nondisclosure agreements are also widely used with suppliers.

The second most cited barrier, not understanding how to pursue early involvement, is usually a result of never having pursued early-involvement activities. Fortunately, published information is available to provide some insight into the topic, although not as much as other supply management topics. It is also recommended that companies that are new to early involvement start out with a pilot program and learn from that experience. Early involvement is also a prime area to benchmark.

Other barriers will likely exist. Design engineers or a unionized workforce may be unwilling to relinquish any type of responsibility to suppliers. Suppliers may also be unwilling to support early-involvement efforts if the account is not large enough. Suppliers may also lack the resources, particularly design engineers, to commit to early-involvement requests. An important part of pursuing early involvement is identifying ways to overcome any barriers that may affect the process.

The Inevitable Issues

Supply managers who are serious about pursuing early-involvement opportunities will inevitably face a number of important issues. While no definitive answers apply to these issues, research and experience help identify possible ways to address them. Table 13.3 identifies the issues that supply managers will likely face as they attempt to make early involvement a reality. The table also presents some possible responses to each issue.

Table 13.3 Early-Involvement Issues and Answers

Issue	How to Address the Issue
What if we are inexperienced at managing early-involvement?	Early involvement is ideal for benchmarking and learning from published research about early involvement. Inexperienced firms should start their involvement efforts with a relatively minor project or application. Conduct lessons learned sessions at the end of each project.
Who should have internal ownership of the process?	This is an area for supply managers to demonstrate leadership by managing the early involvement process. Because many early-involvement opportunities involve technical topics, expect engineering to be an important participant.
What activities should involve suppliers?	Corporate and strategic steering committees should identify opportunity areas for early supplier involvement. Firms should think broadly about when and where to involve suppliers, not just during product development.
Which suppliers should be involved?	The supplier rationalization process should recognize those suppliers who are capable of supporting early-involvement efforts. Supplier selection assessments should also consider a supplier's early involvement willingness and capability.
Who from the suppliers should be involved?	Early involvement often centers on design and technical issues, so the first point to get across to suppliers is to leave the salesperson home. Search for suppliers that are willing to provide support in any functional area required, not just engineering.
Should involvement be physical or virtual?	Firms with separate design facilities often have on-site supplier residency programs. Other firms pursue a combination of on-site and virtual communication. Firms that have restrictions against external parties working on-site might prefer using an off-site location or a virtual exchange of information, particularly when performing design work.
Should early supplier involvement be ad hoc or continuous?	Most early involvement is tied to a specific project or need, making involvement more ad hoc. On-site suppliers may provide support that is continuous.
How can we motivate suppliers to participate?	Buyers should reduce the size of their supply base and offer larger contracts as an enticement for supplies to become involved early. Progressive suppliers want to get closer to their key customers, so convincing them to participate should not be difficult. Buyers can also offer suppliers that provide early design work the production contract (assuming they are capable).

Table 13.3 Early-Involvement Issues and Answers (Continued)

Issue	How to Address the Issue
How can we gain internal acceptance to early involvement?	Executives need to make a clear business case for early involvement. Establish metrics that show the value of early involvement. Publicize success stories.
Do we pay suppliers for early-involvement support?	A majority of firms view early-involvement support as part of the service package suppliers should provide, especially if the supplier receives a longer-term production contract. If the supplier does not receive a production contract, then expect to pay the supplier for design services.
What will be the effect on other suppliers who are not early participants?	Suppliers that are not selected to be early participants may take this as a sign that they are not a preferred supplier, similar to suppliers that are not selected to be part of an alliance. This may result in the supplier redirecting its efforts toward other customers, some of whom may be direct competitors.
How can we protect proprietary information?	Firms extensively use nondisclosure agreements with early-involvement suppliers, particularly when they are less experienced with the process. Also, early involvement should be pursued with suppliers with whom the buyer trusts and has a positive working relationship.

SEPARATING THE BEST FROM THE REST

Imagine sitting at your desk and minding your own business. Suddenly you receive an e-mail from your manager saying she is "intrigued" by the idea of involving suppliers early, especially during product development. She wants you to put together a presentation by the end of the week that will help her better understand how to turn this concept into a reality. Fortunately for you, there is a solid body of knowledge about the practices that leading companies put in place as they pursue early involvement. Let's share that knowledge so you can look good in front of your manager.[5]

Firms that achieve the kinds of outcomes sought from early involvement pursue a set of practices *more extensively* compared with firms that are not as successful. Successful firms, especially during new product development:

1. Follow a formalized process to identify purchased items that would benefit from supplier involvement.
2. Rely more extensively on cross-functional teams for supplier selection and the planning of involvement efforts.

3. Use the same supplier for design work and full volume production.
4. Make suppliers formal project team members.
5. Emphasize more extensive cross-functional and intercompany communication during projects.
6. Are more likely to colocate supplier personnel with buying company personnel.
7. Pursue formal trust development efforts with suppliers.
8. Are more willing to share technology with suppliers.
9. Conduct joint education and training efforts with suppliers.

Understanding these practices will help supply managers focus their efforts and achieve the kinds of performance results that make early involvement a differentiating strategy.

A NEW WAY OF DOING BUSINESS

In the late 1990s supply executives at a leading chemical company were asking a question that should be routinely asked: How can we create advantages from working closer with suppliers? A major concern at this company involved the time and cost required to retrofit or build production facilities, which this company has dozens of around the world. New competitors were entering this company's markets quickly and at a lower cost. For the first time, company executives began to question if perhaps their facility design model might be out of date.

A major part of any process facility involves the control systems that serve as the facility's nerve center (think about oil refineries or nuclear power plants, for example). Historically, the decision about what control system to use was left up to individual business units. And with over 20 business units, it should come as no surprise to end up with an array of custom-designed control systems, each with its own operating, training, and spare-parts requirements. Different operating procedures limited this company's ability to shift operators from one facility to another. The design process also realized few savings from standardization, economies of scale, or spare-parts inventory management. Facility costs, which greatly influence final product costs, were not being managed well.

The current model also did not consider the potential advantages that might arise from involving suppliers early rather than later in facility design. Like most business models, this one worked relatively well until competitive pressure forced the company to search for new ways of doing business.

Although this company had used longer-term agreements to support material and equipments purchases for several years, it had never pursued an alliance relationship that focused primarily on early supplier design support. (Chapter 15 expands on the topic of supply alliances.) After an exhaustive analysis of the capabilities of different control suppliers, one was selected to take the lead for designing control systems for new and retrofitted production facilities. This was a dramatic shift for the buying company—a supplier was now responsible for assuming a leadership role when developing control technology for new and retrofitted facilities. It also represented an unusually long-term commitment, since the building and retrofitting of facilities was not an everyday occurrence.

What did this company receive from early involvement that it did not receive under its current business model? First, the control technology supplier attends corporate-level executive meetings to discuss the future of control technology. This involvement happens well before any facility plans are formally underway. The supplier is also a member of the facility design teams that work at the corporate level. To encourage face-to-face interaction, the supplier has also colocated a full-time manager at the buyer's corporate office.

By working together at higher-level technology meetings and with individual design teams, the supplier better understands the buyer's requirements and capabilities. The chemical company, through its longer-term asset requirements plan, influences how the supplier directs its R&D investment, and the supplier, through its intimate knowledge of control technology, influences retrofit and facility designs. Design teams build in supplier-provided control system technology early rather than relying on custom designed systems after suppliers have bid for a project.

As with any corporate-level initiative, buy-in from the operating sites is essential. Because the supplier supports multiple business units, visibility to each unit's requirements is important. Executive leaders have created a corporate-wide process-planning network that brings together the control supplier and business unit personnel. The process-planning network works to reach a consensus about the technology requirements at each business unit, and the control systems supplier actively participates in this network. It is a forum for communicating the needs of the business units. The network also helps business unit personnel become better acquainted with the control systems supplier.

The Value of Early Involvement

Perhaps the best indicator of the value of early involvement is a reduction by almost half the time it takes to retrofit or build a facility. Previously the facility design model featured the chemical company working with a design contractor on each project. The contractor had responsibility for subcontracting with a control system supplier, often through competitive bidding. Now the chemical company works early on with its control systems supplier and bypasses the design contractor altogether, realizing time and cost savings. Furthermore, the control supplier hears about the company's requirements first-hand rather than filtered through a design contractor.

Besides providing early design support, the supplier has also committed to lowering facility operating costs. The supplier has placed at selected facilities full-time engineers who are responsible for helping control operating costs.

Learning from the Process

This venture into early involvement has resulted in some worthwhile learning. While the chemical company appreciates the value of early supplier involvement, it also knows it should pursue early involvement selectively. Not all suppliers or opportunities are candidates for this approach. Supply managers also acknowledge the importance of information sharing, frequent opportunities for interaction, and the development of trust with early-involvement suppliers. These suppliers gain access early on to the buying company's *corporate* strategy. Early involvement at this level moves way beyond supply strategy.

Early involvement often evolves from longer-term agreements and relationships, making longer-term contracting a vital prerequisite activity. It can take three to five years before a purchaser can fully integrate itself with an early-involvement supplier, making patience a virtue that many managers lack. For the supplier these relationships require a shift from a marketing and selling perspective to a technical support perspective.

Early-involvement relationships are not risk free. The supplier selection process takes on added importance, since an incorrect decision will have longer-term consequences. Furthermore, the buying company is betting that the supplier will remain on the leading edge of control system technology. It is important to continuously access the value of the relationship, including the technological leadership that the supplier provides. This relationship could conceivably last 20 to 30 years.

CONCLUDING THOUGHTS

Progressive firms are making early involvement one of their most important supply management strategies. The challenge is to take what we know to be an inherently good idea and translating it into a set of directives and action plans that make early involvement a reality. Early involvement is an area that really begins to separate the supply leaders from the laggards, and like all the other topics presented throughout this book, it requires an understanding of how to make it work.

SUMMARY OF KEY CHAPTER POINTS

- Early involvement is the process of relying on suppliers, either physically or virtually, to provide support early on during strategic planning, demand and supply planning, continuous-improvement projects, project planning, and the development of new technologies and products.
- Early involvement has the potential to affect the success of important corporate initiatives. Various studies show that early supplier involvement can lead to competitive advantage. Other studies have found that U.S. firms have lagged in capturing the benefits available from early involvement.
- Besides the timing of a supplier's involvement in product and technology development, there are varying degrees this involvement can take, including gray- and black-box product designs.
- A variety of drivers are behind the growth in early involvement. These include the need for continuous improvement; competent suppliers usually have something of value to offer customers; the need to develop new products, services, and processes quickly; extensive outsourcing of noncore capabilities and competencies results in firms losing skills in certain areas; design changes become exponentially more complex and costly as a product moves through product development; and firms that are proficient at early involvement are winning in the marketplace.
- The decision about which supplier to involve is critical. Selecting the wrong supplier may result in performance indicators moving the wrong way. Early involvement should be a consideration during the supplier selection and strategic planning process.
- Some supply managers overestimate how much a supplier wants to commit to the buyer's early-involvement initiatives.
- Research reveals that the two largest barriers holding U.S. firms back from relying on suppliers early are a fear of exposing proprietary information to outsiders and a lack of understanding regarding how to pursue early involvement.
- Firms that achieve the results sought from early involvement follow a formalized process for identifying purchased items for supplier involvement, rely more extensively on cross-functional teams for supplier selection and the planning of involvement efforts, use the same supplier for design work and full volume production, make suppliers formal project team members, emphasize more extensive cross-functional and intercompany communication during projects, are more

likely to colocate supplier personnel with buying company personnel, pursue extensive formal trust development efforts with suppliers, are more willing to share technology with suppliers, and conduct joint education and training efforts with suppliers.

ENDNOTES

1. J. P. Womack, D. T. Jones, and D. Roos, *The Machine That Changed the World.* (New York: Rawson Associates, 1990), 118.
2. R. B. Handfield, G. L. Ragatz, K. J. Petersen, and R. M. Monczka, "Involving Suppliers in New Product Development," *California Management Review* 42, no. 1 (Fall 1999): 59–82.
3. As reported in an article by J. Teresko, "The Tough Get Going," *IndustryWeek,* March 2005, 28.
4. R. M. Monczka and R. J. Trent, "Purchasing and Supply Management: Key Trends and Changes throughout the 1990s," *International Journal of Purchasing and Materials Management* 34, no. 4 (Fall 1998): 2–11.
5. R. B. Handfield, G. L. Ragatz, K. J. Petersen, and R. M. Monczka, 59–82.
6. This case is example is adapted from R. J. Trent, "Strategic Alliances and Partnerships," Chapter 8 in *The Purchasing Handbook* (New York: McGraw-Hill, 2000).

14

SOURCING GLOBALLY

In an attempt to regain some lost competitiveness, a U.S. producer of power tools decided to outsource its lower-end products to a contract manufacturer in Asia. This would allow the U.S. producer to focus on higher-margin products while still offering customers a full range of tools. Unfortunately, the Taiwanese company the U.S. firm contracted with did not seem to know when to turn off its production line. Like the Energizer bunny, the line kept going and going and going, so much so that the contract manufacturer really had no choice but to sell the extra inventory to other companies throughout Asia. The Taiwanese supplier even shared the design with other Asian companies. Before long, the U.S. producer found itself competing in North America against its own product! How could a strategy that was designed to help invigorate a company go so terribly wrong?

Even with increased risks, such as intellectual property theft and variability due to lengthened material pipelines, the growth in worldwide sourcing has been steady over the last 25 years. This growth mirrors the growth in international commerce. While precise numbers are hard to come by, total purchases from non-U.S. sources for larger U.S. firms has increased from 9 percent of total purchases on average in 1993, to over 25 percent in 2000 and now close to 30 percent.[1] This increase encompasses a wide range of purchase categories and industries.

At some point, companies mature beyond basic international purchasing and pursue a coordinated view of their worldwide supply operations, or what is termed global sourcing. While many researchers and practitioners interchange the terms, fundamental differences exist between the two concepts. *International purchasing* relates to a commercial purchase transaction between a buyer and supplier located in different countries. This type of purchase is typically more complex than a domestic purchase. Organizations must contend with lengthened material pipelines, increased rules and regulations, currency fluctuations, customs requirements, and a host of other variables such as language and time differences. *Global sourcing*, which differs dramatically from international buying in scope and complexity, involves integrating and coordinating common materials and services, processes and practices, designs, technologies, and suppliers across worldwide purchasing, engineering, and operating locations.[2]

This chapter addresses some important topics associated with international purchasing and global sourcing. We first explore why international purchasing is so much more complex than domestic purchasing. Next, the evolution toward integrated global sourcing is presented, including the progression along a five-level sourcing continuum, the reasons to source globally, eight factors that affect global sourcing success, and the characteristics that define an effective global sourcing organization.

INTERNATIONAL PURCHASING—IT CAN BE COMPLEX!

Almost all surveys reveal that the primary reason for pursuing international purchasing is to achieve price reductions. The next-highest-rated reasons, which often differ depending on the survey, sometimes hardly register on the scale. Industry surveys will also tell us that the number one pressure that firms face is the relentless pressure to reduce cost. For many companies international purchasing is about price, price, and then price. Once in a while it may be about gaining access to new sources of technology or introducing competition to the domestic supply base. By and large, however, price reduction is the driver.

International purchasing is often way more complex than domestic purchasing, which usually leads to hidden costs. The following reasons, while not meant to be a comprehensive analysis of international purchasing, begin to highlight the issues that add to the complexity of international purchasing. A major topic related to international purchasing is sourcing from China, a topic that is beyond the scope of this book.[3]

Logistical Issues

Perhaps the major reason that international purchasing is more complex than domestic sourcing is due to logistical issues. Invariably, any purchasing transaction, particularly those outside North America, will result in longer material pipelines, additional touch points across the supply chain, and multiple modes of transportation. The following identifies some of the issues related to international logistics:

- Lengthened material pipelines
- Delivery variability

- Increased supply risk due to damage, increased handling, multiple modes of transportation, theft, longer supply chains, and so on
- Reduced ability to plan due to longer ordering cycle times
- More complex shipping terms (international Incoterms versus domestic Uniform Commercial Code terms)
- Increased touch points
- Increased use of agents and other third parties
- Increased documentation requirements, including transportation, insurance, and import documents
- Increased regulations resulting from enhanced security

In addition, some U.S. firms insist that a foreign supplier have a U.S. presence to help manage any issues that might arise.

International Purchasing Costs

As U.S. firms increase their levels of worldwide sourcing, particularly from China and India, unit cost savings never equal total cost savings. For a variety of reasons, a quarter of any unit cost savings derived from international purchasing, on average, "disappear" when the true total landed cost of doing business abroad is calculated.[4] At times all of the expected savings may disappear.

Firms should regularly calculate the *total landed cost* of purchasing internationally. Supply managers should create spreadsheets that enable them to enter the relevant data for various cost categories. This exercise serves two purposes. First, it provides a better measure of the true cost of international purchasing. Second, it identifies the cost elements that might be improved upon. It is difficult to improve something that is not measured. Examples of elements that must be factored into the total landed cost include unit price, tooling, packaging, multiple transportation modes, duties and tariffs, insurance, inventory carrying charges, fees and commissions to third parties, port terminal and handling fees, taxes, delivery variability costs, and currency management fees.

Language and Cultural Differences

It is a mistake to assume the entire world is comfortable with the U.S. version of English. Some words do not translate well, and some suppliers flatly refuse to negotiate except in their own language. Supply managers are urged to work with competent translators whenever they engage a foreign supplier. U.S supply managers should also slow down in their speech, rely on extra presentation graphics, write down large numbers, and avoid the use of profanity, jargon, and acronyms.[5]

Cultural differences are also very real around the world. Culture is the sum of the understandings that govern human interaction in a society. It affects the way people act and the way people think.[6] Knowing where and how culture affects international business will improve a supply manager's effectiveness. For example, while attending a trade mission conference in China, a U.S. representative gave a Chinese dignitary a green hat as a gift. Unfortunately, a green hat in China indicates a man's wife has been unfaithful.[7] Supply managers are urged to consult one of the many books written about doing business internationally. Both language and cultural differences add a level of complexity to foreign buying that is not present with domestic buying.

Different Legal Systems

This may come as a shock, but foreign suppliers are sometimes uncomfortable dealing with the U.S. legal system. Perhaps giant class action lawsuits against businesses and what seems like one lawyer for every two Americans are influencing factors. Furthermore, the United States uses common or case law, which often leads to lengthier contracts than what is found in countries that use code or civil law.[8] For a variety of reasons, U.S. companies should not assume that foreign companies want to rely on the U.S. legal system.

Developed countries will have a legal system that should protect the rights of buyers and sellers. True international contracts exist if the country follows the United Nations Convention on the International Sale of Goods. The same cannot be said for many less-developed countries. Even the concept of a legal system that recognizes private property is still evolving within China. It is highly recommended that even if a formal contract is not in place, the parties should have a written document that outlines the expectations of the buyer and seller.[9]

Currency Fluctuation Risks

Anyone who conducts business or travels internationally understands that most currencies change their value over time compared with other currencies. (Some foreign currencies are pegged to the value of another currency and therefore do not fluctuate.) Fortunately, currency fluctuations, at least those that are not rapid or dramatic, are a risk that most firms can manage. Table 14.1 summarizes some common approaches for managing currency fluctuation risk.

Countertrade Demands

While most supply managers rarely encounter countertrade demands, a general understanding of the concept is worthwhile. Countertrade is a broad term that refers to commercial trade, usually internationally, where the buyer and seller have at least a partial exchange of goods for goods.[10] Five major categories of countertrade exist, although different sources may use other terminology:

Table 14.1 Managing Currency Risks

Hedge Currencies	This involves the buying and selling of currency contracts so a gain in one is offset by a loss in another. Be sure to involve finance.
Adjustment Clauses	Parties agree to review a contract if a currency moves beyond an agreed-upon band or width.
Share Fluctuation Risk	This involves the equal division of a change in price due to a currency fluctuation. While not eliminating risk, this approach helps reduce the impact of any currency changes.
Ignore Currency Risk	For short-term transactions or transactions involving stable currencies, ignoring fluctuation risk may be a viable option. Finance should help when forecasting currency fluctuations.
Buy in U.S. Dollars	While this sounds like the ideal method, a seller may refuse to sell in U.S. dollars. If this approach is taken, a seller may include a risk premium to compensate for assuming 100 percent of the currency fluctuation risk.
Use Pegged Currencies	Some countries maintain or peg their currency to a fixed value against the dollar. As long as rates are pegged at a fixed level, risk fluctuations are minimal.

- *Barter.* The straight exchange of goods for goods.
- *Offset.* The party selling goods to another country agrees to purchase an agreed-upon amount of goods from any supplier within that country.
- *Counterpurchase.* The party selling goods to another country agrees to purchase an agreed-upon amount of goods that are usually unrelated to its primary business and often from suppliers designated by the foreign government.
- *Buy-back.* The party selling goods to another country agrees to take as compensation output from a facility it helped build in that country.
- *Switch trading.* Involves the use of a third party to sell at a discount the counterpurchase goods the purchasing department was forced to buy.

Three important observations must be made about countertrade. First, countertrade demands are made by foreign governments, not foreign companies. Second, supply managers are usually reactive participants in any countertrade arrangement. While marketing managers may view countertrade as an important part of their selling strategy, supply managers often view countertrade demands as restricting their sourcing options. Third, companies that are heavily involved in countertrade usually create a specialized group to manage the process, thereby removing supply managers from the process.

Intellectual Property Protection

The theft of intellectual property (IP) is unfortunately a common occurrence across many parts of the world. IP encompasses copyrights, designs, patents, brands, and trademarks. IP theft likely costs U.S. firms over $100 billion annually. And while items such as movies, music, and clothing have routinely been pirated, industrial designs are also an area of concern. The protection of IP is so important within the U.S. culture that the Founding Fathers addressed this topic specifically in the U.S. Constitution (see Article 1, Section 8, Clause 8).

As the opening to this chapter illustrated, IP protection can be an issue when sourcing from unfamiliar sources. The challenge becomes how to manage this risk. One strategy includes disaggregating requirements so no one producer has access to a complete product design. Other firms rely on their IPOs to closely evaluate and then scrutinize foreign suppliers. These offices can also compile a list of suppliers to avoid. Still other companies establish proprietary assets in a country for greater control. While taking on additional assets is often not a preferred approach, it may be a necessary option when pursuing a joint venture.

Most observers agree that legal experts should play a role in protecting IP. These experts can identify preventive measures such as contract clauses and nondisclosure agreements as well as pursue legal remedies if an infraction occurs. An obvious strategy for managing IP risk is to avoid countries that blatantly steal IP.

EVOLVING FROM INTERNATIONAL PURCHASING TO GLOBAL SOURCING

Dramatic changes take place as firms evolve or progress along a continuum from domestic purchasing to international purchasing and then eventually to global coordination and integration. This continuum, featured in Figure 14.1, summarizes this progression along with the level that firms operate at currently and expect to operate in the future. As defined in this figure, firms that operate at Levels II and III exhibit behaviors that define international purchasing, while firms that operate at Levels IV and V pursue integrated global sourcing.

An organization progresses (usually reactively) toward Level II because it is confronted with a requirement for which no suitable domestic supplier exists, or because competitors are gaining an advantage from their worldwide sourcing activities. First-level firms may also find themselves being driven toward the second level because of triggering events in the supply market. Such events could be a supply disruption, changing currency rates, a declining domestic supply base, or the emergence of worldwide competitors. International purchasing at this level is usually limited or performed on an ad hoc or reactive basis.

Level I	Level II	Level III	Level IV	Level V
Engage in Domestic Purchasing Only	Engage in International Purchasing as Needed	International Purchasing as Part of Sourcing Strategy	Integration and Coordination of Global Sourcing Strategies across Worldwide Locations	Integration and Coordination of Global Sourcing Strategies with Other Functional Groups
	International Purchasing		**Global Sourcing**	
Current*	8.4%	20.1%	18.8%	22.7%	29.9%
Five Years	5.9%	6.5%	7.8%	20.9%	58.8%
Expected Change	-30%	-68%	-59%	-8%	+97%

* Percent of companies operating or expecting to operate at a particular level

Figure 14.1 Current and expected worldwide sourcing levels. (Source: Robert M. Monczka, Robert J. Trent, and Kenneth J. Petersen, *The Global Sourcing Research Project*, 2005.)

Strategies and approaches developed in Level III begin to at least recognize that a properly executed worldwide supply strategy can result in major improvements. However, strategies at this level are not coordinated across worldwide buying locations, operating centers, functional groups, or business units.

Level IV, which is the first of two levels that define global sourcing, represents the integration and coordination of sourcing strategies across worldwide buying locations. Operating at this level requires worldwide information systems, personnel with sophisticated knowledge and skills, extensive coordination and communication mechanisms, an organizational structure that promotes the central coordination of global activities, and executive leadership that endorses a global approach to sourcing. While worldwide integration occurs in Level IV, which is not the case with Level III, the integration is primarily cross-locational rather than cross-functional. The emphasis at this level, at least initially, is usually on forming worldwide supply contracts.

Organizations that operate at Level V have achieved the cross-locational integration that Level IV firms have achieved. The primary distinction is that Level V participants integrate and coordinate common items, processes, designs, technologies, and suppliers across worldwide purchasing centers and with other functional groups, particularly engineering. This integration occurs during new product development as well as during the sourcing of items or services to fulfill continuous demand or aftermarket requirements. Furthermore, supply leaders begin to focus on more than global contracts. They begin to focus on worldwide consistency in practices, systems, measures, and strategies.

Only those firms with worldwide design, development, production, logistics, and procurement capabilities can progress to the more advanced levels within this continuum. While many firms expect to advance toward global sourcing over the next three to five years, the reality is that many will lack the understanding or the willingness to achieve such a sophisticated level. Some will also lack the need. An important part of global sourcing is identifying the appropriate level to operate at and then comparing that level to current levels. Plans are then developed to close any gaps.

The reality today is that few firms truly operate at Level V. Instead, pockets of excellence exist within companies that consider themselves global sourcing organizations. A company may be good at developing global strategies for direct materials but be weak in its services or indirect materials strategy. Other companies may be good at worldwide contracting but have done little to standardize their supply practices across operating and buying units. There are always opportunities to grow.

In some respects, integrated global sourcing represents the pinnacle of supply management strategy. However, evolving toward higher global sourcing levels is not easy. In fact, the features that characterize Level IV and V firms are quite different from the features that characterize Level II and III firms. A sample of these features includes regular strategy review meetings with worldwide managers, IPOs, a worldwide purchasing data warehouse, cross-functional strategy development teams, a worldwide sourcing council, a formally established sourcing process, and extensive electronic communication tools.

The operational complexities associated with international purchasing have not gone away as a firm evolves toward integrated global sourcing. A set of features that support the development of global strategies and practices are now required in addition to the operational complexities brought about by international purchasing. Table 14.2 presents the characteristics of an ideal global sourcing organization. While few organizations match this ideal, these characteristics provide a good benchmark to compare against.

GLOBAL SOURCING—WHY DO IT?

Since global sourcing is a time- and resource-intensive process, why would any company pursue such a demanding approach to sourcing? What does this process offer that domestic or international purchasing does not? Actually, the evidence in favor of integrated global sourcing is quite compelling.

Table 14.2 Characteristics of Best-Practice Global Sourcing Organizations

Executive Leadership

- Cross-functional leaders participate on a global sourcing steering committee.
- An executive position has the authority to translate a global vision into reality.
- Global sourcing leaders make strategy presentations to the executive committee and, on occasion, to the board of directors.
- Executive leaders recruit qualified cross-functional and/or site-based participants to be part of global sourcing project teams.

Process

- A well-defined and understood process is in place that requires participants to establish goals, meet process milestones, and report progress to executive leaders.
- An executive leader or steering committee reviews and proposes process improvements as required.
- Lessons learned sessions are conducted at the conclusion of each global project.
- Global agreements are continuously managed, reviewed, and reestablished as required.

Resources

- Executive leaders identify and make available critical resources to support global initiatives.
- The global process involves individuals who have the ability to take a global perspective.
- Information is made available to project teams, including forecasted requirements, current supplier performance, comparisons of actual prices to baseline prices, and data on potential suppliers.

Information Technology

- Data warehouses provide access to required information on a real-time basis.
- Support documents, guidelines, templates, and progress updates are maintained on a company-wide intranet for easy retrieval.
- Contract repositories store global agreements and provide warning to expiring agreements.

Communication and Coordination

- Global sourcing project teams meet regularly, either face-to-face or virtually, to coordinate efforts.
- Strategy review and coordination sessions occur between functional groups and across sites and buying locations to ensure understanding, alignment, and buy-in to global initiatives.
- Project teams report progress to executive leaders on a regular basis.
- Advanced communication and coordination tools are available, such as Web-based collaboration tools.
- Project updates are posted on a company intranet.

Continued

Table 14.2 Characteristics of Best-Practice Global Sourcing Organizations (Continued)

Organizational Design
• An executive steering committee or council oversees the global sourcing process, including the identification of high-potential global opportunities.
• An executive position is responsible for the success of a centrally led global sourcing process.
• Cross-functional project teams are responsible for the development of global strategies and agreements.
• Organizational design features the separation of strategic and operational activities.
• IPOs support global sourcing requirements within specific regions.

Measurement
• Finance representatives agree on methods to validate savings from global initiatives, including how to establish baseline prices and compare aggregated savings against preestablished targets.
• Supply managers meet regularly with executive leaders to review savings from existing agreements and expected savings from in-process activities.
• Measurement systems calculate the impact that sourcing initiatives have on corporate financial measures (ROI, ROA, EVA) and the impact that global suppliers have on site and buying location performance indicators.

Adapted from R. J. Trent and R. M. Monczka, "Achieving Excellence in Global Sourcing," *Sloan Management Review*, Fall 2005, p. 24.

Perhaps the most revealing difference between international purchasing and global sourcing is the perception the participants in these two groups have regarding the benefits they have realized from their worldwide efforts. Table 14.3 presents these benefits sorted by the largest average difference between those firms engaged in international purchasing and those engaged in global sourcing. Although the differences for only the top eight benefits are reported here, firms that engage in global sourcing reported realizing every benefit (16 benefits evaluated in total) at a statistically higher level than firms that engage in international purchasing.

One benefit that both segments rate highly is the ability to achieve a lower purchase price or cost through worldwide sourcing, which is why this item does not appear on a table that sorts the benefits by their largest differences. Both international and global sourcing companies routinely achieve double-digit price reductions compared with domestic sourcing. The initial benefits from international purchasing are price focused and are often available from international purchasing activities. However, other sought-after benefits are only realized once a firm pursues more advanced global sourcing activities. In particular, greater

Table 14.3 Why Pursue Global Sourcing?

Benefit	Global Sourcing	International Purchasing	Difference
Better management of total supply chain inventory	4.29	2.74	1.55
Great supplier responsiveness to buying unit needs	4.47	3.08	1.39
Greater standardization or consistency of the sourcing process	4.25	3.01	1.24
Greater access to process technology	4.69	3.49	1.23
Improved supplier relationships	4.61	3.46	1.15
Greater access to process technology	4.54	3.46	1.08
Improved sharing of information with suppliers	4.10	3.04	1.06
Greater supplier involvement during product development	3.86	2.80	1.06
	N = 55	N = 83	

1 = Not realized, 4 = Moderately realized, 7 = Extremely realized
Average across 16 benefits = 3.2 for international purchasing segment; 4.23 for global sourcing segment

Source: R. J. Trent and R. M. Monczka, "International Purchasing and Global Sourcing: What Are the Differences?" *Journal of Supply Chain Management*, Fall 2003, p. 26.

access to product and process technology and better management of supply chain inventory are benefits that global sourcing firms enjoy at higher levels compared with firms that pursue international purchasing.

Other benefits that are more readily available from global sourcing include greater supplier responsiveness, greater sourcing process consistency, improved supplier relationships, and improved sharing of information with suppliers. The differential advantages realized by the two groups helps explain why so many firms hope to evolve toward Levels IV and V over the next five years.

If Table 14.3 is not convincing, then perhaps Table 14.4 will be. This table reports on the degree of similarity or difference across geographic locations and buying units for international purchasing and global sourcing organizations. An objective of most supply managers is to eliminate costly and inefficient duplication across locations.

A lack of coordination results in each location developing its own set of methods for supplier selection, contracting, measurement, and strategy development. A desired outcome from integrated global sourcing should be consistency around a set of best practices. That is exactly what the more advanced companies

Table 14.4 Similarity across Segments

Similarity Area	Global Sourcing	International Purchasing	Difference
Strategy development process	4.90	3.68	1.22
Supplier assessment practices	4.90	3.75	1.15
Purchasing or sourcing philosophy	5.04	3.96	1.08
Current purchasing strategies	4.96	3.96	1.00
Problem resolution techniques with suppliers	4.90	3.90	1.00
Contracting approaches	4.54	3.58	.96
	N = 55	N = 83	

1 = Act similar, 4 = Somewhat similar, 7 = Very similar

Source: R. J. Trent and R. M. Monczka, "International Purchasing and Global Sourcing: What Are the Differences?" *Journal of Supply Chain Management*, Fall 2003, p. 26.

are achieving. Global sourcing firms are well ahead of their international purchasing counterparts in the race to eliminate dissimilarity.

In the long run, one of the most important outcomes from global sourcing may be a company-wide consistency that most firms now lack. The items showing the largest difference between the two segments in Table 14.3 relate to sourcing approaches, practices, and beliefs. Global sourcing should lead to greater consistency, which in the final analysis may be the most powerful benefit realized from this process.

EIGHT FACTORS THAT AFFECT GLOBAL SOURCING SUCCESS

Now that we have established that global strategies and approaches should result in differential advantages, the focus becomes one of knowing how to pursue integrated global sourcing. The good news is that a recent research project identified a set of factors that are essential for global sourcing success.[11] The following explains those factors.

Defined Process for Developing Global Strategies

The presence of a defined process to guide global efforts is one of the most important factors affecting global sourcing success. A defined process helps overcome many of the differences inherent across worldwide locations. Social culture and laws, personnel skills and abilities, and business culture are areas where companies indicate they often have widespread differences across geographic locations.

A defined process helps align very different participants and practices around the world. The lack of a process and its enforcement often leads to the self-interests of individual sites and operating locations, rather than broader corporate interests, becoming a priority.

While no standard process exists, an effective global sourcing process contains certain features. These include regular strategy coordination and review meetings with worldwide managers, a formally defined set of steps for developing global strategies (some companies have adapted their commodity strategy development process to assume a more global perspective), and the integration of technical specialists, operations, logistics, and sourcing personnel across worldwide locations. Other features that support a global sourcing process include cross-functional/cross-locational teams to develop and manage worldwide strategies, experienced global sourcing personnel who view sourcing requirements from a worldwide perspective, executive leadership that is capable of communicating a clear vision, and suppliers who are interested in worldwide contracts. Internal customer buy-in to global agreements along with an ability to measure the benefits attained from global sourcing also characterize an effective process.

Advanced organizations will have in place a defined global sourcing process that is communicated and understood throughout an organization. These organizations will also have a process owner who has responsibility for reviewing and improving the process, conducts lessons learned sessions at the end of each project with results forwarded to all global team members, and assumes ownership for managing, reviewing, and reestablishing global agreements as required. And executive leaders will maintain control throughout the process by requiring teams to provide updates and to achieve process milestones.

Centrally Coordinated/Centrally Led Decision Making

An emphasis on centrally led or centralized sourcing governance, coordination, and decision making is clearly taking place today. In fact, almost three-quarters of firms surveyed report their most important purchases are coordinated from a center-led or headquarters group, while over 70 percent indicate that purchasing and supply management decision making authority is centralized or highly centralized. The task becomes one of effectively coordinating and leveraging worldwide requirements while remaining responsive to the needs of business unit and operating sites.

As Chapter 3 noted, an important separation should occur between activities that are maintained at a centrally coordinated or centrally led level and those that are maintained at a decentralized or site level. Activities that are part of a centralized organization include developing worldwide supply strategies, locating potential supply sources, evaluating and selecting suppliers, negotiating and establishing contracts, managing supplier relationships, managing supplier development activities, establishing specifications, developing supplier performance measurement systems, and providing supplier performance feedback.

Site-Based Buy-In and Control of Operational Supply Activities

While a shift toward centrally led, centrally coordinated, and/or centralized global sourcing is occurring across most industries, the reality is this shift applies primarily to strategic planning and development. A major concern whenever companies leverage their purchase volumes across multiple sites, particularly when leveraging is performed at a central level, is gaining buy-in to a new supplier, contract, or practice.

Why should users and other interested parties have a voice or involvement during the global sourcing process? First, local sites must agree to use selected suppliers. It makes sense to gain buy-in to any agreements or changes. Second, site personnel are the supply manager's internal customer. It is important to represent their requirements throughout the development process beyond providing basic updates. Third, some supply activities are simply best left at the local or site level.

Operational activities managed at a decentralized level during global sourcing include issuing material releases to suppliers, expediting goods when necessary, resolving routine performance issues with suppliers, developing and executing requirements schedules, planning inventory levels, developing logistics plans, and providing input for measuring supplier performance.

The question of how to involve internal users and customers is important, although there is no one model that will work for everyone. One leading company relies on different individuals to represent the interests of multiple sites and to act as a liaison between project teams and operating centers. Another model relies on executive steering team members to represent site locations. A creative way to involve users is to provide them with the ability to specify their requirements through an electronic template. It is also possible to create global project teams composed entirely of site personnel (although few firms currently practice this approach). Regardless of the model used, gaining buy-in and involvement is essential for ensuring that operating sites support the process.

Information Sharing with Suppliers

Successful global sourcing requires a willingness to share information on a regular basis with important suppliers. Shared performance information includes timely details about supplier quality, delivery, cycle time, flexibility, and cost performance. Shared information can also include rankings of supplier performance against other suppliers.

A second aspect of information sharing involves other types of information besides performance data. This includes an assessment of a supplier's technology contribution, joint sharing of future technology plans, and sharing of future demand and investment plans. Supplier feedback about the buying company's performance is also included in this category

Real-Time Communication Tools

A process as complex as integrated global sourcing cannot be successful without access to communication tools, particularly when participants are located across geographically dispersed locations. These tools allow real-time sharing of information and coordination of global sourcing activities. Firms that rely extensively on real-time communication tools to support their global efforts are more likely to realize a wide range of desirable performance outcomes. Real-time communication tools include Web-based meeting software, electronic mail, videoconferencing, telephone conferencing, and face-to-face meetings.

Availability of Critical Resources

A set of important variables includes the resources that promote the development of global strategies, including time, budget, external help from others, information, and qualified participants. A commitment of needed resources has the potential to separate marginal from exceptional global initiatives. Unfortunately, a lack of resources often causes participants to question the importance of global sourcing as well as management's commitment to the process.

One theme that is consistent across most companies is the importance of qualified personnel to support the global sourcing process, making this an important resource category. Besides being a highly rated success factor, a lack of qualified personnel to support the sourcing process is also one of the most cited problem areas when sourcing globally.

An inability to recruit qualified personnel to become global participants is often a difficult barrier to overcome. The knowledge and skills required for global sourcing differ dramatically from those required of day-to-day operational purchasing. Many companies have created decentralized procurement organizations staffed with personnel who are proficient at tactically managing transactions and material flows. The ability to take a holistic view of the world within a global sourcing process is not something that comes naturally to most purchasing professionals.

It is hard to imagine a successful global sourcing effort without participants having access to complete, reliable, and timely information, another important resource category. Examples include a listing of existing contracts, reports on supplier capabilities and performance, projected worldwide volumes by commodity or category, information about potential new suppliers, internal customer requirements, and forecasted requirements across buying units. Some companies are addressing this critical need by creating global data warehouses and purchase commodity coding schemes, which the next factor supports.

Sourcing and Contracting Systems

As mentioned previously, the availability of information is a critical resource. One way to ensure access to information is through the development of a data warehouse that makes critical information available on a worldwide basis. The presence of an effective sourcing and contracting system relates directly to global sourcing success.

Systems that provide efficient and easy access to worldwide supply data and contracts are an important enabler. While many companies struggle due to a lack of data and information, companies that have developed these systems find they rapidly become an indispensable tool for global supply managers. A study by one company that developed a sourcing and contracting system found the system helped reduce data collection time from 40 days to 1 day and overall strategy development costs by 95 percent.

One of the most important features of these systems should be their ability to capture all expenditures across operating units with a comparison against a benchmark price. These systems should also serve as contract repositories. As contracts come closer to expiring, these systems should notify the proper supply manager about the need for reviewing and reestablishing a global agreement as required.

International Purchasing Office Support

IPOs are becoming an increasingly important part of what drives global sourcing success. IPOs are a formal part of a firm's organizational design and are expected to increase in importance as the worldwide scope of sourcing expands. Over 85 percent of firms that have IPOs say they are extremely important to global sourcing success, with 10 percent saying IPOs are moderately important. Convincing agreement exists regarding the importance of IPOs.

What types of tasks do IPOs perform? Ranked in order of prevalence, these tasks include identifying potential suppliers; evaluating supplier capabilities; resolving quality, delivery, and other problems or issues directly with suppliers; negotiating and executing contracts with suppliers; developing supplier capabilities; measuring supplier performance; and evaluating product designs and samples. These offices will also help with import/export activities and logistical issues.

The growth in IPOs corresponds directly to the increase in worldwide sourcing over the last five years. These offices provide a wide range of support and essentially act as a full-service procurement center within a geographic region. They are part of a company's footprint within a region. While IPOs will increase in importance as firms expand their focus on worldwide sourcing, challenges to their use will also increase. Anecdotal evidence reveals that U.S. firms are already seeing turnover due to the hiring away of experienced IPO staff by other U.S. companies. This will likely increase the cost of maintaining IPOs.

CONCLUDING THOUGHTS

A survey of CEOs by the Foundation for the Malcolm Baldrige National Quality Award revealed they overwhelmingly indicated that becoming more global was their firm's top challenge as they looked across a three- to five-year planning horizon. Furthermore, almost 80 percent of CEOs indicated that reducing cost and improving global supply chains was a top priority. Given the importance that CEOs place on globalization, understanding how to define this topic, including how it relates to strategic supply management, should be a major area of interest. Since most organizations do not have in place well-developed global sourcing strategies, improvement opportunities are largely unrealized.

Companies that produce and sell worldwide should no longer view global sourcing as an emerging strategy. The pursuit of competitive advantage will increasingly require global processes and strategies that become a major part of a firm's supply management efforts. Understanding the fundamentals of international purchasing and the complexities of integrated global sourcing are essential if supply managers expect to realize the benefits that a worldwide approach to sourcing offers.

SUMMARY OF KEY CHAPTER POINTS

- International purchasing relates to a commercial purchase transaction between a buyer and supplier located in different countries. Global sourcing involves integrating and coordinating common materials and services, processes and practices, designs, technologies, and suppliers across worldwide purchasing, engineering, and operating locations.
- At some point, leading companies mature beyond basic international purchasing and endorse a coordinated view of their worldwide supply operations. Since most organizations do not have in place well-developed global sourcing strategies, improvement opportunities are largely unrealized.

- Almost all surveys reveal that the primary reason for pursuing international purchasing is to achieve price reductions.
- Areas where international purchasing creates complexity compared with domestic purchasing include a wide array of logistical issues; more cost elements to consider; different language, culture, and legal systems; currency fluctuation risks; and IP protection issues.
- Firms should calculate the total landed cost of purchasing internationally, taking into account unit price, tooling, packaging, transportation, duties and tariffs, insurance, inventory carrying charges, fees and commissions to third parties, port terminal and handling fees, taxes, delivery variability costs, and currency management fees
- Only those firms with worldwide design, development, production, logistics, and procurement capabilities can progress to more advanced global sourcing levels. While a majority of firms expect to advance toward global sourcing over the next three to five years, the reality is that many will lack the understanding or the willingness to achieve such a sophisticated sourcing level.
- Certain sought-after benefits are only realized once a firm has evolved toward more advanced global levels. Greater access to product and process technology and better management of supply chain inventory are benefits that global sourcing firms enjoy at higher levels compared with firms that engage in international purchasing.
- One of the most important outcomes from global sourcing may be a company-wide consistency that most firms lack, which in the final analysis may be the most significant benefit realized from this company-wide consistency.
- Given the importance that CEOs place on globalization, understanding how to define this topic, including how it relates to strategic supply management, should be a major area of interest.
- Research has identified a set of factors that are essential for global sourcing success. These include a defined process for developing global strategies, centrally coordinated/centrally led decision making, site-based buy-in and control of operational supply activities, information sharing with suppliers, real-time communication tools, availability of critical resources, the development of sourcing and contracting systems, and IPO support.

ENDNOTES

1. R. M. Monczka and R. J. Trent, "Purchasing and Supply Management: Key Trends and Changes throughout the 1990s," *International Journal of Purchasing and Materials Management* 34, no. 4 (Fall 1998), 2–11; R. M. Monczka, R. J. Trent, and K. J. Petersen, "Effective Global Sourcing and Supply for Superior Results" (Tempe, AZ: CAPS Research, 2006).

2. R. J. Trent and R. M. Monczka, "International Purchasing and Global Sourcing: What Are the Differences?" *Journal of Supply Chain Management* 39, no. 4 (Fall 2003): 26.

3. For recent discussions on sourcing from China, see D. Hannon, "Do's and Don'ts of Doing Business in China," www.purchasing.com; R. B. Handfield and K. McCormack, "What You Need to Know about Sourcing from China," *Supply Chain Management Review* 9, no. 6 (September 2005): 28–36.

4. R. J. Trent and R. M. Monczka, "Pursuing Competitive Advantage through Integrated Global Sourcing," *Academy of Management Executive* 16, no. 2 (May 2002): 66.

5. D. Locke, *Global Supply Management: A Guide to International Purchasing*, (New York: McGraw-Hill, 1996), 45–51.

6. Locke, 7.

7. Hannon, www.purchasing.com.

8. Locke, 54.

9. Locke, 53–65.

10. R. M. Monczka, R. J. Trent, and R. B. Handfield, *Purchasing and Supply Chain Management* (Mason, OH: Thomas Southwestern, 205): 315–316.

11. R. M. Monczka, R. J. Trent, and K. J. Petersen, "Effective Global Sourcing and Supply for Superior Results" (Tempe, AZ: CAPS Research, 2006), 22–31.

15

CREATING NEW VALUE THROUGH SUPPLY ALLIANCES

Several years ago a supply management conference featured a presentation by one of the most respected individuals in the field. During his presentation, this leader meticulously described his company's efforts at crafting and then managing supply alliances. He talked about the need for trust, sharing of information, developing clear measures of success, and pursuing win-win opportunities. After a few minutes one of the attendees asked how many supply alliances his company had in place. Without hesitation the presenter said his company had two but was working toward a third. The group was surprised—only two alliances? Surely the attendees had not heard correctly. This approach to supply management surely must warrant more than a handful of alliances. When asked why only two alliances were in place, the presenter responded with a question of his own. "Do you really know what it takes to establish and manage a *true* alliance?"

While a great deal has been written about supply alliances, and the prevailing view is that alliances can be a good thing, the reality is that a firm should maintain only a few true supply alliances. The resources and commitment required to maintain these special relationships ensure that only a few true supply alliances should be formed.

An appropriate analogy involves friends. While an individual may have many friends, only a few are important enough to be best friends. If someone says he has 20 or 30 best friends, we can safely conclude this individual doesn't quite grasp the concept of a best friend. Accordingly, if a supply manager maintains his firm has

257

20 or 30 supply alliances in place, we can conclude this manager does not quite grasp the concept of an alliance. Alliances, like best friends, are special and unique.

This chapter approaches the topic of supply alliances from several perspectives. First presented is an overview of supply alliances, including why and when to form this special type of relationship. Predictors of alliance success, characteristics of poor alliances, and an eight-step process for forming alliances are discussed next. The chapter concludes with an analysis of a supply alliance that has far exceeded the expectations of its creators.

UNDERSTANDING SUPPLY ALLIANCES

One of the challenges when talking about alliances is that no formal definition of a supply alliance exists. Something all definitions should agree upon is that supply alliances are not just longer-term agreements or relationships that are special. Better definitions address the win-win nature of the relationship, the formal and informal sharing of resources and information between companies, the higher-level visibility these relationships receive, and the need to demonstrate continuous benefits above and beyond those available from traditional relationships.

For our purposes, a *supply alliance* is a longer-term, mutually beneficial relationship between two or more firms that has specific elements unique to that relationship: an agreement (though not necessarily a contract) outlining the expectations and requirements of the parties, an organizational structure that promotes successful interaction, clear measures of success, and a high level of mutual commitment. A key point is that supply alliances, as presented here, do not involve legal ownership of one party over another or legally formed joint ventures.

The fact that an organization has formed a supply alliance in and of itself is no guarantee of better supply performance. As with poorly structured longer-term agreements, poorly structured alliances can lead to some serious unintended consequences, including prohibitively high supplier switching costs or closing out new ideas from nonincumbent suppliers. Companies should form supply alliances because there is a strategic need or competitive benefit from doing so.

A serious mistake when pursuing alliances is to claim success simply because supply alliances are in place. After all, if supply alliances are good, then forming alliances should lead to good outcomes. If a supply manager maintains that her firm has formed some high-level supply alliances, she should immediately be challenged to identify what has been achieved because of these alliances. Forming an alliance is an activity, while reaping the benefits from an alliance is an accomplishment. As mentioned elsewhere throughout this book, believing that activity naturally leads to accomplishment can be risky.

One issue related to alliances involves the overused term *partner*. As touched upon in Chapter 11, there is a tendency by some to describe any close working relationship with suppliers or where a longer-term contract is in place as a partnership. And throughout this book, examples have been provided that do use this term. Part of the problem is that the word *partner* is easy to pronounce and sounds impressive. This overuse is similar to calling any assembled group of people a team or referring to any capability that a firm has as a core competency. We have become very loose when using some important terms.

Some companies prohibit their supply managers from using the words partner or partnership when describing even their most special supply relationships. Lawyers will tell us that a partnership entails certain legal responsibilities. And if you look like a duck, walk like a duck, and quack like a duck, you just might be a partner (or something like that). In order to protect the buying company, so the legal reasoning goes, it is best to avoid using that term. Instead, these firms will use terms like *collaborative relationships* or *supply alliances* to describe their most special relationships. Some view these terms as friendlier from a legal standpoint.

Not all supply alliances are created equally. Lower-level alliances, which are common when a buying company signs an agreement with a maintenance, repair, and operations (MRO) distributor, are characterized by traditional performance metrics, functional rather than executive visibility and involvement, and minimal linkages to organizational goals.

Advanced alliances directly support strategic business needs, often focus on developing innovative technologies, feature the exchange of personnel and resources, and are visible across the highest levels of an organization. Furthermore, the measures used to evaluate alliance success should be different compared with other supply relationships. Revenue from new markets entered, new value from differentiating technologies developed through the alliance, and improvements to return on assets or investment all represent new kinds of metrics that reflect the importance of critical alliances.

Why Pursue Alliances?

Whatever the reason for entering into a formal alliance, all supply alliances should have one overarching objective: to beat the market. An effective alliance delivers or creates outcomes that simply are not as available from other types of supply relationships or contractual governance. Many of the reasons for pursuing strategic supply alliances are the same for pursuing strategic supply management.

By definition, a supply alliance should feature a collaborative relationship. This means a willingness to share information and to work jointly to manage cost drivers and cost elements. Strategic cost management is a major driver of supply alliances.

A fair number of supply alliances address the development of new technology that may eventually work its way into new products. Related to this is gaining access to specialized knowledge controlled by a supplier. For example, Boeing's development of fuselage composite technology with its key supplier is designed to dramatically change the way planes are produced. Engineering resources are critical when forming alliances that focus on technology development.

Another major reason for forming supply alliances is to fill in the gaps across the value chain due to outsourcing. These gaps may be in production, logistics, or even finished goods production. As the magnitude of outsourcing increases, the need to form special supply relationships also increases.

Ensuring access to supply within constrained supply markets and greater sharing of risk and reward, particularly for expensive development projects, are also alliance drivers. Chapter 7 introduced the example of the development of a long-range version of the Boeing 777. General Electric agreed to invest $1 billion in the development of the new 777, knowing that every jet sold comes with two GE engines that also need service over the 25-year life of the plane.

Some firms form supply alliances because of a fear that competitors will gain a competitive advantage from their alliances. Reacting to what others are doing is called the "fashion and fear motive." While most managers will not admit that fashion and fear drive their behavior, this reason for undertaking many supply management activities is probably more popular than anyone cares to admit.

Where Should We See Supply Alliances?

It is certainly not the case that alliances are unique to the supply management arena. Most high-profile alliances are actually on the marketing side of the business. For example, think about the airlines that work together, some of them direct competitors, to form the Star Alliance, an alliance designed to broaden the reach of any one airline. Or consider two complementary firms—Starbucks and Barnes & Noble—that have joined to enhance the total shopping experience. Alliances are not unique to any one part of the value chain.

Where should we see supply alliances? True alliances reside within the critical quadrant of the portfolio matrix presented in Chapter 7. This means the product or service has a high value and that any relationship is collaborative by design. Interestingly, many supply alliances are not even about supply. Instead, they focus on the development of innovative technology that then supports the development of new products. Let's take a look at a supply alliance example involving a critical item.

A number of years ago General Motors entered into a 10-year aluminum contract with Alcan.[1] While GM does not spend nearly as much for aluminum as steel, aluminum earns its position in the critical quadrant for a variety of reasons. First, compared with steel, the supply market for aluminum is quite limited. Only a handful of suppliers have the capability to satisfy the volumes required by GM. Next, GM requires close to 2 billion pounds of aluminum annually, making it a purchase category with some serious dollars attached to it. But perhaps most importantly, unlike steel, GM is trying to find ways to increase the use of lightweight aluminum in its vehicles. GM's use of aluminum in an average vehicle is increasing 7 percent a year. It is a growing purchase category, while steel, which is usually viewed as a leverage item, is a mature and perhaps even declining purchase category.

Several features of the Alcan agreement reveal that GM understands quite well that aluminum is a critical item. GM's chairman considered the agreement so important that he personally signed it. The agreement also calls for extensive sharing of technical resources between the two companies. GM and Alcan have established a joint research program at GM's technical center in Warren, Michigan. At any given time between 15 and 40 engineers drawn from the two companies are working to invent new ways to use aluminum and to make aluminum parts easily recyclable. The agreement also addresses the volatility of aluminum pricing. Aluminum price volatility, sometimes changing 40 percent within a single year, has made it difficult for companies such as GM to plan its use of aluminum effectively. The companies addressed this concern by agreeing on a formula that guarantees Alcan a return on its investment in exchange for pricing stability.

PREDICTORS OF EFFECTIVE ALLIANCES

Organizations that pursue supply alliances should have a keen interest in the factors or characteristics that define success. Fortunately, research and extensive experience with alliances over time has helped identify a set of factors that characterize effective alliances.

Executive Commitment and Visibility. Since many supply managers consider alliances to be the highest form of a supplier relationship, it makes sense that successful alliances receive the executive support their status warrants. Simply stated, executive management has the authority to make alliances a reality by initiating contact with peers at another company, making budget and personnel available to support an alliance, and continuously conveying messages about the importance of the alliance. Alliances cannot succeed without executive and organizational buy-in.

Higher Levels of Trust. It almost goes without saying that successful alliances feature a high degree of trust. Without the presence of trust, some firms will shy away from supply alliances, believing that an alliance will expose them to opportunistic behavior by the other party. Fortunately, the parties to an alliance often have a fairly long operating history before they enter into an alliance, making a lack of trust less of an issue. Refer to Chapter 11 for a discussion of activities that build trust within a supply relationship.

Goal Congruency. Congruency simply means that the parties to an alliance have goals that are compatible rather than conflicting. Goal congruency begins to define the win-win nature of the relationship. The presence of goal congruency is also important because it implies that the parties have thought about their goals.

An example will illustrate goal congruency. A number of years ago, Whirlpool Corporation, located in the same state that is home to the Big Three automotive producers, found itself competing against the auto industry for the attention of steel producers. Unfortunately, Whirlpool's volumes did not command much attention, particularly since Whirlpool was spreading its requirements over a half dozen suppliers. Whirlpool's goal was to work with fewer steel suppliers that would direct investment toward the needs of an appliance rather than an automotive producer.

Not too far away in Chicago, marketing executives at a steel company were considering their own set of issues. These managers had made the decision to reduce their customer base so the company could get enter into longer-term agreements with a smaller set of customers from different industries. Delighting the customer would mean making investments that satisfied each customer's unique requirements. By now the goal congruency between the two companies should be quite obvious. The resulting alliance eventually exceeded expectations.

Clear (and Different) Measures of Success. Traditional measures of success, such as price, quality, and delivery, will not adequately reflect the importance or success of an alliance. Furthermore, traditional supplier scorecard measures are not going to work. Supply alliances must move way beyond traditional measures. Indicators such as market share gained, improvements to return on assets or investment, and the effect on profitability begin to reflect the importance of an alliance.

A study involving MRO distributor partnerships and distributor-customer alliances found that over 56 percent of companies could not quantify the savings realized from these agreements.[2] Failing to capture the rights kinds of data may lead to erroneous assumptions about the success or failure of an alliance.

Rigorous Supplier Selection Process. Selecting an alliance supplier is not like selecting just any other supplier. The buying firm should perform the equivalent of due diligence and act as if it were purchasing the supplier. Poor selection decisions will affect an organization for years. Table 15.1 presents a set of questions a supply manager should ask when evaluating potential alliance candidates.

Table 15.1 Alliance Supplier Selection Questions

Identifying a potential alliance supplier requires a different set of selection questions:

- Has the supplier indicated a willingness or interest to work with the buyer in a formal alliance?
- What is the supplier's motivation for wanting to enter into the alliance?
- What is the supplier bringing to the alliance that is unique?
- Are the cultures of the two companies compatible?
- Will there be a free and open exchange of information, including detailed cost information and future product development plans?
- Does the supplier's technology roadmap align with the buyer's longer-term development needs?
- Is proprietary information safe with this supplier? Can the supplier be trusted?
- Is the supplier's senior management committed to a strategic alliance, or is this the desire of a single individual?
- What will be the relationship-specific investment that the supplier is willing to make?
- What resources is the supplier willing to commit to support the alliance?
- Does the supplier have units that compete with the buyer? If so, how will the buyer manager this risk?
- How well does the supplier know the buyer's business and industry?
- Does the supplier have alliances with any other buying firms, including competitors?

Extensive Sharing of Information. Information sharing creates many opportunities to communicate across organizational boundaries. In fact, frequent, open, and accurate communication correlates directly with the development of trust. Shared information falls primarily into three categories: technology roadmaps and product development plans, industry knowledge, and supplier cost and performance data.

Examples of ways to share information include regular meetings between alliance managers, colocation of personnel between organizations, point-to-point communication between functional groups across the organizations, electronic mail, and video- and teleconferencing.

Joint Activities and Efforts. The essence of an alliance is collaboration, and collaboration is about working together. Successful alliances offer many opportunities for the buyer and seller to work jointly. Examples of joint activities include strategy review meetings, development of technology roadmaps, participation on the buyer's supplier council, establishment of improvement teams, colocation of personnel between companies, early supplier involvement on product development teams, and joint research publications and presentations.

Continuity When Personnel Change. Is a supply alliance between people or companies? Oftentimes the answer is both. Alliances are the creation of people, not companies. The risk is always present that an alliance will change or diminish in importance after those who are responsible for the alliance move away. Effective alliances maintain their intensity even after those that crafted the alliance have moved on.

Committed Resources. The resources required from the buyer and supplier to sustain an alliance take many forms, and the presence of critical resources has the ability to separate successful from less successful efforts. Examples of the resources that are often necessary for supporting an alliance include budget for travel and meetings, executive liaisons between the companies, time for cross-functional participants to commit to alliance projects, and executive commitment. Believing that alliances require only a marginal increase in resources compared with longer-term agreements is a serious mistake.

Continuous Focus on New Opportunities. Perhaps the most serious danger facing alliances is complacency. Perhaps the novelty of the alliance wears thin, personnel move on, or new executives take over. One way to overcome this complacency is to create a culture where a continuous focus on new opportunities becomes a way of life. While the alliance is continuous, the focus of the alliance is finite. So what is a finite focus?

A *finite focus* is one that approaches work as a series of projects. Once a project is complete another, one takes its place. This helps avoid the tendency of a flattening out over time in terms of performance. The alliance is structured as a series of opportunities (i.e., projects) that are reviewed continuously and replaced with new projects as existing projects are completed.

Supporting Documents. Various documents, usually signed by executive managers, underlie successful alliances. Oftentimes these support documents are not contracts, although a contract typically is in place to support the day-to-day supply aspects of the relationship. Rather, these supporting documents are letters of intent, memorandums of understanding, or even covenants—documents that portray the expectations and desires of the alliance members rather than all the legalese.

Research with supply chain alliances reveals that higher levels of *trust* and *greater communication and information sharing* correlate strongly with supply alliance satisfaction. *Joint activities* and *continuous improvement efforts* that create codependency also relate strongly to success and satisfaction.[3] Supply managers are advised to pay close attention to the factors that characterize effective alliances.

Table 15.2 Assessing Supply Alliances

This alliance . . .	Strongly Disagree		Neutral		Strongly Agree
Features competition between the parties.	1	2	3	4	5
Shuts out ideas from nonalliance suppliers.	1	2	3	4	5
Has not achieved its intended purpose.	1	2	3	4	5
Is between people rather than companies.	1	2	3	4	5
Focuses primarily on lower prices.	1	2	3	4	5
Features limited information sharing.	1	2	3	4	5
Has led to complacency.	1	2	3	4	5
Has not resulted in a greater sense of co-destiny.	1	2	3	4	5
Has not satisfied executive management's performance expectations.	1	2	3	4	5
Features a lack of trust.	1	2	3	4	5
Should be evaluated for discontinuance.	1	2	3	4	5

CHARACTERISTICS OF POOR ALLIANCES

It is certainly not the case that all supply alliances satisfy the expectations of their developers. A set of characteristics of poor alliances could be the reverse of the factors presented in the previous section. Simply add "absence of" before each factor. Of course, the ultimate indicator of a poor alliance is one that fails to provide any differential advantage to the parties. Table 15.2 presents a tool to assess the health of a supply alliance.

As with longer-term contracts, perhaps the two biggest characteristics associated with poor alliances are complacency and shutting out new ideas. At times a supplier becomes so entrenched with a buyer that other suppliers conclude there is no chance at gaining new business. When this occurs, new ideas are often presented to other companies, some of whom may be a buying company's direct competitors.

True supply alliances have high maintenance costs. These costs include joint planning meetings, sharing of personnel, executive-to-executive interaction, and a direct budget commitment. High maintenance costs are characteristic of a poor alliance if the alliance fails to produce benefits that outweigh the costs.

EIGHT STEPS TO FORMING AN ALLIANCE

Every major topic presented throughout this book has an underlying process attached to it—and forming a supply alliance certainly qualifies as a major activity. Forming an alliance should follow a set of steps that will help ensure a process that features extremely high supplier switching costs after its completion is performed correctly. While these steps assume the buying company initiates the alliance, alliances can also be initiated by suppliers that are attempting to work more closely with their most important customers.

Step 1. Establish Strategic Business Needs. Alliances are not formed simply for the sake of forming them. Alliances should align directly with the objectives of the buying or selling firm. The key point is that alliances are higher-level agreements that link directly to what the business, rather than purchasing, must do to be successful.

Step 2. Create the Infrastructure to Support Alliance Development. While lower-level alliances may be developed with only functional resources, highly visible alliances require a support structure to oversee the process. This could involve an executive steering team or council that is charged with setting the direction for strategic supply management. This group may also charter a cross-functional team to develop a collaborative agreement.

Step 3. Identify Alliance Opportunities. The portfolio matrix presented in Chapter 7 is ideal for helping to identify alliance opportunities. The critical quadrant includes the most likely candidates for alliance opportunities. Executive leadership is essential for approving those areas where an alliance will be pursued.

Step 4. Identify Alliance Candidates. This step may be, at times, one of the easier steps of the formation process. A supply alliance is sometimes evolutionary between companies that have a long operating history (see the featured case at the end of this chapter). This may speed the development process because the parties should have a solid knowledge of each other and have developed the level of trust necessary for a collaborative relationship.

Step 5. Initiate Executive-to-Executive Contact between Companies. Higher-level alliances should capture the attention of executives at the buyer and supplier. While lower-level alliances usually feature manager-to-manager contact, strategic alliances are often initiated between executives at the vice president level or higher.

Step 6. Evaluate Alliance Candidates. Table 15.1 presented a set of questions that should be asked when considering an alliance candidate. Evaluation should resemble a due diligence process whereby one party acts as if it is buying into the

Table 15.3 Alliance Memorandum of Understanding

The parties to this alliance have a mutual desire to be financially successful, expand their market leadership, and establish and maintain a win-win relationship that creates new value. The foundation of this relationship is trust and mutual cooperation, and each party will work to foster a trusting relationship and challenge the other to improve continuously.

The parties to this alliance agree to:

- Meet at least twice a year to establish goals, prioritize activities, and measure results.
- Work together to improve product quality, process yields, and process costs.
- Maintain a nondisclosure agreement and document control procedures to protect individual interests.
- Share information about internal strategies and future plans.
- Share resources and expertise in a manner that creates the greatest value.

For this alliance to be successful, each party must adhere to certain commitments.

Purchaser's Commitments

- Purchaser will rely upon the supplier to provide engineered materials.
- Purchaser will provide design, technical, and marketing knowledge about industry requirements and how the supplier's products add value in this market. The purchaser will work with the supplier to create solutions to industry-specific problems.

Supplier's Commitments

- Supplier will provide purchaser with access to new technologies.
- Supplier commits to solve material and processing challenges.
- Supplier will provide purchaser with design, technical, and marketing knowledge about the use of engineered material throughout the world, when ethical.
- Supplier will strive to provide materials and technology for use in the purchaser's processes.
- Supplier will benchmark materials and services worldwide, with assistance from the purchaser, and to share the results.

Adapted from Robert J. Trent, "Strategic Alliances and Partnerships, The Purchasing Handbook," Chapter 8 in *The Purchasing Handbook*, McGraw-Hill, 1999, pp. 185–186.

other party. The parties to an alliance are entering into a relationship that should last many years.

Step 7. Reach Agreement with Alliance Supplier. This step involves negotiation or agreement between the parties about issues well beyond price. While all relationships have a win-lose component (the parties must charge something for goods or services provided through the alliance), alliances often focus on higher-level objectives (market share or revenue growth) and issues (sharing of intellectual property, risk, and resources). Table 15.3 presents one company's memorandum of understanding underlying a high-profile supply alliance.

Step 8. Grow the Alliance. A key feature here involves assigning a relationship manager to manage the alliance. As noted in an earlier chapter, the level of the assigned relationship manager should correlate with the importance of the relationship. Growing the alliance also means regular reviews of the outcomes realized from the alliance. The alliance supplier should also have a prominent position on the buyer's supplier council, if one exists. The challenge here is ensuring the reality of the alliance matches its expectations. This step is also critical for avoiding diminished performance over time.

Establishing a true supplier alliance is actually a fairly rare event in the history of a buying company. Making alliances an important part of the supply management process requires a discipline and structured approach rather than an ad hoc approach.

WINNING WITH A TRUE SUPPLY ALLIANCE

The following case example discusses a formal partnership to develop advanced engineered materials. (The parties use the term *partnership* to describe their relationship, so that term will also be used here.) The drivers behind this partnership were a need for faster product development, greater product functionality, lower cost, less electronic packaging, and access to innovative technology. Executive managers conceived the partnership as a way to leapfrog existing market technology and to "beat the market." Although the buyer had the capability to design engineered materials, it did not view this capability as a core part of its business strategy.

The buying company sought some specific outcomes from this partnership. Specifically, the purchaser expected reduced product prices, competitive benchmarking support, new material research that was not available to competitors, and shorter product development cycle times. The buyer also had certain expectations of the supplier—the supplier had to commit capacity to the buyer, provide world-class quality levels, be willing to make relationship-specific investment, sign a letter of understanding and nondisclosure agreement, and provide a period of exclusivity for new materials developed jointly.

The buyer did not go through an extensive selection process to identify its partner. In fact, the two companies had a long history of working together dating to 1964. While not the highest-performing supplier across all product lines, it was the most consistent. Perhaps most importantly, the supplier had research centers located in the major regions of the world, something that was vital to a supply partnership that focused on developing new materials.

The idea for a partnership did not originate with supply managers. Instead, a chief engineer at the purchaser put forth the idea of developing a partnership covering engineered materials. The consensus after an executive meeting between the firms was to further explore the idea. The companies formed a committee with representatives from each company. The committee met four times over a 12-month period to develop the partnership agreement. After signing the agreement, the executive leaders committed themselves to educating internal participants who would be working within the partnership.

The partnership did not initially lead to new business opportunities, something that could certainly cause a questioning of the relationship. However, a project that resulted in a technological advancement showed the value of collaboration. By working together, the parties reduced product development time by one year and were able to enter a new line of business that was eventually worth several hundred million dollars in new sales.

The partners have agreed to work jointly on four projects simultaneously. While some of the projects are "tweaks" to existing applications, others are "blue sky" and represent a higher level of risk and reward. When a project is completed, it is replaced by another project, with project leadership shifting between the parties. Managing the top four projects is where the most intensive interaction occurs within this partnership. The supplier budgets $1 million annually to support project development, which is a perfect example of relationship-specific investment.

A major benefit from the partnership is the synergy that evolves from an intensive level of collaboration. Formal partnership meetings occur three times a year. These meetings, with the location alternating between the buyer and supplier, focus primarily on reporting the progress of joint projects. The partners also evaluate future competitive challenges. At one meeting, they concurred on marketplace trends and generated and ranked over 100 potential project ideas. In another instance, the partners developed a technology roadmap where they identified a competitor's technology. This exercise allowed the partners to leapfrog the competitor's technology during a subsequent project.

Consensus exists among the participants that this relationship represents the highest form of supply collaboration. A simultaneous focus on four projects has helped create an expectation of continued performance. With abundant experience about the partnership well in hand, the participants are able to provide a valuable set of lessons learned. Table 15.4 summarizes these lessons.

What indications are there that this alliance has been successful? First, collaboration now occurs in anticipation of future product requirements. The alliance focuses on leading-edge technology applications, proves these applications to be feasible, and then works with product development teams to apply the applications. And second, new materials developed jointly have contributed to new revenue streams. In fact, a major competitor now purchases items developed jointly through the partnership. The outcomes from this alliance illustrate why some firms put forth the time and energy to pursue this demanding type of relationship.

Table 15.4 Supply Partnership Lessons Learned

One company's experience from its supply partnership . . .

- Both sides must receive value for a partnership or alliance to be successful.

- Overcoming resistance to information sharing takes time.

- The sharing of sensitive documents benefits early on from a procedure to manage the flow of sensitive documents between companies.

- Successful partnerships initially require extensive "marketing" by executive managers at both companies.

- Start with early wins—success leads to more success.

- Development of trust is complicated when the parties also have units that compete.

- A formal agreement (although not necessarily a contract) is critical for identifying expectations.

- Joint intellectual activities strengthen the relationship, help break down communication barriers, and promote trust.

- To benefit from a technology partnership, the purchaser must work with a supplier that has access to technology worldwide, including research centers.

- An understanding of expected outcomes must exist before beginning a project.

- Maintaining a sense of competition is critical for avoiding complacency—suppliers must still earn the purchase contract.

- After completing a project successfully, joint celebration helps bring the parties closer.

- Creating a structure to support the development of the partnership and its growth is critical, including a joint committee to develop the alliance agreement, a memorandum of understanding concerning confidential and proprietary information, and regularly scheduled meetings to identify opportunities.

- A continuous focus on four projects maintains the intensity and continuity of the partnership.

CONCLUDING THOUGHTS

Intense competition is forcing firms toward greater integration and collaboration with a smaller set of suppliers. Since individual firms acting in isolation are often ill equipped to confront relentless global pressures, supply alliances become a logical, perhaps even necessary, response for exceeding the expectations of end customers. The proper use of alliances is an important part of strategic supply management.

SUMMARY OF KEY CHAPTER POINTS

- A supply alliance is a longer-term, mutually beneficial relationship between two or more firms that has specific elements unique to that relationship—an agreement outlining the expectations and requirements of the parties, an organizational structure that promotes successful interaction, clear measures of success, and a high level of mutual commitment.

- While a great deal has been written about supply alliances, the reality is that a firm should maintain only a few true supply alliances.
- Since individual firms acting in isolation are often ill equipped to confront relentless global pressures, supply alliances become a logical, perhaps even necessary, response for exceeding the expectations of end customers.
- The fact that an organization has formed a supply alliance is no guarantee of better supply performance. Establishing the right set of measures that evaluate the performance of an alliance is critical.
- The most common reasons for forming supply alliances include strategic cost management, development of new technology, gaining access to supply, filling in the gaps across the value chain due to outsourcing, and sharing of risk and reward.
- Perhaps the most significant characteristics of poor alliances are complacency and shutting out new ideas.
- Research and experience with alliances over time has helped identify a set of factors that begin to characterize effective alliances, including executive commitment and visibility, higher levels of trust, goal congruency, clear measures of success, rigorous supplier selection process, extensive sharing of information, joint activities, continuity when personnel change, committed resources, continuous focus on new opportunities, and supporting documents that formalize the alliance.
- Forming an alliance should follow a set of steps that will help ensure a process that features extremely high supplier switching costs is performed correctly.

ENDNOTES

1. R. L. Simison, "GM Commits to Aluminum in Alcan Pact," *Wall Street Journal,* (November 9, 1998): B1.
2. R. J. Trent and M. G. Kolchin, "Reducing the Transactions Costs of Purchasing Low Value Goods and Services" (Tempe, AZ: CAPS Research, 1999), 63.

3. R. M. Monczka, "The Global Procurement and Supply Chain Benchmarking Initiative: Strategic Supplier Alliances and Partnerships," *GEBN Pilot Module Report* (East Lansing, MI: Michigan State University, 1995).

16

LOOKING TOWARD THE FUTURE

This book began by saying that today's competitive environment is one where capabilities that win business today only qualify for business tomorrow. It is an environment where global pressures to improve are relentless and severe. And it is an environment where speed, flexibility, and innovation often count for more than sheer muscle. For some, this global environment is full of uncertainty and peril. For others, it offers tremendous opportunities.

The strategic supply management framework presented in Chapter 1 and the discussion presented throughout this book would be incomplete unless we extend our knowledge of where we are today to where we are going tomorrow. What might happen within strategic supply management over the next 3, 5, or even 10 years? How should supply managers respond to the competitive realities of a global economy?

This chapter considers what the future might hold for strategic supply management. The projections presented here are subject to debate, since looking toward the future is a risky business. One observer has commented that business leaders need to be careful about making too many prognostications about the future. Most of the time they are going to be wrong.[1] Something we are not wrong about predicting, however, is that change will be the one constant that all supply managers can count on.

A TOPIC-BY-TOPIC LOOK TOWARD THE FUTURE

The objective when looking toward the future is to identify those changes and trends that have a decent likelihood of occurring. Once those trends are identified, our task becomes one of understanding how to respond. For example, when it became obvious that leading firms were reducing the size of their supply base in the 1990s, supplier managers needed to understand why supply base reduction might be a good idea. The challenge then became one of understanding how to manage this change to achieve higher levels of performance.

The following projects where we are progressing within each of the topics presented throughout this book. For each trend or change, ask yourself two questions. First, do you agree with what is being said? And second, if you agree, how should you respond?

Recognizing the Importance of Supply Leadership

Business leaders must increasingly understand the need to endorse a strategic approach to supply management if they hope to tap into new sources of competitive advantage. Many industry members are revamping their supply models to more closely resemble the electronics and automotive sectors, two industries that have been at the forefront of supply management change. The changes affecting the design and sourcing practices of aerospace companies, for example, are dramatic. One European observer has commented that both Airbus and Boeing are evolving into giant, global, concurrent engineering task forces that also manage shortened-cycle final assembly lines, while subassembly manufacturing, the development of metal or composite materials, and systems design become the responsibility of risk-sharing partners.[2] Dramatic supply management changes are also affecting the pharmaceutical industry. We should expect more and more industries to adopt strategic supply management the way the early-adopting industries have adopted supply management.

Because of the organizational rather than functional nature of supply management, expect future supply leaders to come from all across the organization. In addition to leaders working their way through the ranks of the supply organization, expect future supply leaders to also come from finance, marketing, engineering, and operations. The attractiveness of supply management as a career path will increase.

We should also see a higher percentage of organizational leaders, within and outside of supply management, who appreciate the value of applying a strategic approach to supply management. Their challenge will be to respond quickly to supply opportunities in order to avoid realizing a competitive disadvantage.

Creating the Right Supply Organization

An emphasis on centrally led or centralized sourcing governance, coordination, and decision making will continue to grow over the next three to five years. A recent study revealed that almost 60 percent of supply leaders say their business unit is currently structured and governed centrally, with almost three-quarters saying their most important purchases are coordinated from a center-led or head-quarters group.[3] The trend toward greater center-led supply management will accelerate the formal separation of strategic and tactical supply responsibilities.

Future organizational designs will likely feature different reporting relationships than what has traditionally been the case. We should expect to see an elevation of the reporting level of the highest procurement or supply officer. While some CPOs will argue they want to report directly to the CEO, and in smaller and medium-size companies this may not be an issue, others may not be as confident that this represents the ideal reporting relationship. CEOs must confront many issues beyond supply, and there is always a concern about competing with other areas for the CEO's attention. Reporting to an executive vice president who has the authority to respond directly to supply needs may offer a better "sweet spot" for organizational reporting.

Traditional reporting relationships should also change. The practice of procurement groups reporting through manufacturing will diminish as supply management assumes a position on par with other groups. Assuming the supply group is not reporting to the CEO, then where will the supply group report? Given the increasing amount of funds under the control of supply managers, we should expect a more formal reporting relationship with finance. Also, expanded global supply chains are encouraging a pairing of supply and logistics groups.

A key objective as it relates to future organizational designs will be greater integration, and that integration will be across functional groups, across internal business units, and with customers and suppliers. Organizational design is a tangible way to formally pursue integration across the supply chain. We should expect greater use of organizational design features that include suppliers.

A growing emphasis on supply chain integration should lead to new design features. Figure 16.1 presents a model that will support the integration of the supply and demand sides of the supply chain. An important issue here is whether supply management will be housed under this executive position or will maintain separate autonomy. If supply management is strategically focused at a center-led level, the chances are good that a higher-level executive who is responsible for coordinating supply chain activities and the chief procurement or supply officer will be part of a separate reporting structure.

Figure 16.2 presents an organizational model that should become more widely used. Competition is forcing supply chain participants to work more closely together to understand end customer requirements, perhaps through involvement on a customer advisory board. While few organizations have taken integration this far, this approach logically extends some of the design approaches that include suppliers, such as supplier councils.

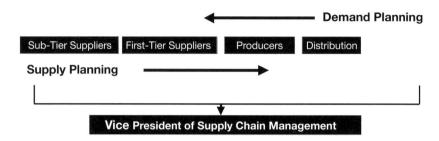

- Responsible for or linked to the worldwide purchasing organization and supply planning
- Responsible for demand and finished finished goods inventory planning and execution
- Responsible for primary customer order fulfillment centers and logistics

Figure 16.1 Integrating supply and demand across the supply chain.

One organizational trend that we can confidently bet on involves the expanded use of teams. This does not mean that supply organizations should not remain selective in how they use this expensive resource. How will using teams change in the future? We will likely see a shift toward full-time teams where participants are organized around distinct supply chain processes, such as new product development, customer order fulfillment, supplier evaluation and selection, and supply management. This contrasts with a team-based model that emphasizes part-time team assignments that are in addition to regular job responsibilities. A growing emphasis on global sourcing will also drive an increased emphasis on virtual teams. Advances in Web-based communication software, along with improvements in videoconferencing technology, will greatly enhance the capabilities of virtual teams.

Measuring across the Supply Network

The broad area of supply measurement is in need of serious attention over the next three to five years. Until supply managers are able to demonstrate the strategic value of their initiatives, it will be difficult to make the case that supply management belongs at the executive table.

Supply leaders will increasingly focus on performance measures that begin to tap into the same set of objectives that are shared by executive managers. This will require a substantial shift from efficiency-based measurement to outcome or effectiveness-based measurement. This transition will require finance to become a more integral part of the supply measurement process. Finance can provide the

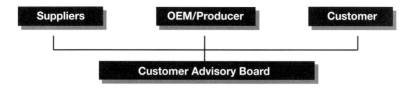

What is the benefit of suppliers participating on a customer advisory board?

- Suppliers better understand end customer requirements.
- Suppliers better understand how they fit within the OEMs business model.
- Suppliers can commit direct investment targeted to the needs of the end customer.
- Suppliers better understand supply chain risks and opportunities.
- Suppliers better understand demand planning data as it is developed and shared upstream.

Figure 16.2 Cross-enterprise integration.

legitimacy that supply management often lacks by validating the savings that result from supply initiatives. This group can also identify the set of corporate indicators that supply managers are impacting. Some organizations will begin to assign finance representatives directly to their strategic supply groups. And more supply organizations will report to the highest executive levels through finance.

While the use of performance scorecards will increase, the scorecards that most firms have in place are in need of some rework. First, we will likely evolve to the point where scorecards are not even issued on a regular basis. Instead, suppliers will enter through a Web portal and see in real time their scores that reflect current information. Second, a variety of scorecards will be in place that reflect different sourcing requirements. Since all supply requirements are not the same, the scorecards that are associated with those requirements should also not be the same. Customized scorecards will become common. Finally, it is likely that more and more supply organizations will compare suppliers against one another by name, and these comparisons will be visible to suppliers. Today, Supplier A might be able to see how it compares to Supplier B, if comparisons occur at all. Anonymous letter designations will be replaced by name designations.

Assessments of the buying company by suppliers should become more commonplace. The growing importance of supplier relationships will serve as an incentive for buying companies to better understand how their suppliers feel about working with them as a customer. The challenge will be one of collecting supplier data objectively and then knowing how to respond to that information.

Using Information Systems to Support Supply Objectives

We should expect progressive supply organizations to take a disciplined approach to their IT applications by focusing their efforts in five primary areas. These include the development or refinement of (1) planning systems, such as demand, supply, and transportation planning modules, (2) execution systems, such as automated material releasing systems and advanced shipping notices, (3) integration systems, such as EDI, (4) e-procurement Web-based tools, and (5) supply management processes, such as contracting and supplier relationship management systems.

The application of systems technology will continue to focus on removing transactions costs and automating the more tactical aspects of procurement. This will result primarily in one of two outcomes. The first is that companies will downsize their supply organization to take advantage of these newfound efficiencies. The second path, and the one that a 1999 study said is slightly more likely to occur, is to redirect these newly available resources toward new value creating activities.[4]

However supply chain systems evolve over the next three to five years, it is safe to conclude their focus will be on data transparency (with appropriate safeguards) and the seamless exchange of information in real time or near real time. EDI, for example, will continue its migration toward Web-based systems rather than third-party value-added networks. This will make the exchange of data through EDI systems even more commonplace than it is today. Supplier visibility to scorecard data should also become a nonevent.

The use of reverse auctions will be used selectively, and hopefully, more properly than in the past. While auctions were the rage just a few years ago, a tightening of supply markets, a better understanding of the limitations of this approach, and an emphasis on developing longer-term relationships with a select group of suppliers should help ensure a more balanced approach to this tool. Supply leaders will increasingly realize that not everything is a candidate for a reverse auction. If they fail to realize this, their more important suppliers will gladly point it out to them.

An interesting unknown involves the future use of radio frequency identification (RFID) to manage the flow of goods and information across the supply chain. If there ever was a case of a technology in search of an application, RFID may be that technology. This does not mean that RFID will not end up having widespread applicability. Unfortunately, at this time many observers are not sure what that applicability will be. It will be important for supply managers to be part of any RFID discussions because suppliers will have to comply with whatever applications a buying company (or industry) decides to pursue.

Developing the Human Side of Supply Management

Supply leaders will continue to encourage their people to expand their educational levels and credentials. The knowledge and skills required as supply management evolves into new areas are likely to be unfamiliar to some. Relationship management, global sourcing, cross-enterprise integration, cost management, contracting, and strategic planning will increasingly become important topics for supply managers to master. Technology will reduce and streamline transactions, allowing supply managers to focus on areas that offer major paybacks. The challenge is to take a workforce that is good at managing transactions and refocusing it so it can manage strategies, total value, and relationships.

Expect progressive supply organizations to have human resource staff committed exclusively to the supply management organization. The importance of human resources to supply management success will drive this focused commitment. Human resource support will often be colocated within the supply organization rather than at a separate human resources location.

Supply leaders will begin to identify the knowledge and skills required for specific supply management career paths. We should then expect to see a systematic evaluation of personnel against the requirements that align with their expected career paths. Customized rather than general training and education to address areas of deficiency will include on-demand modules accessed on a just-in-time basis.

Supply organizations will increasingly focus on the best way to acquire and develop their human resource assets. Turnover due to baby-boomer retirements and the changing nature of supply management guarantee this topic will receive the attention of supply leaders. We should expect leading firms to align with a smaller group (usually six or less) of leading colleges to ensure a consistent pipeline of qualified graduates interested in supply management careers.

Matching Supply Strategies to Supply Needs

The importance of a formal strategic planning process within supply management will increase over the next three to five years. The obvious way to formalize strategic planning is through the development of supply strategies that reflect the needs of not only internal customers but also downstream customers.

The strategic supply management model will increasingly recognize that the needs of customers are becoming more demanding, both at the consumer and industrial level. What this means is that order qualifying and order winning characteristics are constantly evolving. While cost, quality, and on-time delivery will always be important, the ability to quickly mass-customize products through a flexible and responsive supply chain will increasingly define success. A competitive business model that relies on flexibility and responsiveness will require suppliers that are flexible and responsive.

Strategy development will increasingly define the essence of strategic supply management, and it will increasingly become a cross-functional exercise that helps participants better understand their role within the strategic planning process. Supply strategy development will include representatives from different functional groups, and these supply strategies will increasingly be coordinated with the strategies of other groups.

Risk management and prevention will become critical components of the strategy development process. In fact, the inclusion of risk management plans will become a required part of many formal supply strategies. The attention that risk management receives will not diminish in the future.

The segmentation of supply strategies using a quadrant approach is still a relatively new or even unknown concept at many organizations. The use of formal approaches for strategy segmentation should increase over the next three to five years. While there is no standardized segmentation approach, it is important that supply organizations follow some sort of framework to guide their strategy efforts.

Contracting for the Longer Term

There is no reason to believe that the use of longer-term contracts will diminish over the next three to five years. The total dollars under contract should continue to grow, albeit at a rate slower than what has occurred over the last 10 to 15 years. A reliance on a smaller group of suppliers that receive longer-term agreements will continue to be a major part of the strategic supply management model. The consolidation of purchase volumes, increasingly on a global basis, will continue to be emphasized by supply groups and commodity teams. It is unlikely that any firm wants 100 percent of its purchase requirements covered by longer-term agreements. We know that some supply items are best obtained through traditional procurement approaches. Supply managers will also want to maintain some flexibility to take advantage of opportunistic buying.

Switching costs will continue to increase between buyers and sellers as suppliers not only receive longer-term contracts but increasingly receive global contracts. Whether supply leaders like it or not, some of their actions, such as longer-term contracting and transferring design responsibility to suppliers, will continue to shift some power to suppliers. Churning of the supply base will decrease over the next several years.

The pressure to reduce cycle times will affect the time available to craft supply agreements. As a result, supply managers will become increasingly creative in their contracting approaches. The use of preferred suppliers, preapproved contract language, and contract repositories should all become more commonplace as supply managers shorten contract development cycle times.

We should expect negotiating approaches to become less burdensome and adversarial. Progressive supply leaders will increasingly recognize that their most important suppliers do not appreciate doing business with companies that turn their negotiating sessions into a 12-round event.

Outsourcing for Competitive Advantage

More and more firms will include outsourcing analyses as part of their strategic planning process. We should also expect strategic planners to more fully understand and apply the concepts of core capabilities and core competencies. Those areas that are core to the business will likely remain in-house, while those areas where the buying company adds no unique advantage will be candidates for outsourcing. Outsourcing decisions will continue to elevate in importance and move beyond the realm of supply managers.

Outsourcing decisions will often occur even before product development begins. In fact, we should expect outsourcing decisions to be made during the idea generation or concept phases of product development. Supply managers will increasingly play an important role during these decisions. There are simply too many supply issues associated with outsourcing to ignore the direct involvement of supply managers.

The scope of outsourcing will expand to include a wider variety of services. This could even include the possibility of outsourcing that part of the procurement organization that is responsible for obtaining and managing relatively standard items. This would allow the supply organization to focus on strategic rather than operational activities.

While a strategic emphasis on outsourcing should continue, it is not always the case that outsourcing will be the preferred choice. Already we are witnessing an increased willingness by some companies to shift back toward vertical integration, primarily to ensure access of supply within constrained supply markets.

Managing Costs Strategically

The pressure to reduce costs is relentless and severe, and this pressure is not going away anytime soon. The ability to manage supply costs effectively over the next three to five years will become an important *business* imperative. This has been an area where far too many supply managers have demonstrated a lack of creativity. Beating a supplier over the head for price reductions or applying reverse auctions in areas where they should not be applied eventually loses its effectiveness. Chasing lower prices across China, which may provide short-term savings, is also not a cost management technique that applies universally to all requirements.

Supply managers will need to become better at knowing when to apply a wide array of price and cost analytic techniques.

Supply managers will expand their domain of cost management techniques to focus on cooperative cost management. Cooperative cost management is a logical outcome after the development of supplier relationships based on trust. Cost-based pricing, target costing, consignment, supplier suggestion programs, and value analysis are all techniques that should provide payback if buyers and sellers are truly committed to looking after each other's interests rather than narrowly defined self-interests. Risk-sharing models that feature supplier investment in exchange for a share of revenue from each product sold will likely become more commonplace for costly development projects.

Cost management will extend upstream past first-tier suppliers. A true supply chain orientation demands a focus on cost drivers that reside upstream from the buying company or immediate suppliers. The challenge will be one of convincing suppliers that are located several tiers away that it is in their best interests to support the objectives of a buying organization that the supplier does not deal with directly or perhaps did not even know existed.

Building a World-Class Supply Base

Firms that have not already done so will increasingly appreciate the importance of supplier evaluation and selection. Certain trends practically guarantee this will happen. This includes a continued reliance on fewer suppliers, longer-term contracting, and systems outsourcing. For important items, selection decisions will receive organizational rather than functional visibility. And with supplier switching costs becoming ever higher, progressive organizations will approach supplier selection in a fashion that is similar to performing due diligence rather than a cursory assessment.

Supplier selection will become more customized to reflect the unique needs of the supply requirement. Furthermore, the selection process will increasingly include total cost assessments that factor in the many variables that make total cost and unit cost two very different figures. The selection process will also reflect the movement toward a greater reliance on suppliers for design support by paying more attention to a supplier's design capabilities. Supplier capacity will also receive more attention as growing demand in emerging countries creates supply constraints.

Supplier managers will be under extensive pressure to take time out of the selection process. As product and service life cycles become shorter, any process that supports the development of products or services must also decrease. The challenge will be to shorten the selection cycle time without shortening its effectiveness. The use of IPOs or other third parties to evaluate suppliers should become more commonplace.

IT will play a major role in shortening supplier selection cycle time. This includes, but is certainly not limited to, data warehouses and Internet directories that offer a range of information about current and potential suppliers; electronic tools that allow faster processing of RFIs, RFQs, and RFPs; and decision support tools that enhance the speed and effectiveness of the decision-making process.

Third parties should play a greater role in supplier evaluation and selection. This is consistent with the outsourcing of an ever-broader range of services. This expanded role could involve providing data as well as conducting supplier site visits. A possible model is already in place at a high-technology company located in New York. This company routinely uses the staff from an IPO to visit potential Asian suppliers. However, the services are provided on a contract basis. The IPO is not directly part of the buying company's supply organization. This firm has decided to trade fixed costs with variable costs.

Supply base optimization will be a continuing process, but not at the rate it occurred during the 1990s. Most buying organizations will converge on a set of select suppliers that will become part of their long-term supply base. Turnover within the core supply base will become less and less of an occurrence.

Managing Supplier Relationships and Performance

A trend to bet on is the continued growth in the importance of supplier relationships across virtually every industry. Many forces are at work that will ensure suppliers play an increasingly important role in the success of your business. We should expect to see more attention given to matching the importance of a supply relationship with the level of the relationship manager. The role of a relationship manager will increasingly come with formal responsibilities and personal accountability.

Leading companies will make supplier development a more proactive part of supplier performance management. Development efforts need to shift from being predominantly a reaction to supplier problems to pursuing continuous improvement opportunities. This means making the financial and human resource commitments that support supplier development.

The logic why leading supply organizations will take a more proactive view of supplier development is straightforward. Continuous improvement is never ending, and the churn or turnover rate within the supply base for critical items is not likely to increase, and perhaps will even diminish. Supplier development becomes a logical way to ensure access to a continuously improving supply base.

We should expect firms to approach supplier development more systematically. These efforts will be structured as projects, with ROI calculations becoming a required part of the process. Most executives, especially those who are quick to reduce development support when times are lean, will be surprised by the payback of these initiatives.

Customer development on the part of suppliers should also increase. As a sense of co-destiny develops among supply chain members, no where is it written that only buyers can work to develop suppliers. Suppliers have a vested interest in seeing their customers grow. The emphasis should shift toward developing capabilities up and down the supply chain.

Involving Suppliers Early

The early involvement of suppliers beyond product development will increase over the next three to five years. Suppliers should increasingly be early participants during technology planning and development, strategic planning, demand and supply planning, and continuous improvement programs such as value analysis.

An emphasis on system design and sourcing practically guarantees that suppliers will become more critical to success. As mentioned in Chapter 13, a study by Mercer Management Consulting, the Fraunhofer Society for Production Technology and Automation, and the Fraunhofer Society for Materials Management and Logistics predicts that by 2015 automotive suppliers will provide 80 percent of vehicle R&D and production versus 63 percent today.

The extent that buying organizations rely on suppliers to provide design support during product development will grow, and this involvement will increasingly be at the idea generation and concept phases. This means that suppliers will work directly with marketing to better understand the needs of the end customer rather than simply the immediate buyer's needs. Suppliers will also assume greater responsibility for defining product specifications and participating in goal setting, target costing, and joint problem solving.

The extensive involvement of suppliers during product design means closer working relationships will develop between suppliers and engineers. Instead of viewing this as a threat to the role of supply managers, this should provide opportunities to develop even closer working relationships with important suppliers.

We should expect to see greater alignment of IT-based systems, such as computer-aided design (CAD) to promote the smooth exchange of designs and information. Creating aligned systems will be critical for working collaboratively. The much publicized delay in the production of the Airbus 380 can be traced to incompatible wiring as sections of the plan were brought together for final assembly. Airbus's French factories used the latest version of CAD software developed by Dassault, while design engineers in Hamburg used a version of the software dating to the 1980s.[5] The two platforms had very little in common.

Sourcing Globally

The quest for ever-greater benefits from integrated global sourcing is continuous and, for most firms, not yet realized at a meaningful level. Leading supply organizations will view global sourcing as a continuously evolving process that, if managed properly, should provide a steady stream of benefits. Interviews with supply leaders as well as quantitative surveys reveal that companies plan to enhance and expand their global sourcing practices across a number of areas. This includes the continuous refinement of a formal process to guide global sourcing efforts. Supply leaders also recognize the need to accelerate the development of human resources who have the ability to view the supply network from a world-wide rather than local or regional perspective. Other enhancements include the need to develop a set of global performance measures and establish compatible information systems across worldwide locations and with suppliers. Leading firms also expect their global process to promote even greater integration between major functional groups.

We should also expect an emphasis on searching for suppliers that have true global capabilities, which to date has been a struggle. Many buyers are still supported by suppliers that are limited in their worldwide product-service capabilities. This has forced some firms into a regional sourcing perspective even though their intention was to take a global perspective. Pressure to have a worldwide reach and a broad set of performance capabilities will cause consolidation among suppliers in some industries.

The focus of global sourcing will migrate from component sourcing to sub-systems, systems, and services sourcing. And increasingly, the focus of global sourcing will shift from an emphasis on contract development to developing worldwide consistency across supply processes. Developing process and operating consistency across diverse locations may be global sourcing's greatest legacy. Finally, intense cost pressures will lead to in an increased, although sometimes challenging, level of sourcing in emerging markets such as China and Southwest Asia. This willingness to stretch material pipelines thousands of miles will make logistics an important part of the global sourcing process. Stretching pipelines will also ensure that managing risk remains a major supply chain objective.

Creating New Added Value through Supply Alliances

We should expect firms to segment their supply requirements and to rely increasingly on a select group of critical suppliers for ever-increasing amounts of value, including the development of differentiating technologies. It is natural to expect that leading firms will more closely align with a smaller set of progressive suppliers and to develop a collaborative sense of co-destiny with those suppliers. Alliances will happen without so much hype and fanfare as during the 1990s. They will become a more understood part of the supply model and business strategy.

True supply alliances, the relatively few that will exist, will likely focus on two major areas: risk reduction and technology development. Gulfstream's G550 business jet development team, for example, worked at the onset with a group of critical suppliers that were capable of developing technologies that provide a competitive advantage, something that Gulfstream continuously strives to achieve. Honeywell provided major advancements in cockpit avionics, Kollsman designed state-of-the art poor weather and night visioning systems, Rolls-Royce created a new, more powerful engine, and Vought Aircraft Industries developed new wing structures. This maker of premier business jets understands how important it is to align with a premier group of suppliers to exceed the needs of end customers.

Buying organizations hopefully will not use the terms partner and partnership so freely when describing even some of their most common supplier relationships. Not everyone is a partner, and not every relationship is a partnership. Any terms that are as overused as these begin to lose their impact.

OTHER PERSPECTIVES ON THE FUTURE OF SUPPLY MANAGEMENT

A literature search reveals a surprisingly limited amount of research regarding what the supply management domain might look like over the next 3 to 10 years. An exception to this is a 2003 study by Giunipero and Handfield. During their *Purchasing and Education Study II,* published by CAPS Research, these researchers had respondents evaluate their agreement or disagreement with almost 40 procurement and supply management trends. Table 16.1 presents the top 15 trends.[6]

Another solid effort at predicting the future of supply management occurred during a 2005 CAPS Research Delphi study. The Delphi technique offers a carefully designed program of individual interrogations interspersed with information and feedback about responses.[7] Researchers relied on the Delphi technique to overcome the weaknesses found in other forecasting methods that attempt to tap into the knowledge of experts. These weaknesses include relying on a single expert rather than a group of experts, the simple averaging of the responses of more than one expert without synergistic refinements, and relying on face-to-face roundtable discussions and group consensus that may be affected by influential members. The anonymity of the Delphi technique helps overcome these limitations. Table 16.2 presents the Delphi predictions that have an average likelihood of occurring of 6 or higher (where 1= not likely and 7 = very likely). Readers are encouraged to review the entire study to gain a better perspective of the over 75 predictions evaluated.

The projections from both of these studies are consistent with not only what was presented in this chapter but also throughout this book.

Table 16.1 Top 15 Future Supply Trends

Supply Trend	Average Rating
Pressure to reduce costs will increase.	4.51
Strategic cost management will increase.	4.50
Supplier selection will focus on total cost analysis.	4.45
E-commerce applications will replace paper-based systems.	4.38
Sourcing will focus more on strategic issues.	4.36
Global sourcing will increase.	4.34
Strategic sourcing will increase in importance.	4.34
Cross-functional teams will coordinate sourcing efforts.	4.31
Sourcing management will replace order placement.	4.31
Purchasing performance will be more closely monitored.	4.27
There will be more coordinated buying across operating units.	4.27
Tactical purchasing will be automated.	4.26
Use of supplier scorecards will increase.	4.24
Purchasers will manage supplier relationships.	4.23
Two levels of purchasing will evolve—strategic and transactional, day-to-day buying.	4.19

Scale: 1= Strongly disagree, 5= Strongly agree

Adapted from Giunipero and Handfield, "Purchasing Education and Training II," CAPS Research, 2004, p. 64.

CONCLUDING THOUGHTS

Even for firms that have pursued strategic supply management over the last decade, the journey is still evolving and changing. There is always room for growth and improvement. And if we do not think there is, then it is probably time to retire or move on to new pursuits. Those firms that have emphasized early supplier involvement during new product development, for example, know there are opportunities to expand early involvement into other important areas. Those firms that have viewed global sourcing as a means to develop worldwide contracts will start to appreciate the many other outcomes available from that process.

A central theme throughout this book is that it is time for supply managers to step up and become a source of competitive advantage. It is hard to imagine a process that has as much untapped potential as strategic supply management. Part of this is because procurement and supply has been a neglected activity at so many firms. The legacy term called purchasing must give way to supply management, and supply management must become strategic supply management. Hopefully,

Table 16.2 Supply Management Delphi Study Results

Delphi Study Predictions	Likelihood Rating
Your business unit will increasingly collaborate with suppliers to identify and reduce costs throughout the supply chain.	6.67
The ability to integrate and manage strategic suppliers will be considered a core competency and will not be outsourced.	6.58
Your business unit will increasingly emphasize cross-functional sourcing teams to leverage expertise and strategies across your organization.	6.33
High-level information sharing will play an increasing role in future relationships with suppliers.	6.31
Your business unit will develop more comprehensive knowledge of supplier capabilities and will better leverage this knowledge to your advantage.	6.29
Sourcing will become increasingly involved with other functional groups and processes.	6.20
Your business unit will take an active role in ensuring the adequacy and execution of the supply strategies of critical tier one suppliers.	6.17
Suppliers will be expected to take on a greater cost management role based on guidelines/expectations established by your business unit.	6.13
Your business unit's supply strategy will be to enhance cross-enterprise relationships with core suppliers to achieve a higher level of cooperation and enhanced business and technical integration.	6.11
Your purchasing/sourcing/supply activities will increasingly become centrally led with decentralized execution.	6.09
Your business unit's suppliers will be expected to increasingly provide value-adding service in R&D, engineering, manufacturing, order fulfillment, and systems integration.	6.00

Scale: 1= Low likelihood, 7= High likelihood

Source: Ogden, Petersen, Carter, and Monczka, "Supply Management Strategies for the Future: A Delphi Study," *The Journal of Supply Chain Management*, Summer 2005, p. 43.

this book has provided a better understanding of what strategic supply management is all about. With that said, it is time to go forth and conquer!

SUMMARY OF KEY CHAPTER POINTS

- Because of the organizational rather than functional nature of strategic supply management, expect future supply leaders to come from all across the organization.
- An emphasis on centrally led or centralized sourcing governance, coordination, and decision making will continue to grow over the next three to five years. This trend will accelerate the formal separation of strategic and tactical supply responsibilities.
- Supply leaders will increasingly focus on performance measures that begin to tap into the same set of objectives that are shared by executive managers.
- Progressive supply organizations will focus their IT applications in five primary areas—planning systems, execution systems, integration systems, e-procurement Web-based tools, and supply management processes, such as contracting and supplier relationship management systems.
- Strategy development will increasingly define the essence of strategic supply management, and it will become a cross-functional exercise that helps supply leaders better understand their role within the strategic planning process.
- Switching costs will continue to increase between buyer and sellers as suppliers not only receive longer-term contracts, they will increasingly receive global contracts.
- More firms will include outsourcing analyses as part of their strategic planning process.
- Supply managers will expand their domain of cost management techniques to focus on cooperative cost management.
- Supplier selection will become more customized to reflect the unique needs of the supply requirement. Furthermore, supply managers will be under extensive pressure to take time out of the selection process.
- Many forces are at work that will ensure that suppliers play an increasingly important role in the success of your business over the next three to five years.
- The early involvement of suppliers within a broader range of important processes beyond product development will increase.
- Leading supply organizations will view global sourcing as a continuously evolving process that, if managed properly, should provide a steady stream of benefits.

- Supply alliances will happen without so much hype and fanfare as during the 1990s. They will become a more understood part of the supply model and business strategy.

ENDNOTES

1. K. Korth, "Globalization: Myths, Speculations, and What You Need to Think About," *Automotive Design & Production* 117, no. 10 (October 1, 2005): 20.
2. P. Sparaco, "A European Perspective: Two Way Street," *Aviation Week & Space Technology* 21 (November 27, 2006): 68.
3. R. M. Monczka, R. J. Trent, and K. J. Petersen, "Effective Global Sourcing and Supply for Superior Results" (Tempe, AZ: CAPS Research, 2006), 32.
4. R. J. Trent and M. G. Kolchin, "Reducing the Transactions Cost of Purchasing Low-Value Goods and Services" (Tempe, AZ: CAPS Research, 1999), 28.
5. C. Matlack, "Wayward Airbus," *BusinessWeek* 4006 (October 23, 2006), 47.
6. L. Giunipero, and R. B. Handfield, "Purchasing Education and Training II," (Tempe, AZ: CAPS Research, 2004), 64.
7. J. A. Ogden, K. J. Petersen, J. R. Carter, and R. M. Monczka, "Supply Management Strategies for the Future: A Delphi Study," *The Journal of Supply Chain Management* 41, no. 3 (Summer 2005): 26–48.

INDEX